31643

Also by WALTER BERNSTEIN

Keep Your Head Down

INSIDE
OUT

INSIDE OUT

A Memoir of the Blacklist

WALTER BERNSTEIN

Alfred A. Knopf   New York   1996

THIS IS A BORZOI BOOK
PUBLISHED BY ALFRED A. KNOPF, INC.

Copyright © 1996 by Walter Bernstein
All rights reserved under International and
Pan-American Copyright Conventions. Published
in the United States by Alfred A. Knopf, Inc.,
New York, and simultaneously in Canada by
Random House of Canada Limited, Toronto.
Distributed by Random House, Inc., New York.

http://www.randomhouse.com/

Library of Congress Cataloging-in-Publication Data
Bernstein, Walter.
Inside out: a memoir of the blacklist / by
Walter Bernstein.
p. cm.
Includes index.
ISBN 0-394-58341-8 (alk. paper)
1. Bernstein, Walter. 2. Screenwriters—United
States—Biography. 3. Blacklisting of authors—
California—Los Angeles. I. Title.
PN1998.3.B477A3 1996
812'.54—dc20
[B]   96-12569   CIP

Manufactured in the United States of America
First Edition

For my children
and
For Gloria

INSIDE
OUT

The blacklist returns in images.

A man is beating his wife.

The year is 1950 and I am watching them from the window of my living room. It is a hot, sticky New York day and I wear only underwear shorts. The phone is ringing, but I am held by this scene across a courtyard from my apartment. No one else seems to be paying any attention, although both lovebirds are screaming. When he starts dragging her across the room by the hair, I decide to call the police. But then, head yanked back, she spots me through her window. The sight infuriates her. She yells up at me, outraged, "Put on your clothes, you!" I duck away and answer the phone. It is my agent. He wants me to use a pseudonym for a script I have written for television. Until now I have always written under my own name. But he says the climate is changing. He talks vaguely of certain lists. I am known to be left-wing, why take a chance? I agree, needing the work. I hang up and hurry back to the window, peering around a corner. The couple sit lovingly at a table, sharing a beer. I feel betrayed, ashamed, disappointed, guilty. Tragedy has turned to farce.

It would be like that for the next nine years, for me at least, trying to survive as somebody else.

I am walking down a street when I see a man approaching. He is a producer I have worked for in the past, a pleasant man with a lovely wife and two lovely children. He has good taste in all things, rare in a producer, or anyone else for that matter. He is sorry he cannot hire me now, even under a pseudonym or with the protection of a front. His regret is genuine; he hates the blacklist. But now he sees me and ducks his head and crosses the street so we won't meet. His face is set in a rigid half smile. He is angry at me for subjecting him to this.

I am standing on a subway platform when two men approach me. They are dressed conservatively and wear felt hats. They introduce themselves politely; they are from the FBI. They ask if I am now ready to talk to them. It is not the first time the FBI has confronted me with this question, but before they have always come to my home. The fact that they have found me far from my house is unsettling. I know it is done to unsettle me, but this does little to mitigate the fear. I may be followed. My phone is being tapped. Someone is telling them where I go. I shake my head and move away. They do not follow but watch as my train arrives and I get in. Through the closing doors I see them standing there, expressionless, watching me.

The images dissolve, one into the other. None has pride of place. I write movies; focus is all.

I BEGAN writing movies in the summer of 1947, when I went to Hollywood to work at Columbia Pictures for a writer-director-producer named Robert Rossen. At the time, I was on staff at *The New Yorker*, where I had published fiction before the war and reportage later as a soldier in the army and now as a civilian. The war material had been published as a book and received well enough so that I got a ten-week Hollywood contract. I was delighted to go. The best part of my childhood had been lived either on the street, playing ball, or in the movies. That was my real life; the fantasy life was what went on at home. So I flew off with a light, expectant heart, sitting on the plane next to an anxious young actor named Robert Stack. He, too, was a recently returned veteran and doubtful whether he still had a career. Before the war his distinction had been that he was the boy who had given Deanna Durbin her first screen kiss. He was worried now that everyone had forgotten him. I assured him that he would be remembered, and indeed he was. But he spent the flight morosely fearing the worst, while I looked happily out the window at the welcoming country rolling underneath.

Hollywood turned out to be all I had hoped for. The sun shone brightly and the air was soft. You could see mountains. There was no smell to the flowers, but I had had enough smells in New York. The first morning an actor friend drove me to catch a bus to the studio. The only other passenger was a very pretty young woman. She recognized my friend from a movie he had just made and asked if I, too, was an actor. I said I was a writer. She asked if I was working. I said I was under contract to Columbia. She stood up and came over and sat down beside me. She said she was an actress and she had a boyfriend, but he was home in Oregon and she liked writers because they were intelligent. She gave me her phone number. Nothing like that had ever happened to me before. But when I called, either her boyfriend had returned or it was another working writer who answered with some irritation. So that was the end of that, although it seemed a promising start.

For Rossen, I was to write a screenplay based on a Chekhov story called "The Grasshopper," but he soon switched me to a more ambitious project Columbia had given him, an adaptation of the Robert Penn Warren novel *All the King's Men*. I did not write very much. Mainly I sat listening to Rossen as he paced the room, punching the air with his fists. He was a chunky, aggressive New Yorker who had served thirteen years as a contract writer at Warner Bros. In those days, as he told it, two or three writers would be assigned to a staff producer and they would meet every morning to go over the day's newspapers and see what true stories could be turned into movie fiction. They were often gangster stories. The big stars had all been taken by MGM, so Warner's had to develop stars out of plots rather than the other way around. They managed to create Cagney and Bogart and Davis and Robinson and Garfield and Flynn and even Paul Muni, the eminent actor from the Yiddish and Broadway stage, whom they billed as Mr. Paul Muni to show they were stepping up in class. They also developed a style of fast, tough, cynical romanticism that became a Warner's trademark. This was Rossen's specialty and he eventually got his chance to direct a melodrama called *Johnny O'Clock*, although for Columbia rather than Warner's. This led to directing *Body and Soul* with John Garfield, a successful independent movie that led in turn to his present triple-threat capacity at Columbia.

I learned a good deal about movies from Rossen, especially about how they moved. He knew the kinetic nature of the art, the fluidity and combination of images that drove a story. And drive was what interested Rossen; he came from the school of bang-bang storytelling where what counted was what happened next and the sooner the better. He acknowledged the primacy of content, but his heart was in the action. What he mainly wanted from me was someone who would help him make his political ideas palatable to the studio executives. Like myself, Rossen was a Communist. This was no secret to anyone. Once he wanted to move his desk to a more pleasing spot and the two of us began wrestling it around his office. Suddenly an irascible voice called out from the doorway.

"Who's that, Rossen, one of your Commie writers from New York?"

Standing there was a stocky, bald middle-aged man with an irritable look. Rossen laughed and nodded and introduced me to Harry Cohn, the head of the studio. Cohn shook my hand without interest and left after telling Rossen he was putting the desk in the wrong goddamned place. Communists held no terrors for Harry Cohn. He knew who was boss, and nothing got into his pictures that he didn't want in.

Rossen knew that, too. We would discuss some leftist point to be made in a scene and then he would go upstairs and present the scene to Cohn. He would return with the radicalism either deleted or softened to an acceptable liberalism. Sometimes that helped the scene, sometimes it didn't. None of it did anything to dilute Rossen's verbal militancy. The Hollywood Ten—ten writers, directors and producers—had just been called before the House Committee on Un-American Activities, and Rossen was furious at not being one of them. He felt unjustly left out. The Ten had originally been nineteen, Rossen included, but he had not survived the cut. He would complain to me that they were not sending in the first team. On the other hand, he was always failing to pay his Party dues and I was assigned to get them from him. Rossen would promise but rarely pay. Instead, he would get me to box with him in the office. He fancied himself a fighter and would bounce around in front of me, throwing stiff jabs and vicious hooks from a discreet distance. I think in this case I represented the Party as coercive authority to him, although he viewed everyone as some kind of opponent. He was a curious mixture of bluff and talent, but I liked him for reasons I never could figure out. He had an appealing energy, or perhaps it was simply that he was nice to me. I even liked him after he had given names to the committee, although I would not speak to him again.

This was a few years after I had worked for him. Rossen had been subpoenaed some time after the Ten, had testified once and refused to inform, and then later had changed his mind. I thought I understood why. Rossen had no real belief larger than his ego. He saw informing as pure survival, without any of the justifications other informers found necessary to give. He had little existence to himself apart from making studio movies and he went on to make some good ones, such as *The Hustler*. But when I think of him, I think of being at his home one evening before he himself had been called. He was helping his young son write a letter to a friend whose father had just given names to the committee. Rossen was assuring his son that it was hard but necessary to break off the friendship, that what his friend's father had done was unforgivable. I did not see how this extended to the man's family, but Rossen obviously did. It was a difficult, painful moment; the children had been close. Rossen was patient and kind and gently persuasive with his son. But then, I've often wondered, what do you say to your child after you yourself have informed? I wonder if he told him what he told the committee: that in these times you "could no longer indulge yourself in the luxury of individual morality."

After my ten weeks with Rossen I was offered another job by my agent, a nervous ex-dancer named Harold Hecht. He had just formed a producing company with his star client, Burt Lancaster. They raised my salary from $250 to $500 a week and paired me with a more experienced screenwriter named Ben Maddow. We were to adapt an English thriller called *Kiss the Blood off My Hands*. Once again it was a learning experience, only this time I did some actual writing. Maddow was a poet and, under the name of David Wolff, had written a documentary film about civil liberties called *Native Land*. I had liked the film and came to admire Maddow. He had a film sense that was then entirely new to me. He wrote for the eye as well as the mind, while I was still chained to the ear. He was also, like many of the New York writers I met in Hollywood, a product of the Depression. They all seemed touched with some ineffable sadness, as though the world had broken something in them that could never be entirely mended. Maddow had graduated from Columbia with a science degree in the pit of the Depression and had been unable to get any kind of job. For a year, he told me, he left his apartment only at night, roaming the city by himself until dawn. He had a taste for what was bent and melancholy. When he wrote a novel some years later, the final pages were a minute description of the garbage floating in the East River. After our collaboration he went on to write fine scripts for *Intruder in the Dust* and *The Asphalt Jungle*, and then he was blacklisted.

But between us, in that earlier day, we made *Kiss the Blood off My Hands* into an offbeat melodrama that borrowed (stole) heavily from Hitchcock. It was attractive enough to get Joan Fontaine, then a star of some magnitude, as its leading lady and Gregg Toland, who had shot *Citizen Kane,* as the cameraman. The studio approved a start date. Everyone congratulated everyone else. Then, true to hallowed custom, another writer was hired to rewrite the script that had made all this possible. It was my first encounter with the sacred Hollywood principle, still religiously observed, that before drinking any lifesaving liquid, you must first piss in it. This

was based on an old joke about two producers dying of thirst
in the desert, and it was called the pissing-in-the-tomato-soup
story.

But I had enjoyed working with Maddow. I learned from
him and I enjoyed Hollywood. The Universal studio commissary served good food at decent prices. As at most studios,
there was a writers' table, where you could listen to clever
people tell funny, bitter stories about Hollywood. The pace
was slow. There were orange juice stands where you could
drink all the freshly squeezed juice you wanted for a quarter.
I would stand and drink and watch my stomach swell. I liked
riding the streetcars that crisscrossed the city. For a while I
had no car of my own and Lancaster would pick me up on
the way to the studio, where he was making another film. He
would ask me questions about what classical music to listen
to, what art to look at, what books to read. It was not that I
had any special knowledge. He would have asked anyone. He
had not had much education and he was eager to improve
himself. Hecht viewed this with suspicion. He would have
been happier if Lancaster had only wanted to chase women.

Women were often on Hecht's mind. He had been in Hollywood a number of years and I had just arrived, but he kept
asking if I knew any nice girls he could meet. He also liked
pumping Lancaster about his sexual activities. Burt regarded
him with amused contempt but also took his advice. When
Lancaster, feeling himself inadequately trained, wanted to
take acting classes at the Actor's Laboratory Theater, Hecht
vetoed it. The Lab was considered a left-wing organization
and Hecht, although (or because) he was a Communist himself, did not want Lancaster anywhere near the place.

I had come to Hollywood for ten weeks, leaving behind
a   failing wartime marriage. I stayed for six months. I was
having fun. All my life I had wanted secretly to write for

movies—secretly, because if you were serious about writing, you became a novelist or a poet or a playwright. Movies meant Hollywood, a place for selling out. On the other hand, during the hard times it was also a place where you might possibly make a living, which was more than you could do as a serious writer. But I went with hope and remained with pleasure. I loved being inside a studio, watching how a film was made, the craft that went into it, the teamwork among the makers, the unstated pride in their work. I became friends with a film editor named Robert Parrish who had grown up in the movie business. His family had all been extras, hanging out at the studio gates, waiting for some director they knew to summon them for work. Then he had become a child actor (he is the newsboy who bedevils Charlie Chaplin with a peashooter in *City Lights*). Now he was a film editor who had just won an Academy Award for *Body and Soul*. I would walk the back lot with Parrish, stopping to talk to technicians he knew (he seemed to know everyone), listening with interest to the anecdotes and the shoptalk, realizing for the first time there was an industry here, not just a money machine or a dream palace.

I made other friends, but all from the movies; Hollywood was a company town. The cold war was starting, and with it the blacklist, but it was not affecting me and, secure in wish fulfillment, I did not really believe it would. Winston Churchill had made his Iron Curtain speech at Fulton, Missouri. The Hollywood Ten were summoned before the House committee, but the committee members seemed only stupid; I understood their bigotry but not their power. Who, really, could be on their side? I also knew the Communist Party was no menace. After all, I belonged to it. The charge that we wanted to overthrow the government by force and violence was ludicrous. Nothing I had ever done or intended or even thought was designed for that. No one I knew in the Party even dreamed of it. Our meetings might have been less boring if they had. I took for granted that I could be both radical and accepted, since that had always been the case. And yet, while the Party was legal, belonging to it was rapidly becoming dangerous. What had formerly been tolerated was now becoming criminalized. You were not even allowed to come clean without dishonor. If you wanted to escape either the blacklist or criminal contempt, you had to become an informer. You could not tell the committee or the various clearance centers just about yourself; names were what they wanted, calling them information. But they already had all the information they needed, for whatever they needed it for. They also had the names. What they really wanted was *your* name. The need was to demonstrate their power and your subservience. They needed to show that you, too, were on their side.

Still, I had committed no crime, no one seemed to be after me, no one, to my knowledge, had named me as a Communist, my work was well received and rewarded, and however much I felt for the Hollywood Ten, whatever was happening to them (jail, blacklist, exile) was not going to happen to me. I was a war veteran of some small renown, having been the correspondent for *Yank,* the official U.S. Army magazine, who had slipped unauthorized into German-occupied Yugoslavia and obtained the first interview with Marshal Tito. I was a published writer in the exalted *New Yorker*, a family man, an Ivy League graduate. I had been welcomed on public platforms with senators of both parties. I had even belonged to the American Legion, although with subversive intent according to the Legion. In my own admiring eyes, I was socially impeccable. I was very young.

But at the end of the Hecht job, in December 1947, I returned to New York. I arrived at the tail end of a magnificent blizzard. Buried in snow, the city lay as if spellbound. There was no traffic, only an eerie quiet. People strolled in the middle of the white streets past the ghostly stranded cars. They held hands. They threw snowballs. No one was angry. The whole city had a peaceful, postdisaster numbness. I had returned because I was unsure whether or not I wanted to live permanently in Hollywood and also to face my unhappy marriage. The snow, after I had been six months in a city without seasons, settled the first question. I would live in New York and try to work in movies. True, in two days the cars were moving again and the snow had become grime and the people were back to snarling at one another. But it was still New York and some part of me that had not been used in Los Angeles, some essential energy that I had not even noticed was gone (that was the scary part), had returned and made me feel whole again.

The marriage took care of itself, expiring in acrimony and pain, although not before the arrival of another child, this time a son. Having little money and no place to live, I moved in with two friends, Martin and Adele Ritt, who had a small apartment in Chelsea. Ritt was an actor who had recently become a director—a gruff, talented, generous man with an easily ignited temper. Once, acting in the Group Theater's *Golden Boy* and annoyed by an actor named Charles Crisp (later changed for films to Charles McGraw) who was heckling him from the wings, Ritt left the stage, flattened Crisp with a punch and returned in time to pick up his cue. When we played tennis, I soon learned to duck when Marty missed an easy shot, since he would start cursing and hurl the racket without much caring where it went. Usually it went toward my head.

At that time neither Ritt nor I was working. Adele had a

job selling space in the Yellow Pages, but that brought in very little. I slept on the living room couch and did the cooking. Marty supported us with his gambling. He won money playing poker, betting on ball games and handicapping horses. He always knew what he was doing and he was very good at it. He was the only gambler I ever knew who gambled to win. Sentiment never attracted or diverted him; he had no other agenda. He showed as little emotion losing as winning. His temper never interfered. He never exulted when he won or complained when he lost. The only time I ever saw him show emotion while gambling was the first time he took me to the track. I had never been before and knew nothing of horse racing, but I went armed with the picks from the newly installed handicapper for the *Daily Worker*. The Communist newspaper had just decided to broaden its appeal to the masses, and I figured that included me. I won six dollars. Marty lost all his bets. He was enraged by what he saw as a political betrayal, although I was never sure whether he was mad at me or the Communist Party. He was always mad at the Communist Party, usually for the right reasons.

It was a time of not unpleasant dislocation. We awoke early (Marty found it unreasonable to sleep past five-thirty and could not believe anyone else wanted to) and Adele would go off to work, and then Marty and I would walk to the Automat for coffee and crumb cake or, if the morning was cold, a bowl of oatmeal with real cream ladled over it. He would take gambling money out of a savings account he kept for that purpose and go off to the track. I would go do the shopping along nearby Ninth Avenue. In those days Ninth Avenue in Chelsea was a street of amiable temperament. The buildings were low, the stores were family-run, and the shopping always took a little longer than it could have.

At the butcher's, I would sit for a while with old Mr. Gold-

enberg, who had retired and passed his small shop to his two
hearty sons, but who came in every day to talk to the customers. He knew my financial situation and would advise me
on what cuts to buy, always pushing the shoulder instead of
the leg, the chuck instead of the sirloin (just use a little meat
tenderizer). Often he stepped up and carved the meat himself,
treating it with stern affection, a skillful enemy of waste. He
tried teaching me a butcher's knot, but I was too clumsy. Or I
would pass some time at the Little Old Lady's Jam Shop, run
by a genuine little old lady who prided herself not so much on
her superb jams, which she cooked on a small gas range in the
back, as on being a graduate of the first-ever nurses' class at
Bellevue Hospital. In the evenings Adele Ritt was often engaged in political work, mainly for a liberal organization
called the Committee for the Arts, Sciences and Professions,
and Marty and I would stroll up to the theater district, where
friendly managers would let us into a play after the curtain
went up.

I wrote articles for *The New Yorker* and other magazines
during that time. The living was meager, but I enjoyed the
work. The articles were often about sports and I would go to
prizefights with A. J. Liebling, who wrote about them better
than anyone. He was a rotund, erudite man with a bald, egg-
shaped head and a vast store of knowledge. After the fight he
and I would go to dinner and I would listen enthralled as he
talked about past fights and fighters or great meals he had
eaten (he was a serious and gifted eater) or else French me-
dieval literature, which he also knew a thing or two about.
He was the only person I ever saw drink a double martini like
a glass of water, without a stop.

I found a lot those days to be enthralled about. Martin Ritt
introduced me to Elia Kazan and I was enthralled by him,
too. Kazan was Marty's closest friend in the theater. He had

been instrumental in getting Marty into the Group Theater and Marty, realist and sceptic, came as close to idolizing him as he could anyone. Kazan had an idea for a play and was looking for a writer. It was to be the story of a man who rose from gangster to garment manufacturer and was based on a real person who had since moved on to become a successful Broadway producer. Kazan was thinking of John Garfield for the part. I had seen Kazan as a mesmerizing actor on the stage and found him equally so in person. He was short, with a big nose, and he was the most seductive man I had ever met. He made you feel wanted and cared for. He understood you and passed no judgment.

Yet in some way Kazan distrusted this dangerous gift, although he knew how well it worked. Once he talked eloquently to me of wanting to play Richard the Third, knowing the evil uses of charm. He would have made a fascinating Iago. Both women and men responded to him and his ability to seduce was one of the qualities that made him such a good director. He was able to get performances from actors that they themselves did not think they were capable of. But he constantly felt a need to prove this. He thought himself unattractive. Marty told me of standing on a street corner with him, watching a pair of pretty girls across the street, and Kazan saying they wouldn't want anything to do with a pair of funny-looking Jews. Kazan was not Jewish and his looks had nothing to do with his appeal. But it was what he felt. I visited him in New Orleans, where he was directing a movie called *Panic in the Streets*, and watched one night as he primped endlessly in front of a mirror. He was going out with a local young woman who had been hanging around the set, and wanted to know if he looked all right. He could have gone in his bathrobe so far as the young woman was concerned; she wished only to please. But Kazan kept searching in the mirror for his allure, while Zero Mostel, who was in the film, and I tried first kidding him and then, when that didn't work, reassuring him, which worked even less. I started writing the play for Kazan, pleased that he also seemed to share my politics. One day he asked if I would introduce him to a man named Blackie Meyers, a charismatic vice-president of the National Maritime Union. I knew Blackie, who was a Communist, and arranged a saloon meeting one afternoon. Blackie came with two other merchant seamen and they and Kazan and I spent a friendly few hours drinking and talking politics. Later, walking away up the street, Kazan told me that these were the people with whom he belonged, felt at home with, shared beliefs. He might have differences with the left, but it was the side he was on. It was a stirring speech and I believed him. He was enthralling.

A short time later he testified as a friendly witness before the House Committee on Un-American Activities and named his friends from the Group Theater who had been in the Communist Party with him. He continued to insist he was a man of the left. I did not know him well enough to ask him about this. I dropped the play and did not see him again. Marty was stunned; he could not believe Kazan could have done this. He did not believe, any more than I did, the explanation Kazan gave in an ad he took in *The New York Times*, expressing his hatred of communism. There seemed little for him to be afraid of. Kazan was one of the most important and powerful directors in the country, in both theater and films. He had directed *Death of a Salesman* and *A Streetcar Named Desire*. He had won an Academy Award for the movie *Gentleman's Agreement*. He could easily have continued to work on Broadway. The entertainment blacklist existed in direct proportion to the amount of money involved. Since the theater was small change compared with movies and television, the blacklist was porous there.

Many actors felt the same as we did about Kazan, including James Dean, a friend of Marty's. We met Dean on the street one day and Marty introduced me, and the talk inevitably turned to Kazan and his testimony. Dean was contemptuous and vowed never to work with him. Then he did *East of Eden*, directed by Kazan. Shortly after that, we saw Dean again on the street. He came up to us and spoke without slackening his stride. "He made me a star," he said, and walked on.

Kazan enthralled me. Henry Wallace, who ran for president on the Progressive Party ticket in 1948, did not. He was a handsome, distant man, at home with humanity but not necessarily with people. His real passion was hybrid corn. The Wallace family had been scientific farmers for generations and both Wallace and his father had been secretary of agriculture. Henry Wallace had also been vice president under Roosevelt until he was passed over in favor of Harry Truman. Wallace despised Truman, whom he thought smallminded and vindictive. He was worried about the direction in which Truman was taking the country, instituting loyalty oaths for civil servants, creating a subversive activities board, proclaiming the Truman Doctrine to save the world from communism. Wallace believed the doctrine was a sham and would be used to curtail civil liberties. The Progressive Party was founded by disaffected liberals and free-floating radicals to oppose all this, and Wallace agreed to be its candidate. He was enthusiastically supported by the Communist Party, whose members, along with non-Communists, did much of the legwork that went into organizing and campaigning. I wrote speeches for Wallace, believing in his cause and disbelieving in the two major parties, neither of which had enthusiasm for anything but war, cold by preference, hot if necessary.

The 1948 campaign was another failed attempt at creating a third party, but not, I thought, because of my speeches. They were good enough for Harry Truman, who, turning left for votes as his underdog campaign wound to a close, started using their themes, arguments, even phrases. I would write about the need for national health insurance or consumer protection or help for small farmers, and hear it echoed in a Truman speech. The Progressive Party became the last gasp of the movement that had started in the thirties, the coalition of labor and liberals, Socialists and Communists, that flourished as the New Deal during the Depression and as the antifascist Popular Front during the war. It failed to win enough support to become a viable political force and lasted only a few years.

By then the cold war was heating up and a blacklist was needed to keep it stoked. The list included anyone who had belonged to or otherwise supported liberal or radical causes. It was generous in its selection, incorporating, among others, unionists, doctors, dentists, academics, government employees, housewives, artists and performers. Communists were effectively demonized and liberals marginalized; even if the latter jumped on the anti-Communist bandwagon, they were not considered really necessary to the crusade. Spies abounded or were thought to abound. Slogans proliferated: Better Dead than Red; Beware the Red Under Your Bed.

Two FBI agents called on me at Ritt's home to ask about a college acquaintance, William Remington. A woman named Elizabeth Bentley had admitted spying for the Soviet Union and accused Remington of doing the same. He had denied it. I had known Remington only slightly at school. He had graduated two years before me and I had not seen or spoken to him since. I remembered him with appreciation, though. He had spoken out on my behalf when as the movie reviewer for the college newspaper I had come under virulent attack by what seemed like the entire student body. I had panned the movie *Lost Horizon* for, among other things, being too escapist in those grim times. This had not sat well with Dartmouth students, many of whom were majoring in escapism. So Remington's sympathy was welcome, although it did not keep me from being fired.

I told the FBI agents what I knew, which was nothing about Remington's politics, and they left without asking anything more, although I realized later that I had unwittingly told them a good deal about myself and the Ritts. Remington was later convicted on Bentley's testimony and sent to prison, where he was beaten to death by another inmate. I remember him throwing the javelin on the football field on warm spring afternoons, a tall, serious blond young man, older than most students because he had taken time off to work for a while on the Tennessee Valley Authority, a little aloof, a bit mysterious, no hint anywhere of doom.

Still, *The New Yorker* planned to send me back to Yugoslavia to cover the trial of General Draža Mihailović, the Chetnik leader accused of collaborating with the Germans. I was a reasonable choice, having been there during the war. I had preserved my contacts. But Harold Ross, the editor, called me in to say he had received complaints that I was too left-wing for the assignment, that I would be biased in favor of the Yugoslav government. This cut no ice with Ross, who had a vast, pleasing ignorance of politics. He assured me that *The New Yorker* was full of Communists. He knew who they were, he said, naming not only several liberals but also some of the conservatives. Nobody was going to tell him whom to hire, and if he didn't like what I wrote, he would simply not print it. He was reassuringly foulmouthed and I liked him very much. But the State Department stalled on giving me a passport, never giving any reason why it was delayed, its answers to me and the magazine couched in bureaucratic double-talk: The application is under review, there are certain (unspecified) problems, you will hear from us. But we didn't hear and finally the trial was held and I never did get to Yugoslavia.

Then Marty got a job directing on television and offered me work.

Television was new. Television was exciting. Television was free! There was no admission charge; all you had to do was buy a set. Television was this wonderful electronic tabula rasa that everyone was rushing to write on. Is it film? Is it theater? It's television! The fact that it was shot live brought it closer to theater. On the other hand, you did shoot it with a camera. Nobody knew anything. It was unique. You could not stop a show once it started. There were no retakes. You could not edit what you shot; you cut in the camera. And you had to be careful how you moved that camera if you used more than one. A long cable led from each camera to its electrical outlet and you could roll over another camera's cable and produce an alarming bump in the shot. This could not always be explained as an artistic effect. If an actor forgot his lines, everyone else had to improvise. Work was full of surprises, not all of them welcome.

But the air was also full of young, eager talent and many of the shows had the excitement of discovery. Marty was directing a half-hour dramatic show called the *Somerset Maugham Theatre* and I adapted a few Maugham stories. I also wrote for a show called *Charlie Wild, Private Eye*. This half hour had a total budget of five thousand dollars, of which fifteen hundred was skimmed off the top by the packager. The producer, Herbert Brodkin, doubled as the art director and I wrote very fast. Then Marty moved on to produce a dramatic show for CBS called *Danger*. The director was Yul Brynner, who at the time was more interested in the camera than acting (he was an excellent photographer). But Marty's love was then the theater and he left to direct Broadway plays while Yul left to act, reluctantly and with no great expectations, in *The King and I*. His place was taken by his assistant director, Sidney Lumet, and Charles Russell became the producer.

Both Lumet and Russell had been actors, Lumet as a child on the Broadway and Yiddish stage, and Russell briefly as a stiff and embarrassed leading man in Hollywood. There he had been for a while under personal contract to the producer Sam Spiegel, then known as S. P. Eagle, who paid him $125 a week and loaned him out to studios for $750. Lumet and Russell were totally dissimilar. Russell was tall, Lumet short. Lumet bristled with energy, Russell was shy and diffident. Lumet dressed rather like the kid in *Dead End* he had once played on the stage. Russell was elegant, buttoned-down Brooks Brothers. Like most directors, Lumet needed and relished control. Russell accepted it with reluctance. Lumet was ebullient, Russell self-effacing. Lumet had the talent, Russell the taste. They made a happy, successful team. I worked for them with pleasure, turning out half-hour melodramas with tragic endings. The pay was low, the censorship relatively mild. There was nothing we felt we couldn't do. We were creating a new art form. It was a heady, satisfying time.

Until my agent called the day I saw the man beating his wife, and I used a pseudonym for the first time. The pilot script had been for Young & Rubicam, the advertising agency. In those days advertising agencies often produced their own shows and then sold them to a network; this was before the networks figured out where the money was and started producing for themselves. The pseudonym I chose was Paul Bauman. The choice was random; the name had no particular relevance for me. In fact, I rather disliked it. Perhaps that was the reason: If I could not use my own name, I would use a false name I could disdain or even disown. So Bauman went on the script, and it was submitted to the advertising agency.

Then my agent called again. The producer wanted to see the writer. He had in mind a few script changes and would like to see Bauman in his office later that afternoon. I told my agent that was impossible. Too many people at Young & Rubicam knew me as my real self, whoever that was getting to be. He hung up, annoyed. But soon he called back, his spirits lifted. He had fixed it. He had told the producer that he was firing Bauman because he was uncooperative and refused to change anything in his script. He had found the producer another writer to do the changes. I said that was fine with me and asked who was the other writer.

"You," he said.

He told the producer that he had managed to get Walter Bernstein to do the rewrite and that Bernstein would be showing up at five o'clock. I asked politely why he couldn't have put my name on it before, since now there seemed to be no problem.

"You can't be too careful," he said.

So I went to see the producer as myself and sympathized as he told me how unprofessional Bauman was. He would certainly never use him again. The meeting was very pleasant. We agreed on the changes and I quickly did them. The producer was pleased and wondered why the agent had not gotten me in the first place, since I was obviously a much better writer than Bauman.

Until then, in the face of all the evidence, I had never really believed that I would be blacklisted. I still thought in terms of what I deserved. I didn't deserve to be blacklisted. Unfortunately this was not a view shared by those hiring me. Soon after the birth of Paul Bauman, I delivered a *Danger* script to Charles Russell, as usual under my own name. This time he said he had bad news. He did not want to tell me in his office and took me downstairs to a bar. It was still morning, early for drinking, but he ordered a scotch and, realizing there was trouble ahead, so did I. The bar was quiet, dark and empty, perfect for bad news.

Russell said he had received a call from a man named Albert Taylor, head of CBS Business Affairs. Taylor was very friendly and complimented Russell on the quality of his shows. However, he thought Russell was paying his writers too much, especially Walter Bernstein, who had recently gotten a raise from $250 a script to $300. Russell said he thought the payment was fair and Taylor said, well, maybe Russell should think about it. The next call was from Dan O'Shea, the executive in charge of Business Practices. O'Shea also said Russell was paying too much for scripts. On top of that, he was using Walter Bernstein too much. O'Shea said the world was full of writers; why not try a few of those? He was not as friendly as Taylor.

Russell had then consulted his immediate boss, William Dozier, the executive producer of dramatic programs. Dozier was a smooth former movie producer who had once been married to Joan Fontaine. He knew his way around. He told Russell what Russell already knew: that O'Shea's suggestion was not really a suggestion, it was an order. Bernstein was not to be used again. He was on a list. Dozier told Russell to tell anyone who asked that they were changing the style of *Danger* and needed a different kind of writer.

It was a transparent excuse that sounded reasonable. Shows were always being changed and the first move was usually to fire the writer. This was not because executives could tell one writer's style from another, as I had recently discovered with Bauman, but because firing writers was easier and safer than firing anyone else. Executives do not like firing each other because the person fired might one day surface in a position to fire them. Writers, however, are never in a position to fire anyone.

Now, as we sat in the bar, Russell told me the truth. He could use this script under my name, since it had already been contracted for, but subsequent scripts would have to be under Bauman's name. Naturally CBS would not know about this. Russell had no politics himself, only a belief that what was happening was wrong. We were not yet friends. He was taking a very big chance. If found out, he would lose his job and possibly land on a list himself.

I knew these kinds of lists had been compiled. Back in 1947 three ex-FBI agents had formed American Business Consultants (ABC), bankrolled by a businessman named Alfred Kohlberg, best known as a lobbyist for Nationalist China. The "Business" part referred to radio and television networks and the advertising agencies that controlled the casting for the network shows. The "Consultants" determined, for a fee, whether these casts were free of Communist taint. An additional fee could be paid by those accused who wanted to come and clear themselves and so remain employable. In essence, it was a protection racket. ABC also published a newsletter called *Counterattack* that pointed out which tainted performers were appearing on what shows. It gave the names and addresses of the programs' sponsors and urged its readers to help defeat communism by writing in protest to these sponsors. It all had an efficient circularity: First make the accusation; then offer protection against what you had created. And the climate was ripe. Terrified networks, agencies and sponsors fell into line like saloonkeepers during Prohibition when Al Capone came to call.

Later ABC published a booklet called *Red Channels*, subtitled *The Report of Communist Influence in Radio and Television*. This listed 151 actors, writers, directors, producers, painters and musicians, together with their alleged Communist or Communist-front affiliations. *Red Channels* became the bible of the blacklist movement. There were eight listings for me, all of them true. I had written for the *New Masses* and *Mainstream*, both Communist publications; had joined organizations in support of the Republican side in the Spanish Civil War; had joined another organization to demand more rights for black veterans of World War Two; and had been active for Soviet-American friendship and Russian War Relief. I would have felt insulted if I had not been included. On the other hand, inclusion in *Red Channels*, however honorable, meant an automatic blacklisting. No one ever questioned this; it was simply accepted by the networks and movie studios. There was no government edict behind it, no proof of illegality, moral turpitude or, even worse, lack of talent. If you were in *Red Channels*, you were blacklisted. As a network producer testified in a lawsuit, "We cannot take any chances. We quarantine everybody in the book."

Unless you recanted. This could be done publicly or privately, in person or through a signed statement, directly to the studio or network or through one of the anointed experts, such as George Sokolsky, a Hearst newspaper columnist, or Fredric Woltman, a reporter for the *New York World-Telegram*. Usually a simple denunciation of previous activities and beliefs was enough. It was not like being summoned before the House committee, where clearance could be obtained only by informing. But sometimes a more telling action was required. One accused actor prominent in the liberal caucus of AFTRA, the actors' radio and television union, was told by CBS, then engaged in negotiations with the union, that he could prove his Americanism by renouncing the left and joining the right-wing caucus. He did, hating himself, and continued to work, hating unemployment more.

So I was blacklisted. Officially, if without public acknowledgment. For the next eight years in films and the next eleven in television.

But what had brought me here? Was it only politics, or might it also have been movies, the lure of their shadows? Or could it be a mixture of the two, movies and politics, a seductive blend of the real and the more than real, colluding in a fatal synergy?

I embraced them both, secure in revolutionary romanticism.

CHAPTER

2

sit crouched low in my seat at the Century Theater in the Crown Heights section of Brooklyn where I live. I am hiding from my father, who walks up and down the aisles, whistling the familiar theme he uses to summon his children. It is Saturday afternoon and the rabbi is coming to our home for my weekly bar mitzvah lesson. But on Saturdays the Century shows not the normal double feature but a triple feature, plus newsreel, short subject, serial, cartoon and coming attractions. I entered when the doors opened at noon and am not due out until six and I am not about to give that up for learning in Hebrew that now I am a man. After a while my father leaves and I slide back up and give my full attention to Jack Holt and Ralph Graves in *Dirigible*. Or was it *Submarine*? It hardly matters. The two buddies will fight over a woman and then make up when one of them crashes or sinks and the woman will be set aside while men rescue one another. They and I know what being a man means, what is really important, and you don't learn it from Hebrew lessons.

BY THEN I had been going to the movies for some time. The first one I was permitted to see was *The*

Noose, starring Richard Barthelmess. I was five or perhaps six. I have little memory of the film except of being frightened by the villain, an actor named Montagu Love. He was the first in a long line of movie villains who I always knew were indestructible. If the hero won, it was a fluke. The game had been fixed. There was no way in how I saw the world that any hero, crippled by sensitivity and honor, could prevail against such confident villainy. Later, during the thirties, when the heroes lost some of their purity and became more rugged and even corrupt, I could concede their occasional victory. But not then, not yet, not before the great crash that destroyed the innocence of that world. What I mainly remember is how I felt on entering the Albany Theater for the first time, passing out of the known daylight into the enveloping dark with the bright, flickering, enticing, enormous screen at the far end, hearing a kind of strange, tuneless music I had never heard before. It came from a piano below the screen and I knew it was designed for me alone to enhance a sense of pleasurable dread. I let go of my uncle's hand at once, let go of more than that, knowing that in some fundamental way, at least for this short time, regardless of what was up there on that screen, I was safe.

We lived then with my mother's parents and two of her brothers. No one besides me really cared much about movies. My parents preferred the theater, which was unusual in their set, where the standard recreations were movies and card-playing. My uncles, who had both served in France, only liked war movies. My grandmother liked going to the movies in the afternoon, when she had finished cleaning her house and preparing dinner, and she didn't care what was playing; all she wanted was an hour or two of undisturbed rest. She would settle down in the dark theater and go to sleep, lulled by the music and the silent figures on the screen. But she returned home one day upset and angry. She was finished with movies. The figures on the screen were keeping her awake. They were talking out loud. She felt betrayed and never went again.

My grandmother was a shrewd, illiterate, lusty woman whom I adored. She dominated her husband and her children but deferred to me, not only the firstborn grandchild but a boy. She would pick me up and swing me around until I was dizzy. My mother would read the tabloids to her, the *News* and the *Mirror* and the *Graphic*, and my grandmother would nod sagely at the lurid stories of murder and fornication and sudden, undeserved wealth. Nothing really surprised her.

"America *goniff*," she would say with a shrug. America thief. Land of opportunity.

She had a survivor's understanding of her adopted, buccaneer country. Politics for her was the art of knowing whom to bribe and voting the straight Democratic ticket. She had followed my grandfather from Poland or perhaps Lithuania or Russia—no one was exactly sure, the borders were always shifting—and worked in sweatshops with him and she knew which side bread was buttered on. One of her sons, my uncle Nat, was a bit of a scoundrel and stole the car of a young woman he was presumably courting. The woman went to the police, but unfortunately for her, she turned out to be a Communist. This was just after the Palmer raids, a post–World War One period of witch-hunts against immigrants, anarchists, socialists and other riffraff. How my grandmother found out about this, I don't know, but she did and went for the jugular. She managed to smear the young woman enough to exonerate my uncle, the authorities happily conniving. As a sop to justice, however, he was forced to join the navy. The family considered this an act of shame, a Jew in the military (his father, after all, had fled Poland to escape this), but it was marginally less shameful than going to jail, which was what Uncle Nat seemed determined to do.

After the navy, though, he returned and went straight. He had his mother's energy and her nose for what was permissibly illegal, so he went into business. The family had already made the business move from the sweatshop to the store and the social move from the Lower East Side to Brooklyn, and Nat went to work in the store. It was called the National Clothes Shop and was on Delancey Street in Manhattan. I liked Nat because of his loud, good-humored vulgarity and loved visiting the store. It was always full of friendly cops watching amiably while my uncles measured neighborhood gangsters for suits that had to be let out a little around the chest to accommodate their artillery. There was also a movie theater down the street and I could occasionally inveigle an uncle to take me there and leave me for a while, although once they closed the store and all of them came with me because the picture was *The Patent Leather Kid* (also with Richard Barthelmess) and it was about the war and boxing, which was another militant activity my uncles and I both liked.

This was all on my mother's side. My father's impoverished family had arrived from Russian Poland, settled in Brooklyn and remained poor. But my father and his two younger brothers had worked their way through college and two of their sisters had married professional men. My mother's family looked down on anyone who had an education but no money. They were ignorant people who considered themselves canny. They saw no value in learning that did not make a dollar. They tolerated my father because he was a schoolteacher, which at least meant steady employment. But education on his side of the family inevitably brought politics. He had a sister who was a charter member of the Communist

Party. She was rarely talked about, an unseen, rejected presence who I sensed was dangerous to have around. In the early thirties she went to Moscow as a secretary for the Comintern, taking dictation from the likes of Dimitrov and Togliatti, typing her unquestioning way through history. Much later I encountered her on marches for civil rights or against the Vietnam War, a tiny, determined woman, armored in belief, still faithful. But when I was a child, her radicalism was something to be avoided, a stain on the family even worse than Uncle Nat's larceny, which did not compromise his Americanism.

I considered all this irrelevant. Tom Swift was relevant, and Don Sturdy and the Boy Allies and the Brooklyn Dodgers and, above all, the movies. My father loved his sister but had little to do with her, and that was all right with me. He was a careful, thrifty man, who taught night school as well as day and umpired ball games on the weekends to make extra money. He liked umpiring better than teaching, although he rose to be principal of a junior high school. His teachers liked him, though, and gave him gifts. When he became a principal, it turned out that two of his students were the children of the manager of a local movie theater, and that meant I could not only get in free but sit in the mezzanine. I would go after school on Fridays, which still left Friday night free for another movie if I could get one of my uncles to take me. Saturday matinee was when I went alone, standing by the box office with my dime in hand, trying to get some complicitous adult to take me in. I didn't care what I saw, although I had preferences. Love stories were boring because kisses only held up the action. Movies were action to me, images that moved. I loved war movies and sports movies and gangster movies in about that order. My ideal movie was *Corsair*, starring Chester Morris, an actor with a jaw almost as square as that of Richard Dix. Morris played a college football hero who fights in World War One and then comes home to become a rumrunner. I had to be dragged out of the theater.

My father had chosen teaching because it did not then require a graduate degree. He was the eldest of five children and he had his parents and siblings to support. His own father had been an unenthusiastic tailor in the old country but quickly gave that up in the new. He spent his time helping out at the local synagogue. He was the only one there who knew English and he would translate for anyone who needed help. To me, he was an old man who never shaved and who smelled of whiskey. His beard scratched my face when he kissed me. He was considered saintly at the synagogue, but not at home. Saintliness did not put food on the table. He was also a Socialist, although I did not find this out until he was dead, when my Red aunt told me. It seemed he had no use for making money. His children looked down on him, but they came to terms with this when he died. They made him finally respectable, their parental failure, this immigrant who had rejected the dream. They had a small obituary published in *The New York Times* with the heading "Abraham Bernstein—Small Business Man."

After he graduated from Columbia, my father had been offered a position with William Fox, the movie pioneer, but there had seemed no security in that raffish, upstart business. He always regretted not taking the job, but he kept it to himself until very late in life, when he told it to my sister and me sitting around a table, drinking coffee after my mother died. My father felt the job with Fox might have released some adventurous part of himself that being a schoolteacher had not. But he had chosen security and compensated by going to the Elks Club gym after school each day and playing four-wall handball until he was exhausted. Afterward he would come home and nap until dinner, his snores shaking the house. He was a man who embarrassed his children in restaurants by finishing what they left on their plates. But that need, that cold legacy of his early poverty, lessened after he retired. Then my mother died and another burden fell away and the ice broke a little. He became generous. He still took empty containers to restaurants so he could bring home any bread or pickles remaining on the tables, but then everyone his age did. They had won the right in a lawsuit. He died at eighty-nine while on a cruise with his girlfriend and his last words, to the ship's doctor, were whether he would be able to dance that night.

Because my father was protected by civil service, we were not really affected by the Depression. We moved every two years or so, always within our pleasant, middle-class neighborhood, but that was because you could get the first month or even the first two months rent-free. When I was still in grammar school, a troublesome tooth sent me weekly to the dentist for a year and during the long trolley ride I would peer through the window at the lines of silent, patient depositors waiting outside the failed banks. They were there whatever the weather, all through the year. But I was merely curious. I had my own pain to consider. When it was not on my aching tooth, my mind was on my hapless, hopeless Dodgers. I had no time for bank runs.

We lived that year on the edge of an area called Pigtown because the people there raised pigs. They also raised goats and even the occasional cow, and they lived in shacks built from scrap lumber and odd bits of metal they would scavenge. They had tough, wiry children who amused themselves chasing the Jewish kids home from school. I used to wonder how they knew we were Jewish, although I later realized that was no problem for anyone wanting to chase Jews. Most of the time I came to no serious harm. I was not fast, but I was slippery. In the winter we would combat them with snowballs made from a thin layer of snow wrapped around a large piece of coal and then dipped in water so it would freeze. More than one Gentile head was laid satisfyingly open with these.

Grammar school was a nightmare; I was a terrible student. I like to think now that I was probably dyslexic, but maybe I was just dumb—or trying to get even with my father. He knew teachers in my school and, hoping for praise, would come around for information on how I was doing. I hated his showing up, denying he was there for anything other than to walk me home, but actually, as I knew, to get the goods on me. I knew I couldn't trust him. When I had loose baby teeth, he would ask to see them, promising he wouldn't touch, and then, my trusting mouth wide open, he would force the tooth out with his fingers. So it could have been a willful, unconscious trade, my stupidity for his expectations, unprofitable but satisfying.

The agony was slightly less in high school. I went to Erasmus Hall, one of five thousand students on three shifts. My horizons widened even as my formal education continued to lag. Math and science were as Sanskrit to me; only English provided succor. Still, the Astor Theater was immediately next door to the school, and when I caught the six-thirty-to-noon shift, I could squeeze in a movie before going home. I had twenty-five cents for lunch, which bought a hot roast beef sandwich with mashed potatoes and gravy, apple pie and a glass of milk at Bickford's cafeteria, but I could easily forgo that. Admission at the Astor was only a dime during the day and that still left fifteen cents for candy. Nourishment was not a problem.

The rabbi's lessons by then had been changed to midweek, since getting me there on a weekend was too much trouble, and I was finally forced to confront my bar mitzvah. The ceremony was lavish, held in a fancy banquet hall on Eastern Parkway called the Park Manor. There were several hundred guests and a full orchestra. I stood at the entrance in my new blue suit and accepted presents with hypocritical gratitude. There were the inevitable fountain pens, but also a few typewriters and $175, mostly in gold pieces, which I loaded into my pockets. I had been allowed to invite five friends, and we were all quickly bored. After eating everything we could get our hands on, we sat stupefied on the dais, making obscene remarks about the grown-ups. I was having the normal miserable time of a bar mitzvah boy. My stomach ached from too much food, and my cheeks burned from being pinched.

Then I remembered there was a double feature playing down the street at Loew's Kameo. No one would miss me; this whole affair was for them, anyhow. I alerted my comatose friends, and we slunk out without telling anyone. No one noticed us. We stayed for only one feature, though, an enormous and uncharacteristic sacrifice on my part which I hoped my parents would appreciate. But when we came out of the theater, police cars were racing up and down the parkway and I arrived back at the Park Manor to find my parents frantic. My mother tearfully hugged me—she thought I had been kidnapped—while my father instantly went for my pockets. He was relieved to find the $175. No one asked what movie I had seen. I never saw any of the gold pieces again, but I got to keep two of the pens and one typewriter.

Eventually, after what seemed forever, I graduated from Erasmus, to my surprise if not my parents', who took this sort of thing for granted. I was helped by a friendly English teacher who prevailed upon my physics and chemistry teachers to pass me. They might have done this, anyway; I was on the cusp. Or they may have simply recoiled from the idea of having to teach me for another year. By that time I had unaccountably been accepted at Dartmouth College, a mystery considering my marks. But my father had a friend, a Dartmouth alumnus, and that school gave special weight to alumni recommendations. There was, of course, the possibility that someone had been fixed. Where I came from, that was not to be lightly disregarded. Perhaps the college was running low on applicants from Brooklyn. Dartmouth prided itself on its geographical diversity, which meant a uniformly white, middle-class student body except with differing accents. I didn't much care where I went, so long as it was out of town and had a respectable football team. The idea that I could get in anywhere at all was elevating enough.

Then, shortly before I was to graduate in January, my father offered me a chance to go to the University of Grenoble in France for six months before entering college. He knew a teacher who had lived with a French family there, and I could stay with them. Grenoble had a special language course for foreigners. I qualified with my four years of high school French, a language I had successfully battled to a draw. The offer startled and confused me. It came from nowhere. It did not fit into any pattern I knew or even desired. I did not know how to react. My only experience away from home had been summer camp when I was ten and eleven, but there had been no oceans to cross and no language barrier. I knew I would be going away to college, but that was normal and familiar. This was scary.

I did not know what prompted my father to give me this wild, dubious gift. He had never been overly generous with me; I had had to fight him for a subscription to *Boys' Life* and it was my mother who would slip me money for the circulating library. I knew that in some way, like my going to an Ivy League college, the trip meant more to him than it did to me.

If I had had a choice about where to go for six months, I would have picked Hollywood. He had aspirations for me that I did not share. Acceptance was important to him and it could be validated only by some WASP stamp of approval. He had fought so hard to achieve comfort and respectability, but he always felt it circumscribed, restricted by his timidity or simply being Jewish, at peril always of its being taken away. He lived at the discretion of the Gentiles and he wanted to make me secure by giving me advantages, plunging me so deep into the Protestant heart that I could not be dislodged. But acceptance came naturally to me; I took it as my assimilated due. And so I resented him for this generous offer, seeing only his need and not his love.

And yet I could not refuse his largess, frightened as I was. There is a snapshot of me before sailing that bleak winter morning. I stand on the pier next to my friend Stanley Edgar Hyman. The USS *United States* looms in the background. I wear a felt hat and an unhappy smile. Stanley looks skeptical, already a critic. Behind us my family is a looming, unfocused presence. I am sixteen years old.

The trip across justified the unhappiness. I was seasick most of the way and a kind passenger plied me with crystallized ginger as a remedy. All that did was establish a permanent hatred of ginger. My Paris hotel room was gloomy and had no soap. The French word for soap was foreign to me, as were most other French words, and I had thoughtfully neglected to bring a dictionary, so I rang for a chambermaid and acted out furious washing for her. She brought me towels. My French family met me in Grenoble (there was soap on the train) and they were pleasant and kind, but they spoke no English. My classes at the school were also entirely in French and I could not understand a word. The only thing I understood was that when you pronounced the letter *t* in French, you put your tongue behind your bottom teeth rather than behind your upper teeth, as in English. The only reason I got this was that the teacher demonstrated it.

I was also too shy to speak to any of the other students, all of whom were older than I. So, after the first fruitless week, I bought a secondhand bicycle and sped off ostensibly to school every morning and never went near the place again. The school didn't care since it already had my tuition, and my parents didn't care because I never told them. I would just cycle around the city, taking in the sights. I developed an efficient system of shrugs that, added to my few French words, served well enough in stores and restaurants. I was never taken for an American, and that somehow pleased me. My accent seemed to baffle people, most of whom thought for some reason that I was Hungarian. There were movies to see, but they were inconveniently in French. The only one in its original version was the Max Reinhardt rendering of *A Midsummer Night's Dream*. It had an all-star cast that included James Cagney as Bottom and Mickey Rooney as Puck. I thought that Warner Brothers had gone mad. At the end of the day I would cycle back for supper. We lived on a hill about five miles out of town and my room looked out over the Isère Valley. I would sit by the window at twilight, watching Mont Blanc in the distance, its snowy peak glittering white at first and then, as the sun set, slowly shading to pink and then orange and then fading as the mountain disappeared in the dark. After supper I read and then reread the two books I had brought, *The Sun Also Rises* and the Studs Lonigan trilogy. I also drank wine for the first time. The family only drank red wine, which they watered. I spoke very little at meals, too cowardly to expose my limitations, but I shrugged a lot. Everyone was very nice to me. I was desperately lonely.

Then I ran into some English students. They were sitting at a café, talking and laughing. They were a few years older than I and seemed very sure of themselves. I was too shy to approach them, but the next day they were there again. The third time they acknowledged me. They, too, spent little time at the university and preferred roaming the city, looking for action. They were all Communists, which was what had drawn them together. And they introduced me to politics. There was a lot to be political about in that spring of 1936. There was Hitler and there was Mussolini. There was fascism and there was antifascism, mostly led by the left. In France a Popular Front government had just been elected, a coalition of Radical Socialists, Socialists and Communists. Trouble was brewing in Spain. There was still a Depression. Sit-down strikes had broken out. Cycling through the streets of Grenoble, we would wave to strikers hanging over the balconies of their occupied buildings and they would wave back and we would all sing "The International." I knew nothing of Marxism, but I had discovered proletarian internationalism.

I also knew nothing about the proletariat. I knew the little we all knew then about Hitler and the Jews. Relatives had begun arriving from Germany with stories. I had seen the long lines of despairing people outside the shattered banks. And now I knew what I felt singing along with those men and women on the balconies. I felt as I had felt at war movies. There was nothing else with which I could compare this feeling. It made me tingle as I did when my hero went over the top or took his Spad into the air against Richthofen's Flying Circus. Tears came to my eyes. No one was getting killed or performing any obvious feat of heroism here; they were just people laying claim to their workplace. But they moved me the same way. Maybe it was the singing, the hold that music takes on the heart. Maybe it was my desire to please these new, necessary friends I had made. I wanted their approval and they were so certain in their beliefs; I had nothing to go up against them with, even if I had wanted to.

And I didn't want to. I was looking through sixteen-year-old eyes, awash in adolescent sentimentality. But there was something more than that, a feeling that may have been romantic but was not sentimental, a new kind of contact with people, with these strangers on the balconies, a sharing with them of something different and important. Not only the music but the words of "The International" stirred me. We were fighting not just for these strikers but for the whole human race. The idea was staggering. It expressed what I wept for in movies, what moved and thrilled me the most: people fighting not only for themselves but for other people, and now for the whole world. Only this was not on a screen; this was in the streets and the people were real. I did not know what place it all held for me, what those words actually meant, what the sharing would lead to. Any fighting was far in the future for me. But I had found what would form me politically for the rest of my life. I had found an ideal and a cause that I believed was noble.

The closest of my new friends was a lanky, towheaded boy named Robert Conquest, who was preparing to go to Oxford in the fall. He was a very militant Communist and later in life he became an equally militant anti-Communist and the foremost expert on the Soviet gulag. But then he was fervent in his radicalism. Together we cycled from Grenoble to Geneva and around Lake Leman and back to Grenoble. We had a very fine time. We met an Indian youth who was bicycling around the world and went partway with him, and once we were nearly run over by the *Hindenburg* as that doomed dirigible suddenly appeared over us on a low practice run. It looked like some enormous blowup toy escaped from a gi-

ant's nursery, threatening in its mindless bloat. We watched
with a child's wonder as it drifted over our heads, so close we
thought we could touch it, sailing confidently to the next
year's fiery crash at Lakehurst. Our bikes had no gears and
the mountains were high and sometimes it took us four hours
to get up an Alp and ten minutes to get down. If we were
lucky on the ascent, we could catch on to the rear of a truck
and let it pull us to the top.

In this way my truancy continued for the rest of the semes-
ter and then it was time to go home. I had become proficient
in bicycling and shrugging, but not much else. My horizons
had widened a bit further. I had become politicized, if not sophisticated. I said a fond good-bye to my French family, feeling I had not gotten to know them at all. It may have been
because of my shyness or callowness or not having enough of
their language, or perhaps it was just the unrevealing French.
Still, they had been kind to me. Conquest was going on to
Spain, where there was to be a Workers' Olympics as an antifascist alternative to the regular Olympics in Berlin. He asked
me to go with him, but my finances did not allow for this. We
did travel to Paris together and found a cheap room to share
for a week. We walked around during the day and in the
evenings we went to a penny arcade where there was a shooting gallery. If you hit five bull's-eyes, you won a bottle of
cheap champagne. Conquest turned out to be a crack shot
and we would take the champagne to a table and after that it
was up for grabs which came first, finishing the bottle or getting sick.

One night, when we had drunk just enough to be still feeling good, we were approached by a well-dressed Frenchman
in his thirties with the mildly battered face of a prizefighter
who had not taken too many punches. His English was good
and his manner friendly. He bought us a bottle of much bet-

ter champagne. He invited us to his apartment overlooking the Bois de Boulogne. There seemed no good reason not to accept. We were all men of the world. His apartment was full of autographed pictures of movie stars and athletes, all dedicated fondly to him. I recognized Maurice Chevalier and Georges Carpentier. We had more champagne. It was now past midnight and we wondered how late the Métro ran, but he assured us it ran all night. Then he told us about this spot in the Bois where at two o'clock in the morning beautiful women came from all over Paris to have sex with unknown men in the dark. It sounded promising. We were in no shape to question.

We left his apartment and entered the Bois. He led us deeper into what seemed an increasingly dense forest. If what these women wanted was dark, they were certainly getting it. I was not exactly uneasy, but the champagne was wearing off and some little sense returning. It had no chance against the vision of all those pliant, undiscriminating women. I looked over at Conquest but could barely see him. Then we came to a fork in our path. Our helpful guide said either way would take us to our assignation. He suggested we split our forces and meet at the other end. In a flash Conquest disappeared. Our French friend then took me firmly by the arm and started leading me into some bushes. At this point lust sensibly gave way to terror. I tried to pull away, but he was too strong. He assured me I had nothing to fear; he was not going to hurt me. He was getting excited and struggle was getting me nowhere. Desperate, I grasped at reason. I told him I couldn't. He said I could. I said I couldn't. He wanted to know why. I was being outreasoned. I was also being dragged into the bushes. I said the first thing that came into my head.

"My doctor won't let me!" I cried.

It was an inspired fiction. Bringing a medical opinion into

the situation was clearly not what he expected. It had a lunatic plausibility. Disarmed for the moment, he relaxed his grip to think this over and I tore away and ran. He ran after me. I could see nothing in the dark and kept bumping into trees, but so did he. Finally, exhausted, I fell to the ground and huddled under a bush. I could hear him calling, assuring me of his hygienic intentions, and once he passed within a few feet, but finally he gave up and went away. I lay for a while longer until I was sure he had gone and then got up and tried to find my way out of the park. I wandered up one path and down another until I finally saw the shapes of buildings and came out onto a street. In the distance was a Métro station, but of course the subway had stopped running hours ago. So I walked back to the Rue Pont Louis Philippe, arriving along with the sunrise. Conquest was awake in bed reading. He had also gotten lost in the dark but had managed to find his way out while the subway was still running. He was pleased I had retained my virtue.

We parted fondly and reluctantly after that, more men of the world than ever. Conquest went on to Spain, but there was no Workers' Olympics. Franco's rebellion broke out and Bob happily picked up a rifle to fight for the Republican government against the fascists. His family took a different view and yanked him quickly back to England and Oxford. I sailed home to America and Dartmouth, where I had another kind of culture shock. I had seen Brooklyn and Paris and I had seen the Alps, had lived in sight of them, and I had even had a glimpse of the Mediterranean, but I had never seen New England. It was early fall when I arrived in Hanover, New Hampshire, and the blaze of color in the trees stunned me, as did the hard beauty of the countryside in which sat this picture-postcard colonial campus, all that magazine America promised.

I also had never seen young men wearing jackets that

didn't match their pants. In my Brooklyn, at my age, you wore a sweater or a suit. I felt more out of place than I had in France. But going to class in that first tentative week, admiring the easy social graces of these self-assured prep school graduates, I also felt a weight drop off me, a sudden absence of an anxiety that had been with me since first grade, like what I had felt on first entering a movie theater. It was a revelation. School had ceased being a nightmare. I knew I would not have to work to pass courses here. Particularly after Erasmus Hall, with its five thousand scratching, biting, clawing students hungry for a degree, a scholarship, a way to escape the cruel grip of the Depression; after that, Dartmouth was going to be easy. Its standards were lower and the competition was feebler. I might be outclassed sartorially, but otherwise I could relax. There need be no hard studying, no fear of failing. I paid for this attitude, of course, but that rueful understanding came later.

However, even remote, conservative Dartmouth could not entirely escape the outside world. The former editor of the college newspaper had been a left-wing firebrand named Budd Schulberg. He had graduated the year before I arrived, but he had shaken up the campus with news stories and editorials that included support for causes like striking Vermont quarry workers. He left a legacy of political action and now the Spanish Civil War arrived, bringing speakers and rallies to raise money for the Loyalists. I was still full of revolutionary fervor and joined a chapter of the liberal American Student Union and also found a tiny cell of the Young Communist League which, although secret, still managed to be ineffectual. There were never more than four of us and we would meet sporadically and discuss underground what we had already discussed overground. Occasionally a Party organizer would appear to find out what we were doing, but we weren't doing anything but talk. Sometimes he tried to get us to distribute the *Daily Worker* on campus, a request we chose to regard as a joke. It was hard enough getting students to read the *Daily Dartmouth*. And while I was interested in politics, I was more interested in movies and getting on the humor magazine and finding a varsity sport I could play. Dartmouth was all male and three hours from the nearest women's college, so there were no women to get interested in.

I got lucky with the movies when the graduating critic for the *Daily Dartmouth* recommended me to take his place. The job also came with a free pass to the local theater. The only catch was that there were no screenings or previews, so you had to write the review before seeing the movie. I found this no real impediment. I considered it a challenge, a spur to the imagination. Anyone could review a movie after seeing it; that was mere criticism. Doing it this way made it art. You had to read the publicity handout from the studio, make an educated guess at what the movie was about, decide how good or bad it probably was, and write the review. There was a certain purity about the process. It was unsullied by reality. Also, I quickly found that my batting average was as good as or better than that of critics who had actually seen the movie first.

So I sailed along happily until I panned *Lost Horizon*, a movie beloved by the rest of the student body. I didn't just call it bad, I called it escapist, irresponsible in these perilous times when action, not Hollywood escape, was wanted. The review was righteous and very high-minded. It carefully omitted any reference to all the other Hollywood escapist movies that I dearly loved.

The response was immediate. It was as though I had awakened some sleeping undergraduate beast. Letters to the editor poured in, calling me a Red. They called me other things as well, but that predominated. No one mentioned that perhaps I had not seen the picture. The editor, a gentle young man named Harold Berman, thought it best that I be replaced. No one objected. I had few supporters besides Bill Remington. No one considered it a civil liberties issue. No one missed me. I was sorry to lose the job, especially since I was really right about that one. It meant that I would now have to pay to go to the movies.

Getting on the magazine had not been difficult, since there were few applicants. Finding a sport to play was harder; I was small and I was slow. But I was quick of hand and eye and so I became a fencer. The chief advantage of this was that it got me out of Hanover during the spring mud season. Our manager was canny enough to make most of our matches away and we visited Harvard, Yale, Columbia and Princeton, getting trounced at each stop but enjoying the trip. We were not very good. Still, I did enter a state tournament and won possibly the most qualified trophy in sport. I became the 1937 New Hampshire YMCA Grade B Foils Champion, a title that just managed to fit on a very small loving cup.

I lived those college days in a state of amiable schizophrenia, split between the wish to belong to this congenial elite and a growing political radicalism. The college gave me room for both. It was a time when that was possible. Being radical was considered a not totally unreasonable response to a system gone murderously out of control. The Depression continued with millions of unemployed. Hitler grew more powerful, aided by the willed torpor of the democracies, while Maxim Litvinov of the Soviet Union called vainly at the League of Nations for collective security against fascism. Radical ideas were in the air and taken seriously, so long as they remained in the classroom.

I belonged to an official college group that brought guest

speakers to Dartmouth. Liberal and even Marxist speakers
were welcome. The best ones were English and the best ones
of those were Harold Laski, who taught at the London
School of Economics and had a little black mustache and
stood very straight and dissected capitalism drily in words
that burned like dry ice; and the very young Auden, looking
like the village idiot, who gave a dazzling speech on Kipling
and afterward sat drinking endless cups of black coffee before chasing his student hosts around their dormitory rooms.
The president of the college had once said that if Leon Trot-
sky came to America (he had recently been expelled from the
Soviet Union), Dartmouth would invite him to teach. I
quoted this in the humor magazine after the college had dis-
invited Earl Browder, the head of the American Communist
Party, when our student group contracted for him to speak. It
didn't get Browder to Dartmouth, but it got me quickly summoned to the dean for an apology.

Otherwise the college was tolerant of radical opinion.
Communism was not yet a threat in the Connecticut River
Valley. And I was in love with New England. Frequently, on
clement weekends, I would take off at daybreak and start
walking along one of the back roads, thumbing rides when I
grew tired. People picked me up without suspicion and I went
wherever they took me. They were farmers mostly, friendly
without condescension, drily curious about where I came
from, often sharing a sandwich or an apple with me. Most
were poor. Many lived in the kind of shacks I remembered
from Pigtown in Brooklyn. But this was a more isolated kind
of poverty, less voluble and more austere, pitiless in its rural
desolation. I had thought, in my provincialism, that poverty
like this did not exist north of New York. Sometimes I wandered too far and found myself at night on a dark road with
no idea where I was. Then I would try to find a barn or an

empty farmhouse, its owners dispossessed, the bank's For Sale sign sagging on the unmowed lawn, and sleep there on the floor or on some abandoned furniture, a pair of legless chairs or a worn-out sofa too ruined to take along, until it was light enough to start off again.

When I had classes I could safely cut, I would hitchhike across Vermont and New York to Syracuse, where my friend Stanley Edgar Hyman was enrolled at the university. It was an arduous trip, but I could usually do it in a day. The roads were full of lonesome salesmen who drove long distances and liked to talk. They were generous, too, like the farmers who picked me up on the back roads. In those days hard times brought out the generosity in people and the salesmen would buy me lunch and even sometimes go out of their way to drop me in a spot more conducive to my being picked up again. Only once, in Utica, was I hassled by cops, but all they did was drive me to the city limits and leave me there.

At Syracuse I would sleep in Stanley's fraternity house and we would eat at a truckers' restaurant called Koegels, where for thirty-five cents you had a choice of three eggs with ham or a T-bone steak, together with toast, cabbage salad, french fried potatoes and Pepsi-Cola. Stanley had become by then an open Communist. He had also started a love affair with another student named Shirley Jackson, an alarmingly thin, eager girl who wanted to be a writer, but who wanted even more to have Stanley's approval, and who would urge me to convince him to let her into the Party. Shirley had no interest in politics, which baffled her; she preferred dealing in the occult, where she felt at home. But she was willing to try if it meant getting closer to Stanley. He refused, claiming she was not ready yet. Fortunately for her kind of writing, she was never ready.

Budd Schulberg returned to live near Dartmouth while he

finished his novel *What Makes Sammy Run?* We met at a professor's house and he became a friend and mentor. His father had been head of Paramount at one time and this gave him great prestige in my eyes. He was one of a string of young Hollywood princes whose fathers, regal studio executives, had sent them to Dartmouth for no reason anyone could figure out. Perhaps it was because of Walter Wanger, a Dartmouth alumnus and movie producer, who boosted the college whenever he could. Wanger was a sincere, humorless man who produced sincere, humorless movies, but his real fame came from shooting a talent agent he suspected of having an affair with his wife, the actress Joan Bennett. Shooting an agent was not in itself enough to make him famous; what did it was Wanger's marksmanship: He had shot the man in the balls. Actually he had shot him near the balls, but close enough so that a certain creative license could be taken. This enabled the story to become part of Hollywood folklore.

Before that Wanger donated film scripts to start a Dartmouth film library and occasionally sent cameramen, editors and other technicians to lecture on the craft. I attended all the lectures and longed to follow these people back to Hollywood and become like Schulberg. Budd was a true prince, attractive in his kindness and good sense. He also spoke with a stammer that added gravity to his opinions. He was still as militantly left-wing as he had been as a student and I looked up to him, feeling this was what one should aspire to, this life that could embrace art and politics, each serving the other with stern moral purpose.

There were other influences. I decided that to be a proper Marxist I should probably read Marx. *Capital*, however, proved impenetrable. The economics eluded me totally, except for the theory of surplus value. That had been explained to me at the age of twelve by my uncle Irving, the socialist, while we were walking along the lake at Camp Copake, The Island Paradise, where my family summered. An amateur boxer, Uncle Irving had also shown me how to close my fist when I threw a punch, which actually came in handier. *The Communist Manifesto* was another matter. That hit me like a thunderbolt with its great hammering phrases, its wrath and coruscating wit, its combination of praise and contempt for a capitalism that could produce so much wealth yet so much poverty, its promise of another system, inevitable in its coming, that would finally make men human in the truest, highest sense.

I lay in my off-campus room, cutting classes, reading Marx and Engels and Lenin. I read the social novelists, Dreiser and Norris and Dos Passos and Steinbeck and Louis Aragon and anyone similar I could get my hands on. I read Upton Sinclair and Lincoln Steffens, *Pelle the Conqueror* by Martin Andersen Nex and *Jean Christophe* by Romain Rolland, which made me think I understood what it meant to be Beethoven. I read until I was sodden with words. On vacations, I searched out Russian movies, becoming dazzled by Eisenstein, impressed by Pudovkin, moved by Dovzhenko. These were directors as good as my idol, John Ford. It was gratifying to know that one of my favorite Ford films, *The Lost Patrol,* had been taken from a Russian movie called *These Thirteen.* And like his movies, theirs were heroic. They validated my romanticism. The books had opened my head. The movies opened my heart. A new world was being created and I wanted to be active in the creation. Meanwhile, back at school, I became editor of the magazine, won my letter on the fencing team, learned about classical music, looked at modern art for the first time, took a course in Proust that by itself made college seem worthwhile and in the long spring twilights lay on the grass of my arcadian campus and listened to the fraternity glee clubs compete in song. There was no contradiction anywhere. I was where I belonged.

I graduated in June 1940. In the four protected years I had spent at college, the Spanish war had been lost and the Holocaust begun. Czechoslovakia had been abandoned to Germany. The Soviet Union had then signed a nonaggression pact with Hitler, stunning everyone. How could the land of socialism make peace with Hitler? Liberals decried it; radicals split over it. I saw the pact as self-preservation, loathsome but necessary. And then, Hitler invaded Poland. I was at a summer arts school in Massachusetts, preparing to return for my senior year, when the piano teacher brought me the news. He was an Austrian refugee, a plump, sweet-faced man who had conducted symphony orchestras in Vienna. In America he taught piano to surly children and fell in love with motels. He could not get over the fact that instead of an impersonal hotel room, you could stay in your own little house. It had some important American meaning for him.

When he told me, I was picking raspberries, half going into my hat to be taken back for pies, the rest into my mouth. My hands were stained purple from the juice. Our immediate feeling was a sense of guilty relief. At last the issue had been joined. Hitler would have to be confronted and I had no doubt that eventually he would be beaten. I could already see the war movies in my head. But the Communist Party saw the war, without the Soviet Union, as an imperialist war and not to be supported. Back in my Young Communist cell, reduced to three by graduation, we agreed this policy was stupid and immoral. Hitler was still Hitler and we had to be for anyone who fought him. Another Party organizer came to convince us differently. He had a friendly smile and a dent in the side of his head where he had been beaten by company goons while on a picket line. He was very patient with us and totally unconvincing, perhaps because he spoke with so little conviction himself. After our meeting we took him out for a few beers and he confessed he did not believe in the policy either, but it had been decided and had to be carried out. Then, happy to change the subject, he talked about his days organizing Pennsylvania coal miners. He had been beaten up and jailed many times, but he spoke of his work there with fondness and regret, remembering a simpler past when the lines were clearer. He was very likable and later died on Guadalcanal.

But I believed in the Soviet Union. I believed in antifascism and international solidarity and brotherhood and the liberation of man, and the Soviet Union stood for all of these. These were not cant phrases for me. They thrilled and touched me. I listened over and over to the poignant songs of the International Brigade in Spain, haunted by knowledge of that tragic defeat, avoidable if the democracies had helped the Spanish government, and then listened to the Russian Red Army Chorus, stirring in a different, rousing, confident way, the team that knew it was going to win. I was in the grip of a new kind of patriotism, one that transcended borders and unified disparate peoples. It insulated me from another reality: In those same four years Stalin had arrested millions of people in Russia. Millions had either been shot or died in prison. Founding members of the Bolshevik Party were tried and executed as enemies of the state. I knew of the trials but not the terror; still, I paid little attention. I did not read or inquire further or question. The Soviet Union had been under constant attack since being formed; it was natural that there would be spies and saboteurs, agents of a vengeful capitalism. It was my first example of what horror can be perpetrated in the name of security and how easy then to apologize for it. The example was lost on me.

I graduated into a world of anxiety and anticipation. The war hovered over everything. People seemed to move in a kind of slow motion; the air itself seemed listless. Hitler overran France and blitzed England. Charles Lindbergh and his America First organization called on Americans to stay out. It was none of our business, and besides, Germany was too strong. The Nazi Bund, an American organization friendly to Hitler, announced a demonstration in Yorkville, the German section of Manhattan. A demonstration was organized against them, Communists, Socialists, Trotskyists and liberals coming reluctantly together in a common cause. We lined the sidewalks along the Bund's route, milling around under our various banners, eyeing one another with suspicion. The Bund appeared, marching down a wide street lined with German restaurants. They did not look formidable; they looked ordinary. But some wore uniforms with swastika armbands and that was enough to create unity on the left. We started jeering at them, calling them Nazis and Fascists. They yelled back, calling us dirty Jew Communists. A small gray-haired woman dashed out of our ranks and began hitting Bund members with her pocketbook. Someone pushed her to the ground and then the ranks broke and the fighting began. The watching police waded in, swinging nightsticks without discrimination. I learned the uses of a tightly rolled newspaper, not to whack but to jab at the eyes. It felt good having the enemy before me; there were no ambiguities here.

Otherwise I stayed clear of the Communist Party, preserving a remote allegiance. I trusted its principles, if not its practices. The Germans and the Russians split Poland in half, but I grasped at what was positive: People would be better off under the Soviets than the Nazis. Certainly the Jews would. Increasingly refugees were arriving in America with horror stories about concentration camps and their information was even getting into the mainstream press, which had so far not been paying any particular attention. The Russians would save the Jews from the Gestapo. My belief in the Soviet Union was boundless. I argued with my friend Stanley Hyman, who had gone to work for the *New Republic*, then a liberal magazine. He and Shirley Jackson had married and were living in a ground-floor apartment in Chelsea. Stanley and I would walk down to the Hudson River and sit on the end of a pier and talk late into the night. Shirley had no interest in our discussions and stayed home and wrote her stories. Afterward, she would show Stanley what she had written and he would explain to her what it meant. She professed not to know; in her own mind she simply sat down and wrote whatever came into her head.

Stanley was no longer a Communist, despising the Party's subservience to Moscow, but to me its lack of independence was less important than the rightness of the Soviet cause. Red was still the color of hope. Also, I had more parochial concerns. I had gotten a job rewriting a play for a theatrical producer who had known me since I was a child. He paid me fifteen dollars a week. For eight a week I found a furnished room in a brownstone on Fifty-second Street off Fifth Avenue. This left a dollar a day for food and movies, which seemed ample. I had long become expert at trading calories for screen time. There was a bar called the Metropole on Seventh Avenue where for twenty cents you got an enormous corned beef or pastrami sandwich, enough to sustain a horse, plus all the pickles and coleslaw you could scavenge from large bowls on the bartop. A nourishing beer was a nickel and the friendly bartender sometimes put a head on it for free. Heartburn was no problem; my digestive tract had been seasoned since childhood by infusions of delicatessen. The play was a manic, shapeless comedy and I worked hard to give it structure and coherence without losing its lunacy. I felt I was earning my money.

Then came the draft. It was not a surprise. Everyone knew the war would come to us sooner or later and we had better be prepared. The Hitler-Stalin pact was still in force and so the Communist Party disagreed, coming out with a slogan: The Yanks Are Not Coming! What did surprise me was my high number in the lottery. It meant I would soon be drafted. Suddenly the menace of fascism seemed remote; self arose in its basest form. I cared about little except that I was headed for the army. It was not as though I were being sent into combat. We were not yet at war; I would just be in uniform somewhere, having a miserable time. But the military to me was still what you only entered, like my Uncle Nat, out of disgrace.

I reported to the draft board at five-thirty on a cold February morning, filled with self-pity. Other draftees trickled in, equally unhappy. The room was in an unheated school basement, and we stamped our feet to keep warm. Eventually a member of the draft board showed up to welcome us—a small, round, hairless man who came in smiling. No one smiled back. He called our names from a piece of paper and then led the way outside, walking ahead of us through the still-dark streets to a subway. There he gave us government transit tickets, told us where to go and wished us luck. The subway took us to an armory, where we lined up with other inductees in a cavernous drill room. There was no heat here either. The line wound past bored doctors in little cubicles, who had us sit down, stand up, bend over and cough. They were followed by the psychiatrists, one of whom kept me longer than usual because I bit my nails. Then we all raised our right hands before an equally bored officer and took the oath that made us soldiers. Our voices echoed hollowly in the huge, dank room. I felt as if I were being sent to prison. The officer left and was replaced by a friendly sergeant. He beamed at us and asked warmly if anyone knew how to work a typewriter. He hinted at privileges. I raised my hand but was elbowed aside in the rush. Later I saw the volunteers sweeping out the room. The example was not lost on me. I had learned one of the great trio of army lessons: Keep your bowels open, your mouth shut, and never volunteer.

I was sent to Fort Benning, Georgia, to become an inefficient part of the Eighth Infantry Regiment of the Fourth Division. Basic training seemed to me essentially ridiculous. We wore World War One helmets and puttees and carried ancient Springfield rifles that were a menace more to the shooter than the shot. Nothing fit, the clothes itched, and the food was inedible. The army seemed totally unprepared for us or anything else. There was no sense of urgency. There seemed no necessity for anything we did. We had been snatched from our homes and abandoned in this freezing, red-dirt wilderness, at the mercy of those who couldn't make it in civilian life. Our indenture was for a year and all anyone thought about was getting out. Most of the recruits in the division were from the North, while the regular army personnel were mainly from the South. This made for interesting cultural exchanges. The most intense of these were the weekly boxing matches, where the finer points of each culture could be demonstrated. The contests were happily uneven. We had among our ranks not only a number of professional fighters and Golden Glovers but also many alumni of neighborhoods like Hell's Kitchen and the New York docks for whom fighting with gloves was considered effeminate. We also had the advantage that while the regulars only despised us, we truly loathed them, along with the army that nurtured and protected them. This added ferocity to skill. The combination made for gratifying revenge.

But I got lucky. One of the company commanders, a

stagestruck West Pointer, decided that what the regiment needed was a show for the troops. We had movies, but he thought there should be entertainment for soldiers by soldiers. The USO had not begun to send out troupes for our amusement; since there was no war, there was no need to uplift our morale. The captain scoured the personnel files and found several of us who had literary or theatrical experience. He had us transferred to his company and I had the agreeable experience of writing a musical comedy instead of going off on maneuvers. Another lucky soldier was commandeered for the music and lyrics. We requisitioned former actors, singers and dancers. This happy pursuit continued throughout the summer while less fortunate draftees fought off chiggers and mosquitoes in the swamps of Louisiana. But the Germans invaded Russia and the war crept closer. I followed their swift, savage advance with apprehension and bewilderment, unable to understand how they could cut through the Red Army with such ease, not knowing how that army had been decimated by purges.

For the Communist Party, the war immediately became one of national liberation. It quickly dropped its slogan about the Yanks not coming, and started forming committees for Russian war relief. Otherwise, the news had scant reverberation where we were. We concentrated on a much more immediate concern: casting the female parts for our show. Fortunately, we found comely young ladies from the nearby town of Columbus. They were all very gracious and invited us to their homes for tea. They had charming southern accents that we often found impenetrable, but this only added to the charm. Each side seemed equally exotic to the other. To us, they were the friendly inhabitants of an alien country, while we seemed to them like arrivals from Mars, albeit with good intentions. This being Georgia, one of the ladies was afloat in Coca-Cola money and would invite us to her summer house for swimming and barbecue. We lived a life that had nothing to do with the army, feeling in some surreal way that we, too, were part of a show, our uniforms only costumes, a temporary obligation.

Our musical was to be the first soldier show of its kind and began to attract attention. *The New York Times* and *Newsweek* planned to send their first-string drama critics to cover the opening, which was scheduled for December 10, 1941. Unfortunately, December 7 came first. I was outside our rehearsal hall that quiet Sunday morning, watching teams of officers play polo and reflecting on how well regular army officers lived in peacetime. Someone called out that I should come inside and I returned, thinking it concerned the show. But everyone was clustered around a radio. The Japanese had bombed Pearl Harbor. An announcer kept repeating, unnecessarily, that this meant war. He kept having to lower his voice as it rose with excitement. We listened silently while from outside came the faint sounds of galloping horses and clicking mallets. Someone said they guessed that now we probably wouldn't get out in a year.

"The hell with that," an actor said. "Now we won't get the critics."

The show went on without the critics and was considered a success, although half the audience got up to leave at intermission since they had never seen a live show before and thought it was over. We had to stand at the door and drive them back. The show did get me transferred to the main post, where I was assigned to the combined intelligence and public relations office. Troops were now pouring into Fort Benning, and journalists descending. There were no more polo matches. A parachute school was formed. The war was going badly, especially in the Pacific, but we were joined with

Britain and France and now Russia, and I felt even more strongly that we were going to win. I was in the grip of a strange, unmerited euphoria, unseemly to express while we were losing. But it was now possible both to cherish the ideal of socialism and to welcome the power of capitalism, to believe in both Stalin and Roosevelt. The enemy was clearly evil. He had attacked us. We had no choice but to resist. The cause was just. We were all in it together. There was something enormously comforting about this. It was also, five thousand miles from any killing, very safe. It was true as well. For the moment.

My new commanding officer was a career colonel who had previously been provost marshal of Hawaii. He was a handsome man with a white, waxed mustache and he wore his campaign hat at a rakish angle. He loved the ladies and the army in about that order. The work was simple and easy: writing press releases and escorting visitors around the post. A woman I knew came down from New York and we rented a tiny house in town and I spent nights there. This was against regulations, since I was supposed to sleep in my barracks, and one day the colonel called me into his office and told me to shut the door. His face was cold as he consulted a file on his desk and asked if I had ever lived at a certain address in Brooklyn. I said that had been my home while I was at college. He then read from the file that a person of my name living at that address was known to be a member of the Communist Party. He didn't ask for an explanation and I didn't tell him it wasn't the real Communist Party, just the Young Communist League. I just stood there. He then asked sternly where I had been spending my nights. I started to lie, and then changed my mind and told him I had been spending them with a woman. It was the best thing I could have said. His face softened; this was the sort of subversion he understood. His tone became avuncular as he explained that I had to sleep in the barracks if I was single, but that a married soldier could live off the base. He advised me to get married. He said he would give me a three-day pass so I could have a honeymoon. Communism was no longer mentioned.

We had not really thought of getting married, but the colonel's suggestion seemed apt. There was a war on, even though it was far away, and no one knew what would happen. There was no clear civilian future anymore, only the uncertain present. Part of me felt I was too young to get married, but I was also too young to die and that had become a definite possibility, however remote. I took the pass and borrowed a car, and we were married in Dothan, Alabama, after we stopped there for lunch. We went to the city clerk's office, where the clerk said I would first have to pass a physical. He gave me the name of a doctor and said it would cost two dollars. The doctor's office was on the top floor of a two-story wooden building. I climbed the sagging stairs, knocked on a flyspecked door and was told to come in. The office was a large, dusty room with an examining table at one end. The doctor sat at a rolltop desk across the room from the door. He wore shirtsleeves and suspenders and wire-rimmed glasses. I stood at the door and told him why I was there.

"Take it out," he said.

I took it out. He looked at it over his glasses from across the room and then muttered that it looked all right to him. I wondered how he knew from that distance but decided not to ask. He signed a certificate, I paid the two dollars and went back to the clerk's office. He rounded up a couple of witnesses and married us. We spent the next two days on a lovely beach in Panama City, Florida, and then drove back to Fort Benning. But getting married had the same dislocated sense of everything else at the time. It did not seem quite real. What was real was that now I could sleep off the base.

What was also real was that I was afterward excluded from any contact with intelligence matters. We may have been allied with Russia, but clearly that went only so far. It was an embrace of mutual dependence and mistrust. The colonel remained friendly, but the dossier on his desk had changed our relationship. I was no longer allowed into restricted files. My contacts were confined to the journalists who came down to write glowing stories about how we were getting ready for war. This was fine with me, since they were nice people, often interesting, and manageable unless they were drunk. Then they would start chasing women or picking fights in bars. At night I went home to the tiny house we rented. Friends would come over or we would visit them or go to the movies. One friend was a black soldier from a truck company whom I had met when he drove some of the visitors around. His name was Avery and he came from Baton Rouge. But he could not chance visiting us until it was dark. There would have been trouble if white people on our block had noticed him coming in our front door. So he would come at night, having parked his truck a few blocks away, and slip in and out unobserved.

Then another transfer came through, unexpected and welcome. An old friend of my family, the playwright Moss Hart, had asked me to look up a soldier who had danced in a musical he had written, *Lady in the Dark*. I had done so and we had become friends. His name was Nelson and he was a beautiful young man from Virginia. His biggest fear was not the war, which he barely acknowledged, but that he would get fat and lose his allure, which was considerable. His next biggest fear surfaced when he crossed streets in traffic. He was certain that a car would run over his toes. I would have to hold his arm and walk between him and the oncoming traffic. One of his lovers in New York was the son of a general and he arranged for Nelson to be transferred to a new army show that was in rehearsal, a musical revue written by Irving Berlin, called *This Is the Army*. While a soldier in World War One, Berlin had written a famous army show called *Yip, Yip, Yaphank*, and this was to be a sequel. All the performers were soldiers, but it was to open on Broadway, with the proceeds going to Army Emergency Relief. When Nelson left, leaving behind a trail of broken military hearts, he promised to get me up there. I never thought he could do it, but, much to my surprise, he did.

I left Fort Benning without regret but with a touch of sadness. Except for basic training, my life there had been pleasant and even rewarding. People had been kind; I felt I had become slightly less provincial. The colonel patted me on the back and told me to stay out of trouble. He said to be careful whom I palled around with. My wife went ahead to find an apartment in New York and I reported to Camp Upton on Long Island. There I found two hundred actors in uniform. Some had been in the army for months, others for just weeks or even days. Their complexions ranged from a deep, healthy tan to the light green of those who had performed where the sun never shone. I recognized some I had seen on the stage or in nightclubs. They all seemed to be enjoying themselves, which was understandable—this was as close to civilian life as a soldier could possibly get. Discipline was healthily lax, although Regular Army noncoms and officers abounded. The tone was generally set by the comics. If a sergeant called for a formation to fall out, you could usually count on someone falling flat on his face.

I was assigned an office and given publicity duties, which again consisted of writing press releases and ushering around visiting reporters. I looked up Nelson, already dancing in a chorus, and thanked him. He was very happy to be back in the dance world, especially since he was going to perform a number in drag. My office was a room in a Quonset hut and I was no sooner installed than a middle-aged civilian came in without knocking. He was small and dapper with a thin city child's face. We had never seen each other before, but he held out a sheet of paper. On it were the lyrics for a song.

"What do you think of this?" he asked without preamble.

I didn't know what to think. The man was Irving Berlin. I thought at first he was joking, but he stood there patiently, waiting for an answer. I looked at the lyrics. The words seemed simple and banal and I made a few hesitant suggestions. He nodded, thanked me and went out again. He ignored the suggestions and the song became another one of his hits. Berlin repeated this several times in the next weeks as he wrote the score for the show. He never took my suggestions, not only because they were inapt but because they were irrelevant. He knew exactly what he had and what he was doing. I don't think he even heard what I said. It was simply some kind of necessary ritual. But if we were both working late at night, he would send out for sandwiches or a roast chicken and we would sit in his office, as bare as mine except for his special piano, and share this bounty. His manner was friendly and regal. He, too, had once been an enlisted man, but that was a long time ago.

This Is the Army opened on Broadway (the critics present this time) to great success. The first number included the entire cast singing to the audience from bleachers on the stage. At the last minute an actor from this section fell sick, leaving a space like a smile with a tooth missing. I was pressed into service and told, after the director had heard me sing, that if I did lift my voice in song, I would be shot. I was allowed to mouth the lyrics, but that was all. Since I didn't know the routines, the actors on either side of me each took hold of my uniform and raised and lowered me according to cue. No one noticed the ensemble had a ringer and I was congratulated for my nonperformance.

Afterward I wrote an article for *The New Yorker* about actors in uniform rehearsing for the show. The magazine prepared to print it quickly, while we were still news, but I was summoned before the Regular Army colonel in charge of our outfit and told this was not possible. I had cleared the piece with my immediate superior, a lieutenant, but the colonel had heard that the article ridiculed the army and he wanted it stopped. He had not read the piece and had no intention of reading anything that scurrilous, but he made it plain that if it were published, I would be punished, possibly by a court-martial, certainly by banishment to someplace distant and uncomfortable.

I went immediately to Harold Ross with this news. He was delighted. As a private in World War One he had edited the army newspaper, *Stars and Stripes*, and relished any fight with the brass. He told me how once he had even been thrown into the guardhouse for insubordination. He assured me that no chickenshit colonel was going to tell him what to print in his magazine. I explained that what was true for him was not necessarily true for me. He said not to worry. He had the cheery tone of a fight manager assuring his boy that they can't hurt us. I knew that whatever happened, the colonel would not be forgiving. What loomed in my future was, at the very least, assignment somewhere around the Arctic Circle.

But while I waited in his office, Ross got on the phone to General George Marshall, the army chief of staff in Washington. Marshall had been an aide to General John J. Pershing, who commanded the American Expeditionary Force in the

First War, and Ross had known him then. What I could hear
of the conversation was jovially profane. When he hung
up, Ross turned to me with a big, gap-toothed smile and
announced it was all taken care of. The article would run
without any further interference. General Marshall had also
promised that I would not be court-martialed. He had said
nothing about transfer, however. I asked with some bitterness
if Ross would like an article from the Aleutians, but he said
not to worry about that, either. The army was setting up a
weekly magazine called *Yank* and the supervising officer had
been on *Stars and Stripes* with him and Ross was sure he
could get me transferred there.

So my luck held. Ross's pull was real and I was assigned to
Yank. Its offices were on Forty-second Street in New York
and I reported there to settle in for the duration. The officer
in charge was a colonel named Forsberg who had been a
magazine publisher in civilian life and his assistant was a major named Weeks who had been a reporter on a Detroit newspaper. The magazine itself was written and edited by enlisted
men. Most of the staff either had worked on newspapers or
had some kind of writing experience. The picture editor had
held the same job at the *New York Daily News*. The copy editor took pride in having held what he considered one of the
most useless jobs in the newspaper business: He had been day
city editor of a morning newspaper, in his case the *Chicago
Sun*. The poetry editor was a poet himself whose ancestor
had been secretary to Abraham Lincoln. The editor in chief
was an amiable, slow-moving, quick-witted former sports-
writer from Boston. His name was McCarthy and he reigned
over us with warmth and wit and a rare generosity of spirit.

Forsberg and Weeks ran interference with the higher-ups.
Because of them, we had a rather astonishing freedom. Censorship was minimal and confined to military security, and

we were able to become a forum for the soldier's opinions and complaints, as well as a source of information. We were a motley, privileged group unified by a belief in the war. For the most part we liked one another. We would lunch together at steakhouses like the Palm or Pietro's or go across the street to an Automat. After work we would wander up under the Third Avenue El to Costello's saloon and drink for a while before going home. Costello's had Thurber cartoons on the wall and was always filled with newspapermen, many of them just back from overseas or preparing to go, and there was an air of excitement and anticipation. It was my first taste of war as aphrodisiac. There were also excellent french fried potatoes you could order with your drink, cut in large chunks but very light for their size. Once a month we had to go and drill somewhere to demonstrate that we were still soldiers. We would assemble shortly after dawn and take the ferry to Governor's Island, where we drilled raggedly for a few minutes and then played softball or touch football, according to the season. If the weather was too terrible, we went to a nearby YMCA and shot baskets.

I still went to the movies whenever I could. Many of the younger stars were already in the service, but there was still Cary Grant to command a submarine in *Destination Tokyo*, and Errol Flynn to foil the Japanese in *Objective Burma*, and Humphrey Bogart to foil the Germans in *Sahara*, and Brian Donlevy and William Bendix to die gallantly in *Wake Island*. And there was always John Wayne as a flying leatherneck or a crawling infantryman or simply back on his civilian horse, riding the range. Many of the war movies were written by left-wing writers who suddenly found themselves in demand. Now that we were friends with Russia, the studios figured that the left had some special insight. The studios were always looking for insights that could be reflected at the box office. This uneasy alliance produced movies like *North Star*, written by Lillian Hellman, about Russian resistance to the Germans, and *Mission to Moscow*, based on a book by our ambassador to the Soviet Union. He was played by Walter Huston as he had played *Dodsworth*, a capitalist you could trust.

What these movies said was that the Russians were really just like us and there was good reason why Stalin was called Uncle Joe. I went to them all, checking my brains at the door, and enjoyed most of them. Brains can be a hindrance during a war and they are not necessary to enjoy movies either. It depends which movie you really want to see, the one on the screen or the one inside your head. They are not necessarily the same. These were like the war movies I had loved as a child, had taken to bed with me, running them over and over again in the private theater of my mind, protection against the dark until I could sleep. There was not much difference between Richard Barthelmess, the slacker turned hero in *The Patent Leather Kid*, and James Cagney, the coward turned hero in *The Fighting Sixty-ninth*. The new ones talked and so had more boring speeches, but there were still good guys, bad guys and lots of action. In any case, I thought the Russians were swell. They were taking most of the casualties and saving our ass. All they needed was for us to help them out by opening a second front.

I also had the nattiest uniforms on *Yank*. This was because they were made to order. My uncles had gone from making suits for civilians to making uniforms for police and firemen, and with the war had branched out into making uniforms for the military. They insisted on making them for me. I would ordinarily have been pleased, except that the pants were always too short in the crotch. Quality control was not a high priority at the Strong Uniform Company. Profits came first, and these were generously provided by a lax government eager to clothe a growing army. But whenever I saw a policeman tugging irritably at his trousers, I wondered whether he had been outfitted by my uncles.

Gradually, as the war expanded, *Yank* began sending correspondents overseas. I was eager to go, even after one of our photographers was killed on a Pacific beach. Finally I got my chance and it was even better than I expected. I was to be the *Yank* correspondent in Moscow. Since there were few flights into Russia, excluding the Luftwaffe, I was to fly to Teheran in what was then Persia, and proceed from there. My only concern was that my wife had just discovered she was pregnant, but my parents were there to help. I received various inoculations for exotic diseases and was handed my orders. These said I was to "proceed to Teheran and such other places as may be necessary for the accomplishment of your mission." It didn't say what the mission was. I wondered why they couldn't have said Russia, but this was the army in its infinite wisdom and I was pleased that I seemed to be some kind of military secret.

A crowded civilian train took me to Miami, where I reported to the former Battle Creek Sanitarium at Hialeah, which the army was using as a staging post. I was given a bed in a dormitory and told to shape up every morning to see whether I was on that day's list to fly out. I did this eagerly. I did it for six weeks until it sank in that perhaps something was wrong. Even for the army, the wait seemed excessive. I had not given much thought to this because after the first week my wife had come down and I could always get a pass and meet her at the beach and this did not allow for serious thinking about the war. Finally, though, I asked the commanding officer why my name was never called. He looked up my file and said the problem was simple. Everyone flying out had to have an assigned priority; the higher your priority, the sooner you got out. Unfortunately it was not that my priority was low; *Yank* had simply neglected to get me any priority at all.

I hastily called the *Yank* office in New York. They were surprised to hear where I was. They took for granted that it was my fault, that I had fucked up in some novel way, but when I explained what had happened—or what had not happened—they assured me cheerfully that they would get on it at once and I would be out of there tomorrow. Meanwhile, I was not to go anywhere. I said there was nowhere I could go. This time they acted properly, but sent me back where I'd come from. A telegram came from Washington giving me the highest priority to fly at once to New York and report no later than seven o'clock the next morning to an embarkation point at the Brooklyn Navy Yard. It was marked "urgent" and signed by a general.

So I flew for the first time in my life. The experience was thrilling, especially since I had been told that a full colonel had been bumped to make room for me. I boarded a two-engine TWA plane at eleven-thirty that night and arrived at La Guardia at six-thirty the next morning. The ride was bumpy and we made several stops on the way. I was too excited to sleep and sorry I couldn't see anything. I found a taxi at the airport and raced to the Navy Yard, remembering the urgency of the telegram, the signature of the general and the bumping of the colonel. Surely there must be a plane waiting to take off exactly at seven, probably on a mission vital to the war effort. I arrived just before the hour, raced into the embarkation office and threw my orders and the telegram at the officer in charge. He looked at them without interest. He had never heard of me. Panting, I pointed out that I was supposed to fly to Teheran.

"Are you fucking blind?" he asked rhetorically.

He pointed out the window, showing me that this was a shipyard, not an airport. No one flew out of here. They sailed. He didn't know what I was doing there and cared less. I called *Yank*. They were still cheerful. They said they had arranged something better for me than mere flying. I was going to Teheran by boat. They said I would be sailing in a week. I asked why the urgency to get me back to New York. That, they said, was the only way to get anything done in the army.

The boat was a small, modern Dutch freighter that in peacetime made the run from Holland to Java. The captain was a huge Dutchman named Rommel. He had an enormous belly and a shaven head, and he always wore black patent leather pumps. The other passengers were three newly commissioned engineer lieutenants going to China, two civilian oil men going to Bahrain Island and three Mexican diplomats. Mexico had just recognized the Soviet Union and was going to open an embassy in Moscow. There was also another *Yank* correspondent, Sergeant Marion Hargrove, on his way to India. Hargrove was a witty young Southerner who had written a humorous book about his basic training called *See Here, Private Hargrove* which had become a best seller. He was good company and treated his fame with quiet diffidence. There was also a navy gun crew for our protection, headed by a soft-spoken ensign named Berkeley who had been a research librarian at the University of Virginia. We carried a cargo of high explosives, most of it in the holds but some in crates strapped on the deck. We were to travel without a convoy. The ship was young and fast and could outrun most submarines, at least those we knew anything about.

We sailed from Philadelphia, through the Panama Canal, around Australia and up to Khorramshahr on the Persian

Gulf. The trip took forty-two days. We saw no submarines, although there were a few scares. We did see a lot of flying fish and magnificent sunsets in the Indian Ocean that lasted for hours, filling the sky with Technicolor brilliance, another kind of movie. We slept two to a cabin. Meals were served by a tiny Javanese steward. Most of the time he served us a Dutch version of an Indonesian dish called rijsttafel, a collection of what seemed different meats served with a great deal of rice. This was deliciously novel at first, but after a couple of weeks the novelty wore off. Also, after a month all the liquor gave out except for champagne. This did not seem too terrible in the abstract, but in the actual drinking it led to monumental hangovers. The passengers had no duties and were expected only to stay out of the way of the crew. During the day we read or slept or walked the deck and stared out at the endless sea, looking nervously for submarines. Everyone was aware of the cargo we carried. Look at it crossly and it could go off. We were torn between wanting to see a submarine, if only to break the monotony, and being scared to death one might appear. We were not so much bored—after a while we were beyond boredom—as suspended. Time had no meaning in the absence of volition.

Still, there were actions to be taken. I made friends with one of the gun crew, an Italian boy named Tony who had had his first professional prizefight just before being drafted. Tony had a long nose and eyebrows that met in a tangle of black hair and on the back of his life jacket he had painted "Tony from Brooklyn." When he heard I came from there, he clapped his hands in delight. He would tell anyone who would listen that Brooklyn was God's country and turn to me for confirmation. He could not walk without shadowboxing and he would get so involved throwing jabs and hooks that he would forget where he was and had to be watched carefully so he wouldn't fall overboard. Tony was studying to take the naval examination that would advance him to the next grade, but he had not had much schooling and the lessons were giving him trouble. We made a trade: I would tutor him in exchange for boxing lessons. He was a patient, gentle teacher and always apologized when he rapped me a little too hard. He would urge me to hit him harder. He had hopes for me; he had a friend, Maxie Shapiro, who had turned professional at my late age. But once I caught him with a right hand under the heart and stepped back, seeing that I had hurt him. He urged me on and I hit him there again. He told me to keep coming, but I was halfhearted after that. He shook his head sadly, sensing the lack of a killer instinct; there was obviously no future in the ring for me.

The Mexican diplomats also gave me lessons. Their passion was bridge, a game I had never learned, but they enlisted me as a fourth, generously and amiably teaching me how to play. I learned poorly; bridge was like chess in that it filled me not with pleasure but anxiety. But they were courtly men who overlooked my mistakes. Otherwise, I would talk literature with Ensign Berkeley or lie in the bow of the ship, watching the flying fish. The seas were calm except when we passed between New Zealand and Australia, and then we hit storms. We sat on the floor in the saloon, yelling like kids as the ship pitched and yawed and we slid steeply up and down from wall to wall, pursued by the furniture.

We made our first stop at Perth, Australia, the little city full of little houses with umber-colored roofs, and I ventured out in search of a bookstore since I had exhausted the ship's scant reading matter. But it was a holiday celebrating labor and the only bookstore open was a left-wing one. I bought pamphlets by Marx and Engels and Lenin and carried them happily back to the ship. From there to the Persian Gulf, I lay out on the bow, reading about how history occurs twice, first as tragedy and then as farce; how man creates his own history, but not as he pleases, only under conditions laid down for him; how the state will wither away under communism. The words and thoughts exploded the world I knew, forming new, crystalline ways of seeing and understanding. I married them to the war, feeling they were part of a final, necessary struggle that would end with a new and better world.

We landed in heat that made Georgia seem like Alaska. The air shimmered with it. Our clothes were clammy with sweat as soon as we stepped off the ship. The hot breath caught in your throat. A waiting port officer told us with relish how his men were dropping like flies. Locked in this hell-hole, he took disaster as a compliment. I said good-bye to Tony, who assured me that I had a possible future in the Golden Gloves, but to forget about turning pro. Hargrove and the other passengers were flying to their various destinations and we said our farewells with varying degrees of fondness. I would miss Hargrove and the Mexicans. I was booked to take the train to Teheran, but the port officer offered me the alternative of riding up in one of the army trucks bringing lend-lease supplies to the Russians. He said it might make a good story since what passed for roads were so rough that after a few trips the truck drivers would begin pissing blood. I took the train. The trip lasted ten interminable hours, the train creaking through a parched and desolate landscape. Occasionally horseback riders would race alongside, bearded men waving rifles at us. I had seen pictures of beautiful, scenic Persia, but this roadbed had not been laid out for tourists.

Teheran was a relief, the city sparkling, the air warm but not too humid, snow-clad mountains seen sharply in the distance. My orders called for me to report to the American military attaché at our embassy and I did so with alacrity. The attaché was a dour man who looked at me with vague distaste. He said he had never heard of me. No one had told him I was coming or what to do with me once I got there. I was starting to get used to this. My orders meant nothing to him. Getting into Russia was out of the question. The border was two hundred miles north and, so far as he was concerned, I could go there and look at Russia, but that was as far as I was going to get.

There was no way to call the *Yank* office, so I cabled for clarification. They cabled back that they were sorry no one had told the attaché, but in the meantime the Russians had changed their minds and would not allow a military correspondent into their country. I was to remain attached to the Persian Gulf Command until further notice. This was marginally better than being sent to Devil's Island. The American troops in Persia were there only to ferry supplies to Russia. The work was monotonous and backbreaking, conducted for the most part in frightful heat or bitter cold. If it didn't get your kidneys, it got your head. Each week saw men shipped out as psychiatric cases. When you were not working, there was nothing to do except wish you were somewhere else. I located the local *Yank* correspondent, a sweet, enthusiastic Irishman named O'Neill who turned out to be a fight fan. When he heard that I had been tutored by Tony from Brooklyn, he decided that a good way for us to keep from going crazy was for me to enter the local boxing tournament. He would be my manager. It would give us something to do until my further notice.

I went into training. We decided it was too hot to run unless I got up at three in the morning, and that seemed extreme. A Quonset hut on the base had been turned into a gym, so I went there to work out. I kept asking O'Neill whom

I was going to fight, but he professed not to know. Then, one day as I was doing sit-ups, the door of the hut opened and a soldier came in. He was about my size, but his shoulders filled the room. He had a broken nose and he needed a shave. He looked ominous. As he walked down the hut to greet a friend, he passed one of the light punching bags and carelessly swiped at it as he went past. The bag flew off its mooring and crashed against a wall. My heart fell into my sneakers. I called O'Neill over and asked if this was the guy I was going to fight. He nodded sympathetically but assured me I would have no problem. All this guy was was tough. I would jab him to death, stick him silly. He wouldn't lay a glove on me.

"All you have to do is keep running," he said encouragingly.

I asked how I could both run and stick him silly, but logic did not interest O'Neill. He was into Irish mysticism. As the day of the fight drew nearer, terror finally gave way to resignation. I would be killed and the army would ship my body home. Or, less terminal, I would be maimed and get an honorable discharge. I wished Tony were at my side. No one knew what I looked like; he could fight under my name.

Then the cavalry appeared. A telegram from *Yank* ordered me to Jerusalem. NBC was preparing a special program to celebrate the first anniversary of the magazine. *Yank* foreign correspondents were to broadcast from around the world and I would represent the Middle East. With salvation came fantasy. As I packed my barracks bag, I was certain I could have taken that guy. True, he had had forty-seven amateur fights, but what was experience against talent? I would have stuck and moved and made a monkey out of him. Tony would have been proud of me. I left with visions of glory, flying to Cairo sick as a dog after a night of debauchery with O'Neill. From Cairo I caught a flight to Jerusalem on a

British transport plane. I arrived after dark and checked into the YMCA, where the Red Cross had taken over the third floor for Americans. The building was pure Kansas City Gothic but very comfortable.

And in the morning, I stepped out into a bleached ancient city that held the smell of history as some cities hold the smell of the ocean or the automobile. Looking out at the spare hills, empty except for a few Bedouin shepherds with their flocks, I felt as though I were looking through time instead of space, and backward through time. History had done its work here. The light was sharp and pitiless; all of Jerusalem's tortured history seemed contained in its light. I walked through the old part of the city, stopping at the bazaars to smell perfumes and taste spices and try on handmade leather slippers. The merchants smiled and offered thick, sweet Turkish coffee with the bargaining. They could afford to smile. Palestine had been selected by the American Army as a rest center and this meant the suckers were coming to town. Peddlers were already selling pieces of the original cross. There were four different Golgothas, each claiming to be the real one. Three of them were tarted up and unconvincing. The exception was a simple hilltop covered with scrub grass. You could stand at the bottom of this hill and look up at the grass and the quiet sky and almost believe something had happened there. I visited the Western Wall and watched old bearded men rock in prayer before it and tried to identify with them, without success. I was a nonreligious, self-loving Jew, sure of my Jewishness, comfortable in the Diaspora.

Still, I was proud of the Jews in Palestine. Riding through the countryside, I would see harsh desert on one side of the road and orange groves on the other and feel pride in the struggle and achievement that had made this bleak land bear fruit. I went to a concert in a graceful amphitheater on top of

Mount Scopus next to the Hebrew University. The orchestra was superb; the string section alone was full of first violinists from the orchestras of Europe. The program began with the playing of "Hatikvah," the Jewish anthem, and I suddenly found myself weeping. Somehow, in some way, as much as I might deny it, I was connected here. Mozart and Beethoven followed, played sublimely, and I listened with my throat caught, looking out to the Dead Sea in the distance, thinking, Such a long, bitter road for such a stubborn, difficult people, and still to play like this.

I was proud of the Jews smuggling in illegal European refugees who would otherwise have gone to the gas chamber. I admired how they outwitted the British army and I attended a British military trial of seven Jewish collective farmers who had been arrested in a raid on their kibbutz. Homemade explosives had been found, but what worried the British were the grenades that had not been found, since the captured ones had tested out more powerful than those the British army used and they were worried about where the others might show up. Palestine was a British mandate and its police were to the Jewish community as the Black and Tans had been to the Irish. There was always tension in the air, a feeling that something very big and bad could happen at any moment.

But there were other factors at work here. There were the people who had occupied this land before these recent arrivals. I was not taken with the Zionist slogan, A Land Without People for a People Without Land. Jewish chauvinism made me uneasy. Jewish racism appalled me. The Arabs were simply considered inferior, an ignorant, backward race with no claim to Palestine. I met and took a walk with Gershon Agronsky, a cultivated, charming man who was the publisher of the *Palestine Post*, the daily English-language newspaper. We wandered through an old Arab quarter of the city and he explained how after the war this would all be Jewish. I asked about the people who were living there now and whose ancestors had lived there for hundreds of years, but he dismissed them. They had no right to this land; it belonged to the Jews. The Arabs would have to leave, by force if necessary. He did not even use the biblical argument that God had given this land to the Jews. He was too sophisticated for that. He simply asserted it as a fact.

The broadcast went well and I was then faced with return to Persia. I was saved by the vagueness of my orders. To go to such places as may be necessary for the accomplishment of an unstated mission meant being able to go anywhere. I inquired of *Yank*. They didn't care where I went so long as I sent back stories and stayed out of trouble. I went to Tel Aviv. It was totally different from Jerusalem. It was like Miami Beach without the big hotels. There I found the writer Irwin Shaw, whom I had met briefly in New York. He, too, was in the army. He had belonged to a Signal Corps unit led by the director George Stevens which had been headed for the dreaded Persian Gulf, but he had managed to escape. He was living at the home of a Mrs. Feichenfeld, previously of Berlin, and writing a play while waiting for the army to catch up to him. He graciously invited me to share his quarters, which consisted of one large room with cots on either side. We could work there together, he on his play and I on stories about the weary American fliers brought to Palestine to relax on the warm sands and drink pasteurized milk. I moved in gratefully.

In the mornings Mrs. Feichenfeld, a friendly middle-aged lady, would serve us a Mediterranean breakfast of cheese and olives and tomatoes and peppers with the occasional herring thrown in so we would not forget our origins. Then Irwin and I would sit down at opposite ends of the room, backs to each other, and start writing. That is, he would start writing. From behind me I would hear his typewriter furiously clacking away while I sat increasingly paralyzed. Eventually, not hearing any equivalent sound, he would turn around and ask with some irritation what was the matter with me. Writing, for Irwin, like the rest of life, was appetite. He approached it with relish, admitting no impediments. Writer's block was foreign to him. He just sat down and wrote, as if he were sitting down to a good meal. I would have hated him if I hadn't liked him so much.

In the afternoons we would go to the beach and swim and throw a ball around. Irwin had played quarterback for Brooklyn College, a school not noted for its athleticism, but years of being tackled behind the line of scrimmage had not dulled his fierce love of sport. When we had no ball, he threw himself around. In swimming trunks he rather resembled a genial, clean-cut American gorilla, and little Palestinian children would watch wide-eyed as Irwin lumbered with heavy grace around the beach. He knew a girl, another illegal refugee, and she had a sister and occasionally we would all have dinner together. Tel Aviv was blacked out at night and we would eat outside in restaurant gardens because of the heat, sitting in total darkness, and I never did get to know what either of the women looked like. But the food was good and we ate well as the women told us stories that five years before would have been unbearable but that by now had become routine. Their family had all been killed by the Nazis. They had lived in cellars and forests, had been raped and tortured; they were lucky; they were here.

But there were not enough stories in Palestine for an army weekly magazine and I decided to move on to Cairo. Irwin came with me and we found separate rooms in a pension. We followed the same routine, except that there was no beach for swimming. Instead we would play tennis at the Gezira Sporting Club, a British colonial institution on an island in the Nile. Enlisted men were not allowed there except as servants, but the American military command in the Middle East unexpectedly gave us both civilian correspondent status, which accorded us officer privileges. We would play during lunchtime. The courts were empty then, not only because everyone was eating but also because it was the hottest time of the day. The temperature was usually over a hundred degrees and everyone thought we were insane. The Arab ball boys shook their heads knowingly, waiting for us to topple over. After tennis we would take a refreshing dip in the club pool. I took an adolescent pleasure in feeling I was there in disguise. As a concession to the war effort, the club was letting enlisted men use the pool after five in the afternoon, but, as I heard one dowager explain to another while they sipped their gin on the veranda, it was all right because the pool was cleaned immediately after.

But there were few American troops in Cairo and few opportunities for stories and I wanted to join the war. The invasion of Sicily had just started and so I said good-bye to Irwin and went out to the local airport. I showed my mystery orders to an impressed officer, who put me on a DC-3 going to Algiers. There I tried to find out how to get to Sicily. Unfortunately, because of some high-level military feud, the local command had said no *Yank* correspondents were to be allowed to cover the Sicily campaign. This seemed not only unreasonable but, on my low level, unenforceable. I went back out to the airport and waited for a ride to Sicily.

The airport was hot and dusty and there were more than a thousand men sitting on the ground, being entertained by Al Jolson. He stood on a platform with a piano and a piano player. I had never liked Jolson or his style of performing, which reminded me of chicken fat. He came from a long line of Yiddish performers I had seen too many times, hard-eyed comedians and throbby-voiced song belters who could make my grandmother cry but left me unmoved. Their craft had been honed before killer audiences in nightclubs and the Borscht Belt, where performing was like a Roman circus. It was either thumbs up or thumbs down, and if down you were dead. These homesick soldiers were not in that league. Jolson had them transfixed; they were completely his. Sitting uncomfortably on the hard ground under that blazing sun, they listened and laughed and applauded, forgetful of where they were. He was on for more than two hours. He told bad, dirty jokes. He got down on his knees to sing his trademark mammy song. He was shameless. He had the guts of a blind burglar. I loathed what he was doing and couldn't stop watching.

Afterward a friendly pilot gave me a lift on an attack bomber he was ferrying to Sicily. He stuck me in the nose cone and I lay there watching the waves rush past, slapping against the plane as we flew about ten feet off the water. We landed at Agrigento and I hitched a ride on a supply truck going toward the front. The Americans were moving east along the coast from Palermo to Messina, while the British were paralleling them inland. I figured that the kind of officer coming to throw me out would not be anxious to go anywhere near the fighting, so I headed for the action. I was exhilarated as I reached the coast. The sun was hot and the sea sparkled and I was finally in the war. I stopped at an MP post outside a farmhouse and they gave me C rations to eat and I ate sitting in the doorway, leaning back against the warm stone of the house, feeling again that sense of belonging, of being completely where I wanted to be. There was a whining noise as something passed over my head and then a faint, clumping sound about a mile back of us. I paid no attention. The noise came again, only this time the clump sounded closer. I looked inquiringly at one of the MPs and he shrugged. Then there was the whine and a great crash as a shell landed about fifty feet away and everyone was on his feet, running. Another shell bracketed the house, dirt flying in the air, and I ran into a field with the others and crouched, looking around, not knowing what I expected to see. The whine and crash came again, but this time moving away from us. An MP said the Germans were going after a bridge farther up the road and we were all right now. They were just shortening the range. The MPs stood up and walked back to the farmhouse, which had not been touched. I stayed where I was. My bowels were too loose for me to move. My feelings about war had suddenly and abruptly changed. They had stopped being political or social or idealistic. They had become personal. You could get killed here. In time those other feelings would return—they were too much a part of me—but for the moment they were buried in sweat and fear and the shameful struggle to keep from soiling myself.

I spent the rest of the Sicily campaign with a reconnaissance unit at the tip of the advance. The men in the unit accepted me with some bemusement; they found it hard to believe anyone would be there voluntarily. But they took me along on their actions. The Germans were slowly retreating along the north coast road and the unit's job was to see where they were and what they were doing. They were doing what any normal army would be doing in retreat: trying to cause as many casualties as possible. The road made a series of S-turns and the Germans would mount one of their 88 mm cannons at the head of one of these turns and wait for us to come around the bend. If we went full speed in our jeeps, we had about ten seconds in the open before being under cover again.

During that time they had a clear shot at us. It made for an interesting ten seconds. They never did hit us, but they came close.

The Germans would also lay mines as they retreated. They would mine the fruit trees so that picking a lemon or an orange had to be done very carefully. They mined the tomato plants and the cactus pears that were just getting ripe and they mined the beaches and, of course, the roads. At any hour you could hear a sudden explosion and then the screaming. The local people would warn us about the mines and the presence of Germans in the area. Once we drove up a mountain to an ancient town called Ficarra and had a brief firefight before capturing four German soldiers. They were older men, left behind as a rear guard, and they looked seedy and frightened. They believed we were going to shoot them. They were very anxious to please and kept smiling at us apologetically. I found it difficult to hate them, although I tried. The people of Ficarra had no difficulty at all. The Germans had occupied their town and executed some villagers, and the people wanted to kill them. They were nice to us, though. Ficarra was a poor town, living meagerly off its steep, terraced fields, and the war had made it poorer, but when the shooting stopped, the people came out of their shuttered stone houses with bread and cheese and wine and hugged and kissed us, and as I found wherever I went, there was always someone with a relative in New York.

From time to time I left the unit and roamed the division looking for stories that I would then write and mail off to *Yank*. Once, wandering at night, looking for a place to sleep, I came upon an outdoor movie being shown to weary infantrymen. They sat on wooden benches lined up before a small screen. I joined them to watch a musical called *You Were Never Lovelier*. The print was dim and the sound scratchy, but Fred Astaire was singing to Rita Hayworth and then dancing with her and then dancing by himself, and that was all that mattered. Magic was being performed in this sacred grove as it probably had been for millennia. Only the form was different.

One day a cable was smuggled to me from the press office. It said I was the father of a baby girl. Mother and daughter were doing well in an army hospital on Governor's Island. I felt pleased and detached. The news was both real and unreal. It had nothing to do with where I was and what I was doing. Then an envelope reached me with a picture of the baby. She had black hair and almond eyes. There had been a picture of me when I was a year old, sitting naked on a bearskin rug, and I had had eyes like that. It made me feel less detached, even if I still could not think of myself as a father.

The stories I sent back were usually not about heroics, unless you would call heroic what men subject themselves to in war every day. I would get out on the road with my bedroll and typewriter and pistol and wander until I found a unit that promised a story. It could be an artillery unit's fondness for its cannon or an account of a battle or any of the boring, dreary, monotonous, frightening moments that make up a war. The main thing was to get the men's names and hometowns right. Sometimes I would get taken along on an action and could write directly about it. One day, I got a ride with the pilot of a tiny one-engine Piper Cub that was used for reconnaissance. The troops called these planes "Maytag Messerschmitts" because with their one small engine they sounded like a washing machine. This time my plane was serving as an artillery spotter.

We flew low over the German lines while the pilot radioed back their positions. No one shot at us and it all seemed very recreational, the sea calm and silvery beneath us, no signs of harmful action. On the other hand, the plane was slow and unarmed, and I wondered what would happen if a German fighter plane spotted us. The pilot assured me there was no problem: He could always turn inside any fighter plane and get down lower than it could and, as a matter of fact, he had a kill to his credit for having lured a real Messerschmitt lower and lower until it could not pull up in time and had crashed. He felt we were in more danger from our own antiaircraft. They tended to be trigger-happy and would often shoot at any plane they saw, regardless of which side it was on. I witnessed that myself when I saw an American P-47 shot down by American gunners. The pilot bailed out safely but had to be restrained when he landed because he had his gun out and was looking for the battery that had got him.

Priggish censors killed a story I particularly cherished. Word had circulated that there was a large brewery in Messina and this had become an obsession among the troops. They lived in fear that it might be bombed by mistake and agonized over ways to protect it. One suggestion was to send in commandos to paint a big red cross on its roof. The summer heat had kept everyone thirsty as well as a little crazed. All the men could think about was that cold beer waiting for them. Messina was the end of the campaign, the port we had to secure as a jumping-off point for the invasion of the Italian mainland. The order was to get to the docks as quickly as possible and cut off the German retreat. The first troops to arrive headed straight for the brewery. But they found the British had got there ahead of them and were not only into the beer barrels but swimming happily in the vats. Little was left but to remain sober and get on with the war. Messina was secured and preparations were begun to invade Italy.

I returned to Cairo. My excuse was simple: Sicily was conquered and I needed a rest. More important, I received a per diem allowance from the Middle East Command, which was not true anywhere else. Normally I received my base pay in the local currency and was expected to eat in an army mess. But in Cairo I could afford to sit on the terrace of Shepheard's Hotel and receive the benefits of British colonialism. These included being served by native waiters and watching field-grade officers with high-priced whores. There was more pleasure from watching the arrival of two Red Army officers who appeared one afternoon. This was very rare; almost no one there had ever seen a Russian soldier before. These looked as if they had been selected to make an impression on the bourgeoisie. They looked like movie stars—both of them tall and clean-shaven with high Slavic cheekbones. Medals glittered on their starched uniforms. They looked neither left nor right as they strode confidently into the hotel. Everyone stopped what they were doing to stare at them. The Red Army was not supposed to look like that. These two looked as if they had a right to be anywhere. A few people wondered nervously what they were doing here. Everyone knew about the siege of Stalingrad and the extraordinary defeat of the Germans. The Red Army was now advancing on all fronts, pushing the Germans back toward Berlin. It was possible that the Russians might not stop there. A slight uneasiness hung over the whiskeys and the pink gins.

I also had ideas for *New Yorker* articles that were not suitable for *Yank*, and Cairo proved a congenial place in which to write them. Irwin was still there, finishing his play, and we resumed our grueling routine—writing in the morning, tennis in the afternoon, drinks and dinner in the evening. This time I lived in a room on the top floor of a large building the Red Cross had taken over. The elevator was always breaking down, which meant climbing twelve flights of stairs. At those times I stayed in and ate stale Red Cross cookies and read

Crime and Punishment for the first time. Cairo was not the rest center for American troops that Palestine was; there were only a few supply troops here. The soldiers roaming the streets were mostly British or Australian or New Zealanders, lean and tanned from years of fighting in the desert. They were very friendly and insisted on buying the drinks if they met you in a bar. The New Zealanders included many Maoris and sometimes American soldiers would resent their drinking where white Americans drank. There were cases of racial insults. Finally, the other New Zealanders tired of this and one night they came into town and beat up every American soldier they could find. After this the insults ceased.

In Sicily the brewery at Messina had been placed safely off limits and so the invasion of Italy proceeded with only its normal share of confusion. The British landed first, without too much opposition, and fanned out across the mainland. The Americans landed six days later at Salerno. They were led by General Mark Clark, whom the troops had taken to calling "Mark Time Clark" because of his dilatory nature. But he was helped enormously by General Kesselring, the German commander, who made the mistake in his counterattack of committing his six hundred tanks piecemeal instead of all together. He could not believe the Americans were so stupid as to attack with a force so inferior to his own. But they were and they did, and Kesselring's misplaced confidence in us made Clark a hero and the invasion another famous victory. I finished my articles, hitched a ride to the airport, flashed my convenient orders and piggybacked plane rides from Cairo to Benghazi and then to Naples.

The Germans had just abandoned Naples after destroying as much as they could. They burned down schools and churches and looted the hospitals. They sank ships in the harbor and wrecked the port facilities. They opened up the prisons in the hope that an augmented criminal class would contribute to the chaos. They also, as expected, mined everything they could think of. They were very thorough. They mined the streets. They mined abandoned vehicles. They mined houses, setting explosives so they would go off when someone sat on a chair. They mined bedsprings. They even mined doorbells. They had shot or hanged civilians for their resistance or as retaliation for attacks on German soldiers, and they had left the bodies dangling from trees and lampposts, carefully booby-trapped. I drove in from the airport past the hulks of ships sunk in the harbor, past the bombed-out houses, the air pungent with a mixture of sea smell and cordite, unmindful of the beauty of this ancient city, echoing now with the rumble of tanks and trucks and the blasts of explosions.

I found the *Stars and Stripes* office and the staff invited me to live with them. They had liberated a large apartment in the Galleria, a huge, stunning glass-domed arcade near the waterfront. Miraculously it had not been too damaged by the bombing. The apartment belonged to a high-ranking Fascist official who had fled with the Germans. The *Stars and Stripes* staff was a friendly, vigorous group, led in spirit by their circulation manager, a bald, gravel-voiced ex-bookie named Estoff. He had been assigned to the newspaper because on his induction form he had listed his occupation as bookmaker and the army had naturally thought this qualified him for the print medium. They also employed a translator, a small, thin middle-aged man who always looked hungry. He had been a philosophy professor at the University of Naples until he was fired for suspected antifascism. I would ask him questions about Italian political life which he would answer patiently. I made no secret of my own convictions, and one day he asked if I would care to go with him to a political meeting—the first

open Communist Party meeting in Naples since Mussolini
had seized power.

He took me to a small hall in a side street. The meeting was
in progress when we got there. About twenty men were listening to a speaker who stood under a red flag with a ham-
mer and sickle. They were mostly older men with worn faces.
Their clothes were threadbare, as were those of most Nea-
politans. They listened closely as the speaker talked about the
need to build the Party, contact the young men returning
from the army, organize openly now among the workers. It
was necessary to continue work with the partisans in the
countryside. The imperative was to win the war. The Americans must be helped, the Soviet Union supported. There
should be agitation for a second front.

Some of the men had fought in Spain. Most had been in
jail, many for years. They had fought against fascism, had remained true to their socialist vision. They had never given up.
Defeat and terror had driven them underground, but now
they had emerged, blinking a little at the unaccustomed light,
still defiant. I was very moved by them. My friend translated
as best he could as questions were asked, points debated, arguments hurled. They were making up for lost time. I sat
apart in that hot, smoky room, unrelated to these men who
had fought and suffered and lost and still were here, yet feeling a connection as powerful as I had felt sitting in that
Jerusalem amphitheater, feeling that both connections were
true and necessary for me but that this connection, this vision
shorn of tribalism, embracing the world without distinction,
was what held me most strongly.

I left Naples after a short while and followed the war
north. This meant getting out on the road and scrounging
rides. The roads were full of refugees fleeing the war or trying
to return to their homes in a liberated area. Families pulled

carts and carried chairs and tables on their heads. Many of the women seemed to me very beautiful. They had olive skin and black hair and an air of great dignity. The kids were not so dignified. They would cling to the jeeps and trucks creeping by or run after them, begging for cigarettes and candy. All the towns had been heavily shelled, and we rode through rubble and past houses with their sides blasted open. You could see rooms with the furniture still in place. One room had a table still set for a meal; a large picture of Rudolph Valentino hung on the wall. The war did not stop children from doing what they always did, using whatever they could find as a playground. They played tag in the rubble or killed imaginary Germans or, on the rare warm day, swam in the deep shell holes that had filled with rainwater. Some of the houses had blankets hung over their exposed sides and it was startling to see a small figure suddenly burst through to leap into some newly created swimming hole. Sometimes a child dived perilously off a roof. Once I saw two little boys patiently fishing in one of the shell holes. There could not be any fish in there and I did not want to think what else they might bring up.

The front was long and viscous at that time, twisting all across Italy, the Allies slowly pushing forward as the Germans stubbornly retreated. When they made a stand, it was very bloody. This kind of war was different from Sicily. That had been affectionately described by the British general Bernard Montgomery as "a model fifty-eight-day campaign." This campaign was a model for slaughter. Every advance was paid for in bits and pieces of flesh. The weather didn't help. The autumn rains whipped down and seemed never to end. Tanks and trucks stalled in the mud. Mules were brought up to take their place. Rations were eaten cold out of tins and the men slept wrapped in their groundsheets, huddled in the mud or shivering on stones. No enlisted man was ever completely dry and no one was ever warm. One night I stumbled into a cow barn where a platoon had taken refuge and lay luxuriantly in straw, warmed by the heat of the animals and lulled to sleep by the comforting splash of cows pissing throughout the night. Battles were fought for a mountaintop, men lugging their weapons up steep, treacherous trails, hoping the air force had cleared the way for them, knowing the planes could not do what they would finally have to do. And when they had gained the mountaintop, what they saw ahead was another valley to be crossed under fire and another mountain waiting to be climbed and conquered.

I wrote about these men and their heroism. I did not write about cowardice or doubt or the mistakes of generals or the killing of prisoners or the alliance with the Mafia in the towns we took. Or about the corruption that always follows war. Or about my own fear or the shame I felt when I refused the chance to go with a unit stringing wire under heavy bombardment, knowing the casualties it would take. No one forced me to go anywhere; these men were the ones who had no choice.

But then, as if to demonstrate the murderous indifference of war, that particular bombardment reached back to the command headquarters where I stayed, forcing everyone to leap for cover. I dived into a ravine and cowered while shells fell with a gleeful lack of discrimination. A man wearing a correspondent's patch and three cameras around his neck jumped in beside me. Instead of cowering, he stood and smiled at me. He ignored the death raining around us. It seemed not to be worth his attention. There was something very graceful about him. Even in this bedlam of artillery fire, he had an air of delicacy and tact. He noticed my fright—not difficult to do—and started gently talking to me. He wanted to know if I had read much Tolstoy. He made it seem as though given the circumstances, the question was entirely natural. I have no memory of how I answered, but he eased me through my terror. When the bombardment finally stopped and there were only the shouts and groans of the wounded, he smiled at me again and climbed nimbly out of the ravine. Afterward I found out his name was Robert Capa. I remembered his photographs of the Spanish Civil War. I never saw him again and was saddened, but not surprised, when years later I heard that he had been blown up covering the war in Vietnam.

I wandered through the war, picking my spots. I was lucky to see *You Were Never Lovelier* twice more, once under a tent at a field hospital among wounded men watching with dead eyes and again in a small, ruined town where the army had commandeered the movie theater. Fred Astaire still danced and sang to Rita Hayworth while Adolphe Menjou fumed. I found myself watching with a lump in my throat. Nothing had changed; the screen still knew the secrets of my heart.

There was a battle for Monte Cassino and I went to see what that was all about. It was about a monastery on top of a mountain. The Germans were in it and we wanted it. Several probing attacks had been repelled and now everyone was more or less waiting to see if we were going to have planes try to bomb the Germans out of there. This was more a problem of politics than simple warfare. The monastery was not only sacred but a treasure-house of art. It contained the culture of fifteen centuries. No one wanted the responsibility of destroying this. Proposals were made to outflank Monte Cassino and leave the Germans sitting there useless, but this seemed too sensible for the military mind. So the small attacks continued while the advance stalled. I drifted around the base of the mountain, ducking the occasional fire from above, and fell upon a British unit where I was introduced to hot, sweet, life-giving tea drunk safely in the lee of a hill while artillery crashed all around us.

Later I joined part of a mountain division that had unwittingly penetrated far ahead of the rest of the war. We ended in a small village recently occupied by Germans who had hanged the mayor and six others because a peasant had killed a German soldier who had been stealing his chickens. We stayed there for six days, waiting for the rest of the army to catch up, and I slept in a real house in a bed with sheets. There was even a sit-down toilet. The villagers greeted us with great enthusiasm and cooked us spaghetti and made us pizzas, apologizing for the quality of the flour, which was brown instead of white. They happily reported the top local Fascist, claiming he had helped the Germans, but the battalion commander said he had no evidence of that, and besides, we were bringing democracy to them and that meant anyone could be anything he wanted to be. They thought we were crazy. The village had been occupied but otherwise spared. It had not been shelled or fought over and the buildings were all intact. But the day we pulled out, the Germans had located us, and as we trudged out of the village, we heard the low, rising whine of a shell. Everyone ducked, but the shell landed behind us in the village. It was followed by several others. We continued on, the shells passing over and hitting the houses we had just left. An old man ran after us, cursing Americans and Germans both. Behind us, in the village, the familiar screaming had begun.

Then I hurt my leg jumping out of a jeep into a ditch as a German plane flew over our road. It was after an ammunition dump farther ahead and flew very low and I could see the pilot clearly, young and blond, as he banked and a bomb flew out in a spiral like a perfectly thrown pass. It missed the dump and the plane flew off. I limped out of the ditch, but the leg hurt badly enough to give me an excuse to return to Naples and then, deciding I still couldn't move around too well, I hitched a ride back to recuperative Cairo. I could have moved well enough to cover a war. I had just had enough for a while.

What really decided me was a visit from a poet. I knew him only from his work, which I admired, but we had a mutual friend who had told him to look me up. He found me at the *Yank* office which had just been opened in Naples. The poet had been in the army for only six weeks, but that had qualified him as an infantryman and he had been sent over as a combat replacement. He was very frightened. He had heard that replacements right now had a very short life span. This was true. The new men were sent into units where the surviving members knew and looked after one another, and where recruits were more of a liability than an asset. Their inexperience could get you killed. They were avoided as much as possible and left to fend for themselves, and this only added to the casualties. Replacements died so quickly that they were often ordered to write their names in large letters on their helmets because they were not around long enough for anyone to get to know them by name. So the poet was right to be scared. He wanted to know if I could help get him out of combat. I knew someone in special services and managed to get him transferred to a theater unit doing plays. He survived the war—but he never spoke to me again. When we met on social occasions, he would not look at me. He did not want to be reminded of how he had been. He had been only human, but I knew how he felt.

Cairo was pleasant, sociable and safe from artillery and planes, and I was able to catch *You Were Never Lovelier* again, this time in a large theater crowded with troops from many nations, so that before the performance everyone had to stand and sing or listen to at least five national anthems. The movie was a little hard to see because there were subtitles in French, taking up space along the bottom, and in Arabic, running down the sides. This did not matter too much except when Astaire danced and you couldn't see his feet. This movie had by now become a kind of talisman for me, a small defiance of death. As long as the two of us could meet in this enchanted symbiosis, I was safe. Irwin had left Cairo to find his brother, who was stationed somewhere in North Africa, but there were drinking friends to be made among the British and Australians and even the Africans, who did not drink but smiled a lot. And then there were the Yugoslavs.

I knew very little about what was happening in the Balkans. It was a British sphere of influence and they kept a tight lid on news. I knew the Allies backed a Serbian group called the Chetniks, but it seemed there was a larger group of partisans led by a Communist called Tito. Two of Tito's high command had been seriously wounded and the British had flown them to Cairo for brain operations. Now they were sufficiently recovered to give a press conference. I attended with other members of the Cairo press corps. The two Yugoslavs, Vladimir Dedijer and Milentje Popovic, were large men in gray uniforms with red stars on their shoulders. Dedijer spoke fluent English and was the spokesman. He had a craggy face with a prognathous jaw and a confident manner. Popovic had a long face with fine features and the look of a dreamer. They answered questions easily. Their partisan army had come together from isolated guerrilla bands resisting the German invasion of Yugoslavia. It now had about three hundred thousand troops composed of Serbs, Croats, Slovenes, Macedonians and Montenegrins. There were Jews, Muslims and Christians. There was an Italian division, a Czech brigade, a Hungarian battalion, a Bulgarian battalion and even a company of Germans. They called it a people's army, led by Communists but including anyone willing to fight the fascists. Tito's real name was Josip Broz and during the Spanish Civil War he had worked in Paris recruiting troops for the Loyalists. By this time the partisans had liberated half the country; the Germans held the cities and major towns, but the partisans controlled the rest.

Finally a British officer called a halt to the conference and led them away. This was the only time reporters were to be allowed to see them. There was to be no further contact; any questions would be channeled through the British and answered in writing. The excuse was that the Yugoslavs were still recuperating. I thought they were being kept away for political reasons. I had no reason to think this except distrust of the British. We might all be Allies, this might indeed be a common war of national liberation, but the lion was not yet ready to lie down with what might be another lion.

Dedijer and Popovic lived secluded in a suburb, their location a secret. But I found the British corporal who drove them, and after I bought him a few drinks and shared scornful stories about officers, he gave me the address. I wrote them a letter asking for an interview. I made it plain that I represented an enlisted man's paper and I larded it with phrases culled from the works of Marx, Engels and Lenin, making it obvious where I stood politically. My phone rang the next day with an invitation to call on them. They greeted me warmly, amused by how I had gotten to them, and asked a lot of personal questions. When they were satisfied, they got down to business. They were grateful for what the British had done for them, not just for them personally but for their army, to which the Allies had begun sending supplies. But they wanted as much publicity as possible for their cause. The more people knew about them, the more guns and ammuni-

tion they would be sent. They thought the Allies did not quite
know how to handle them and would like to keep them on
hold until they figured it out. The partisans were necessary
for the war effort, but after the war Yugoslavia seemed likely
to be a Communist-led country and this did not thrill either
the British or the Americans. Dedijer thought the British were
trying to get as much control over the situation as they could.
Everyone knew the second front was due to be opened soon
in France, and Dedijer thought that news about the partisans
was going to be held back until then. After that no one would
care very much about the Yugoslavs. They would be buried
on the back pages.

The solution to this seemed to me simple and elegant. I said
if I could get into Yugoslavia, I could interview Tito and report on their fight. No outside reporter had interviewed him
yet; it would necessarily get big play even if first printed in a
military paper. I was not bound by the same restrictions as
civilian reporters. I was answerable only to the American
army. All I needed was a way in. They thought this a splendid
idea. If I could get to the Italian port of Bari, they would
arrange to get me across the Adriatic to Tito's headquarters
deep in Yugoslavia. True, Yugoslavia was occupied by the
German army, but that was a technical matter.

We shook hands all around and I went to the officer in
charge of *Yank*'s Middle Eastern bureau and asked his permission. He also thought the idea splendid but said we
needed higher authority, so we went to a colonel in charge of
an obscure intelligence section. We chose him because he was
a well-known fuckup. He had been sent to Cairo in the optimistic belief that the further from action he was, the less damage he could do. He was pleased to see us, since he had few
demands on his attention. He saw no reason why I should not
go to Yugoslavia if I had been invited. It was, after all, their

country and they could invite anyone they pleased. He also took a dim view of candy-assed Limeys telling an American soldier where he could or couldn't go. He offered us drinks and said that when I got to Bari, I should check in with the Special Balkan Section of the OSS and tell them what I was going to do. He would write to the commanding officer and pave the way for me.

I left Cairo thrilled. Flying into Naples, our two-engine transport plane developed serious engine trouble, but all that meant to me was that maybe we could get down faster. I was in a hurry. Most of the other passengers were panicked, but I sat serenely talking to a calm black colonel with pilot's wings. His name was Benjamin Davis and he commanded the Tuskegee squadron of black fighter pilots. They called themselves the Spookwaffe. His expert opinion was that the odds of our landing safely were about 70–30 in favor of crashing. He was very cool about this and oddly reassuring. But we landed without incident and I was lucky to find a B-25 bomber pilot flying to Bari. He was ferrying a war correspondent, a handsome blond woman named Martha Gellhorn, who was going to do a story about the Special Balkan Section. The pilot was obviously besotted with Miss Gellhorn and locked me in the back with the bombs while she sat up front with him and the copilot. As soon as he reached altitude, he began showing off, making the plane do tricks. I flew around like a bowling ball, caroming off bomb racks. At Bari he forgot I was in there and I could hear the three of them getting into a jeep and driving off. Finally, after much yelling and banging, I was released by an irritable mechanic.

In Bari I found the Special Balkan Section housed in a large villa. The commanding officer was a major named Koch who had formerly been a buyer for Bamberger's department store in Newark, New Jersey. He said he had never heard of me.

The colonel in Cairo had never written. Even if he had, there was no way I would be allowed into Yugoslavia. The idea was preposterous. No reporters were allowed into Yugoslavia, at least not yet. Two had been chosen from the correspondents' pool, one American and one British, along with an American and a British photographer. They had been sent to Palestine for parachute training and at some time convenient to the Allied high command they would be dropped into Yugoslavia for an authorized interview with Tito. Major Koch did not know when this would happen, only that it would be after the second front had opened. However, I had come a long way and he would be magnanimous. I was welcome to stay and interview him. I could also write about the SBS and how it was bravely running guns across the Adriatic to the partisans. I had already noticed one of his officers who was doing that, a young, good-looking marine lieutenant named Hamilton whom I had seen in the movies as Sterling Hayden.

My getting into Yugoslavia may have seemed preposterous to Major Koch but not to me. The Allied high command had its priorities and I had mine. I also had permission from my commanding officer. True, his permission was meaningless— he had no jurisdiction here—but that was a mere legalism. The partisans had set up a mission in Bari and I went there at once. Dedijer had also flown in from Cairo and I told him what Koch had said and he told me the invitation still stood. If I wanted to go in, they would take me. He thought the parachute training was a stall. The partisans had carved out landing strips and it was perfectly feasible for the Allies to fly in anyone they pleased whenever they wanted. No one had to jump in. He said a group was being organized to return to Yugoslavia and I could join them. They were mostly partisans who had been wounded and ferried over to Italy for treatment and who were now well enough to return. First, though, I would have to go to the island of Vis, not far off the Dalmatian coast, and stay there until the time was ripe to go in.

I traveled to Vis at night on a launch carrying supplies. Also on the boat was an American captain from the SBS, part of a small American detachment stationed on the island to expedite the movement of arms. He would have taken a dim view of my being there, so the Yugoslavs gave me one of their uniforms to wear instead of mine and I lay in a berth with my face turned to the wall and a blanket over my head. I could hear the American asking what was the matter with me. Someone said I was drunk. When we docked on the island, the American captain got off and the Yugoslavs waited awhile and then took me off. They put me in a car and drove into the interior and turned me over to another group of partisans. By that time it was late at night and they showed me to a room in a farmhouse and I went to sleep.

The next morning I awoke to find myself in an old stone house at the edge of an old stone village. Even the hills seemed made of stone. There were stones lying everywhere. It was hard to think anything could grow here. The house was the headquarters of a partisan newspaper called *Free Dalmatia,* a hand-set six-page weekly printed here and then smuggled onto the mainland for secret distribution. The staff lived in the house and I met them at breakfast: an ex-lawyer, a young architect, a couple of students, an ex-professor of something I couldn't understand, an office worker and a poet. They were all men. There were also five women: a cook and her assistant, two stenographers and the elderly mother of one of the staff who helped around the house. Only the former lawyer, whose name was Lukin, spoke any English. He was a skinny, shy man with glasses and a sunburn. His English was fluent but bookish. He used words like *peruse* instead of *read*. He said that the newspaper was small but much perused. He had bad lungs and had to rest every day after lunch, and he was a devoted Communist.

I stayed on Vis for ten days or perhaps it was two weeks; I lost track of the time. The days were always the same. I would get up and have breakfast with the staff at a long bare table in the attic. Breakfast was bread and tea, the bread fresh from the oven, hot and moist and sweet-smelling, the tea hot and sweet and taken with a spoon, like soup. Then we would all go outside, where people from the village and other partisan detachments had gathered around a public address system the staff had rigged up. They came every morning to hear the Croatian news broadcast from London. There were men and women in gray partisan uniforms with red stars and grenades hanging from their belts. There were children who acted as ammunition carriers. There were always old men who came on donkeys and women who came with clothes they were mending and sewed as they listened. After the broadcast the staff would go to work and I would wander through the village or walk out across the stone fields to the sea. It was spring by the calendar, but there was always a chill wind and no promise of warmth. In the mornings there was ice on the well where we had to wash. The sea was sullen and uninviting. If Lukin were free, he would join me on my walks and we would talk politics or he would try to teach me Serbo-Croatian, a thankless task under any circumstances.

I would return for supper, a one-dish meal usually of vegetables with occasional pieces of fish thrown in or some American delicacy filched from supplies going to the mainland. Once there was a case of chowchow, not, as some thought, a kind of dog food but mixed pickles in mustard sauce. No one had ever tasted anything remotely like this before, but they ate it with gratitude, wanting to know if everyone in America ate so exotically. They wanted to know everything about America and I was pleased to see how many of their ideas came from the movies. They were particularly interested in the present status of gangsters and cowboys and what had happened to Laurel and Hardy. After supper there was more listening to Croatian broadcasts from London and Moscow and then more talk. The poet and architect argued frequently about the relative merits of liberal and classical education. Everyone argued about modern art. When light becomes heat was the subject of one passionate discussion. They were passionate people; no subject lacked emotion.

They also sang a lot. They sang folk songs and European popular songs and songs that came out of the war. They sang about heroes who had died in battle and what their country was going to be like after the war. They were very proud of this, and when they didn't sing about it, they talked about it. Yugoslavia would be a new kind of socialist democracy, free of racism and chauvinism and exploitation, home to its many nationalities, which would have no further need of their ancient tribal hatreds. Their talk was like their songs, fervent and romantic. One song was dedicated to their rifles and another to Tito, in which the girls asked him when he would send the boys home and he replied, "It is not yet time. It is not yet time." But when I suggested one of the Loyalist songs from the Spanish Civil War, they refused. Those songs were beautiful, but they were songs of a defeated army and a lost war. They did not want to be reminded of defeat.

Everyone accepted me and treated me as a friend. They loaned me their sole typewriter and supplied me with precious paper so I could write a story for *Yank* about where I was (disguising the exact location) and what I was doing. When the story was finished, they assured me they would find a way to get it to the *Yank* office in Naples. I was still dressed in a partisan uniform in case any American saw me on the road and they even gave me a bad, chopped-up haircut, shaven on the sides, so I would look the part. They tried to keep me from being bored. There was nothing to read in English, but Lukin dug up Stefan Zweig's biography of Tolstoy in French and I plowed my way through that, thinking of Capa. The radio was kept on all day and I listened to a piano recital from Moscow, opera from Italy, an RAF dance band from London and a talk from Berlin (translated for me) on the senselessness of aerial warfare. From America a plummy voice spoke sincerely to the people of Europe about the pros and cons of bombing Rome and the abbey at Monte Cassino. The speaker thought there was a moral question involved. The Yugoslavs thought this could come only from a country that had not been invaded by the fascists. It was clear to them that if German soldiers were there, they should be bombed.

This set off a spirited discussion about how you treated the enemy. Obviously you tried to kill as many as possible, but how about if you only captured them? Regulations said you did not kill prisoners unless you knew they had committed atrocities. The lawyer had been a military judge in Dalmatia before his lungs went bad and he had had cases in which captured Ustachi, the Croatian fascists, had been young and repentant and had not, as he put it, pillaged with the fascists, and he had released those and sent them home. He was immediately attacked as soft, especially by those who had a personal connection to Ustachi atrocities. The poet's village had been burned after all the men had been shot; the cook's husband and son had been tortured and killed; the architect had an aunt and a cousin who had been raped and then stabbed to death. The brother of one of the students had died in the Ustachi camp at Jasenovac in Croatia. They explained to me that this was the camp notorious for burning men alive; its record was fifteen hundred in one night. There seemed something special about the Ustachi; they made the Nazis seem almost benign.

Then, one morning, we had a visit from a young woman I had not seen before. She had long brown hair and looked as if she belonged on the campus of a good midwestern university. I was with Lukin at the time, listening to him tell me sadly of his unrequited love for a partisan woman in another village. He said that our visitor was something of a heroine, having held a hill alone with a machine gun against repeated German counterattacks. Everyone was deferential to her. She had come to tell me I was to move out with a group that had finally been formed. We were to rendezvous on the mainland with another group and go on foot to a mountain town in Bosnia called Drvar, where Tito had his headquarters. She said the trip would take about a week unless the Germans or Ustachi found us; then it might take longer. The group we were meeting were young partisans going to Drvar for an antifascist youth congress. This was to be the second congress; the first had been held two years before. Many of the delegates to the first congress would not be at the second, she explained, because they had been killed in the fighting. Still, she thought the congress would be a success, since it expected delegates from the other Balkan countries and even the Soviet Union.

The night I left, the staff of the paper produced a bottle of a fiery local brandy and saw me off with toasts to my safety and the brotherhood of all peace-loving people. I assured Lukin that if he could overcome his shyness, his love might not continue unrequited. We embraced; we had become friends. My group of about fifteen people was to leave on a fishing boat, but the boat was late and the leader of the group, an ex–bank clerk from Sarajevo, invited me to dine with him and his staff as guests of a local fisherman. Dinner was a plate of octopus. All octopus meant to me was something large and nasty, hiding in the deep and eager to wrap its tentacles around whatever movie hero was foolish enough to go down there. I was scared stiff of any octopus, even dead on a plate. On the other hand, this fisherman was offering us his own scarce food and it would have been insulting to refuse. I ate the octopus and then went outside and threw up. The boat finally arrived and we all piled in and set out across the dark Adriatic, running without lights to avoid German patrol boats. Fortunately there was no moon. The trip seemed to take forever. There was not enough room to go inside and we huddled together on the slippery deck, turning our backs to the cold, biting wind. No one spoke.

Finally, land appeared as a black mass rising on the horizon. The boat slid into a small dark cove, with a makeshift dock and high cliffs rising behind it, and suddenly there were partisans slipping out of the woods to make the boat fast. They helped us out and the first thing I did was replace the partisan uniform I was wearing with my own. I was an American soldier, and if the Germans had caught me in any other uniform, I could have been shot as a spy. There were whispered conversations between our leader and these new partisans. Then the boat pulled silently out again and I followed the others to a steep path at the base of a cliff and we started to climb. At the top of the cliff another group of partisans was waiting for us and our captain conferred with them in whispers as we stopped to catch our breath. Far to our left I could see a signal light going on and off with steady regularity. Someone said it was a German garrison.

We marched the rest of the night, stopping occasionally to rest, passing farmhouses that gleamed whitely in the dark and seemed fine until you noticed their roofs had been blown away. We stopped only when the sun came up, and then camped in a pine grove. I stretched out on the ground and fell instantly asleep, to be awakened at noon by a very tall, lean young partisan who spoke English. His name was Srdjan and he had been a college student in the Dalmatian city of Split until he had left to go up into the mountains and join the partisans. He had been assigned as my interpreter. Our group was now up to about fifty, mostly young people going to the congress but also including several middle-aged men being transferred to different units and six young girls who had just finished training as nurses and were being assigned to combat units. Everyone was armed.

We walked for seven days, moving only at night except when we were high on a mountain where we knew the Germans didn't patrol. During the day we rested and slept. We carried no food. Peasants and villagers fed us along the way. We would camp outside a village and the people would bring us bread or cereal or sometimes hot, thick soup. Nothing had any salt, but hunger was the issue, not taste. My feet swelled and I didn't dare take off my boots when I slept because I knew I wouldn't be able to get them on again. We walked up mountains and down mountains, all full of false crests. It was like Italy. I would stumble to the top of a crest, figuring it was downhill after that, and there would be another crest just ahead. After a while it became personal. It was not the Germans out to get you, it was the mountains. What I could see of the country during the day was stark and beautiful, minor compensation for being tired, wet, hungry and scared. Planes were our greatest fear, since we had only pistols and rifles to combat them. But they were usually after bigger game, and we were strafed only once by a fighter plane and then we were lucky because we were on a trail flanked by deep ravines and were able to hide.

Sometimes, when we were able to march by day, one of the partisans would start singing and the others would join in. They were a great people for song. Like the people on Vis, they sang about war and politics and love, and they sang the folk ballads that seem the same for every country. I sang "The Battle Hymn of the Republic" and "Yankee Doodle" and "I've Been Working on the Railroad" and "Buckle Down, Winsocki." I had to teach them "I've Been Working on the Railroad," which they liked the best. I would sing a line as we marched, then speak it slowly, Srdjan translating so they would know what they were singing. It worked fine and they insisted on doing the same for me. Soon I was singing their songs and they were singing mine. My favorite was a song called "Republic," which went, "Republic, we want you. You belong to us. We have won you with our blood."

All the villages we walked through had been hit by the war. Most were small, poor and primitive. They had been shelled or bombed and the roofs were blown off and the sides of many of the old stone houses gaped open. The children would see us coming and wait for us at the edge, their eyes huge and liquid, their bellies swollen with hunger. None of them begged. They were different from the wartime children I had seen in other places, the children in Egypt and North Africa sitting silently with their mothers, their hands out, flies clustered on their diseased eyelids, or the feral Italian children running after the jeeps. At first I thought they were too traumatized. But they answered shyly when we spoke to them and became like children I had known outside this war. All I heard them ask for was pencils. We passed literacy classes being held in open fields, old men and women and little children sitting in a semicircle around a partisan teacher.

Eventually the mountains became too steep even for singing. Some of them had snow on their peaks. We would collapse when we reached the summit and I would rub snow on my face and down the back of my neck to wake myself up. We were walking mostly by day now and then one day we came to the top of a mountain and looked down on a valley different from any we had seen. It was very green and very long. In the center was a lovely village, looking peaceful and normal and not quite real. It looked like a movie village where I would find Will Rogers as Judge Priest or Lewis Stone as Judge Hardy, the kind of town where a judge was simply a kind, knowing parent. But it was Drvar, Tito's headquarters.

The village was real enough when we got into it. Only a few houses were still intact, the others had been bombed in the usual way. All of them were pocked with bullet holes. We passed a row of storefronts, the names still over the missing doorways. There was a tailor shop, a butcher shop, a barber shop and what seemed to have been a grocery. They were all empty. Also empty were the streets. You might have thought everyone was having a siesta except that the stillness was somehow expectant, as though the place were waiting for the bombers to come again. Our ranks thinned as we walked through the town, dropping people off. First the nurses left us, and then the men going to the combat units. The young people for the youth congress left for a village on the other side of the mountain. The partings were emotional; everyone embraced everyone else. We had been through something together. Then Srdjan and I were left off at an isolated farmhouse. Since I was here illegally, at least so far as the Allies were concerned, it was thought best to keep me where I wouldn't be seen. The British had a mission in Drvar, and the Americans a meteorological station to inform Allied bombers flying to and from the Romanian oil fields. I did not want to risk bumping into anyone who would want to know what I was doing here, although the American station seemed a promising story since it was on top of a mountain and sounded just like what Cary Grant had set up for his fliers in *Only Angels Have Wings.*

I spent a few days in the farmhouse recovering from the walk. My head ached and I had trouble getting my eyes to focus. I slept a lot. In the mornings Srdjan and I would be awakened by a little boy bringing us goat's milk, bread and honey. He wore a partisan cap with the red star and he would stand in the doorway and watch us eat, giggling at the American. During the day, as I had on the island, I wandered off by myself. Spring had finally arrived and the air was heavy with the rich turned-earth smell of planting. Beyond the village, peasants plowed their fields as if there were no war. I felt peaceful and content. People nodded and waved to me as I passed. If I grew thirsty, I would stop at a farmhouse and a peasant woman would draw me water from a well or offer a cup of goat's milk. Once I helped a farmer dig out a large rock and it was good to feel sweat that was not cold with fear.

I was taken to meet the Minister of Information, a middle-aged man named Ribnika who had been publisher of *Politika,* the largest Belgrade daily, before joining the partisans. With him was his secretary, a polite, taciturn man who had been imprisoned as a Communist for twelve years before the war and had written a novel about it. Like all the other Yugoslavs, they wanted to tell the world what their country would be like after the war. The vision was heady: a federal republic freely elected and respecting everyone's rights, a popular-front government in which the Communists, because of their leadership in the war, would have the leading role. It seemed reasonable to me. Crossing the valley on the way back, I heard the roar of a plane and a Dornier suddenly appeared, flying very low. I dived for a ditch, but it just cruised around, big and black and insolent, and then went on its way.

The Germans could send slow planes like that because there was no real opposition in the air. The partisan ground fire was ineffectual and so they sent ancient Dorniers and obsolete Stukas and even training planes whose pilots would hold the bombs in their laps and throw them out by hand.

One night I was taken to a movie, a Russian film shown in a gymnasium that had been converted to a theater. Srdjan said the Russians had sent in three films, the British one feature and some newsreels, and the Americans none as yet, but he had heard that something called *Sun Valley Serenade* was on its way. He thought it was about ice skating. The former gymnasium, now called the House of Culture, was jammed when we got there and we had to stand. Srdjan was apologetic, but I didn't care if I sat or stood; I was at the movies. I leaned back against a wall, waiting for the wrinkled screen to come alive, feeling the warm, familiar relief I always felt in a movie house. The audience seemed evenly divided between peasants from the village and partisan men and women soldiers. The walls were decorated with slogans and pictures of Tito, Roosevelt, Churchill and Stalin. The movie was about a Russian town invaded by the Germans and how the townspeople took to the hills and became guerrillas. The audience ate it up. The movie was about them. When the guerrilla leader shot the German commander three times at close range, they yelled so loud you couldn't hear the dialogue. The movie was not very good, but that seemed beside the point.

The next night was the youth congress. This was held in a large bombed-out building that had been restored and decorated for the occasion. The usual pictures of Tito, Roosevelt and the others hung on the walls. Slogans were painted everywhere: Long Live Tito! Long Live the Allies! Long Live a Free Federal Yugoslavia! The delegates sat by sections. Belgrade was on one side, Zagreb next to them, assorted Serbs in front,

Croats and Montenegrins behind. A hundred Montenegrins had started out two months before, but only fifty had survived. When I got there with Srdjan, everyone seemed to be singing. Since each section sang its own song, the result was a loud, not unpleasant cacophony.

We sat in the Dalmatian section with people from our march, and there was a happy reunion. Everyone embraced everyone else all over again. The youth delegates said the village they had gone to had been Fifth Corps headquarters and while they were there, the Germans had attacked with Stukas and destroyed the whole village. Many people had been killed and now Fifth Corps headquarters was somewhere in the woods. Fortunately no one from our group had been hurt. We were sitting in the rear of the hall, luckily for me since the front row soon filled up with British and Russian officers. I crouched low in my seat, which made it a little difficult to see what was going on. When the hall was filled, a young man stood up on a dais and waited until the singing died away and then shouted, "Death to fascism!" Everyone roared back, "Freedom to the people!" Then the congress began.

First were the inevitable cables from those who couldn't come. The Bulgarian, Greek and Italian resistance movements had not been able to get through the German lines. There were also cables from those who had come, like the Russians, but who still wished to send congratulations. Then there was a stir in the hall and people began to clap their hands and crane their necks and Tito walked in. He was shorter than I expected. The clapping grew to a roar and then a chant of "Ti-to! Ti-to! Ti-to!" He paused to shake hands with the British and Russian officers and the chanting and foot-stamping went on, building finally to a great yell and burst of applause. I found myself yelling and applauding along with everyone else. Tito stepped up onto the dais and I could get a good look at him. He wore a gray uniform, very well cut, with gold oak leaves on the sleeve and collar. He looked handsome in it, like an actor. His face was strong, with high cheekbones. I had been told that in the clandestine days before the war, when he was on business for the Communist Party, he would sometimes travel disguised as a rich banker. I could see how he could get away with this. He talked for about twenty minutes, quietly. The audience listened with respect. Srdjan translated for me. Tito talked mostly about how glad he was to see the delegates, how important their work was, how important they were. At the end the applause was loud, but not at the pitch it had been before.

The rest of the congress consisted of reports from the delegates. They ranged from a thirteen-year-old boy who had set records for killing Germans to a baby-faced major general who had been a peasant in Bosnia before the war. Many were shy and embarrassed, unused to speaking in public. A Serbian girl spoke about rebuilding her village after Chetniks had burned it. A skinny little boy from Herzegovina spoke about agricultural brigades. A confident young man from Croatia told how he and two others had slipped into Zagreb and killed a Nazi general. He proudly showed the medals they had taken off the general's chest, including one from King Boris of Bulgaria. There was a great emphasis on statistics: so many German trucks destroyed, so many miles of railroad tracks torn up, bridges blown, rifles captured, enemy killed. They spoke about killing and they spoke about building. They all seemed very normal, like kids talking about how their team had done this season. I was with them all the way, cheering from the bleachers.

Speech followed speech and I applauded with enthusiasm. The British and Russian officers applauded with polite correctness. One of the Russians kept falling asleep. I watched

them tolerantly. My clandestinity made me feel privileged. I
had gotten here because I was also part of another, larger
movement. I had given the password and been let in. I was
both soldier and confidant. It was better than the movies. It
was real and I was part of it, sharing the beliefs, if not the suffering. I was part of a promise that a better world would be
built when we had won this necessary war. It made me feel I
wanted to be more than what I was.

The speeches went on until two in the morning. Afterward
the congress was adjourned, the dais cleared of chairs so that
it became a stage, and an announcement made that we would
now be entertained by members of the national ballet company. All the lights went out except for those over the stage.
A group of men and women in native costume appeared and
the entertainment began. There were singers and dancers and
a man who recited his own poem very energetically. After the
entertainment there was an attempt at more speeches, but no
one paid much attention. Srdjan and I left with our delegates.
Outside we said good-bye to them again with more embraces.
It was dawn by now and the valley was taking shape out of
the darkness. From the other side of the mountain I could
hear the faint rumble of cannon fire.

But I was anxious to get my interview with Tito, especially
since there were rumors of a coming German offensive. I
hung around the house for three more days, waiting to be
summoned, and at last a young woman arrived who spoke
English and told me I could see Tito that night. It would be
late, so perhaps I should take a nap first. I tried but couldn't
sleep, and finally, around midnight, a tough-looking, mild-
mannered partisan lieutenant came for me. He led me silently
through the blackness. The location of Tito's house was a secret and I had no idea where I was going. Once we crossed a
stream over a slippery log. Several times we were stopped by

soldiers who materialized ghostlike out of the dark. The lieutenant would show them something and we would go on. In the distance there was the sound of a waterfall and then I could see it, the water churning white and phosphorescent in the night. Tito's house was next to the waterfall, sheltered in a mountain that hid it from air raids.

Tito himself was in a small room, seated behind a desk. With him was the young woman who had come to tell me I could see him. Her name was Olga and she was the interpreter. The room had a patterned red rug on the floor and the walls were covered with what seemed like wrapping paper, reinforced by strips of parachute silk. One wall had a large map of Yugoslavia. A potbellied stove stood in a corner. Sleeping by Tito's chair was a huge dog that looked like an innocent wolf. Tito rose from his desk when I came in, shook hands pleasantly, and I had my interview. He talked about his army, how it had been formed, what it needed (food mostly), how the partisans had succeeded in welding the different racial and religious elements of Yugoslavia into one harmonious whole, and how that would be reflected in the federal state they would form after the war. He said how much he admired America, how he had wanted, like many Yugoslavs, to go there when he was young but had been too poor. He was an attractive, compelling man, very sure of himself and what he was doing. He talked softly, without hesitation, and smoked steadily, putting cigarettes into a holder shaped like a small pipe. As he talked, he fingered some of the objects on his desk: a GI flashlight, a packet of British cigarettes, a copy of *Essential English*. From outside I could still hear the dull roar of the waterfall.

After about an hour Olga stood up and the interview was over. I still had questions to ask and Tito said we would schedule another meeting soon. Meanwhile, he suggested, I should pay a visit to the front and see how the partisans fought. I thanked him and we shook hands (no embracing here), and Olga took me outside and turned me over to the waiting lieutenant, who walked me home. I spent the next few days writing out the interview in longhand. Srdjan had disappeared somewhere and I was left pretty much to myself.

Then, one night, the lieutenant reappeared to escort me to the battlefront. We were to take a small logging railroad that ran from Drvar up into the mountains where the fighting was. I put on my pack and followed him to the railroad station. Several flatcars stood there, waiting to be pulled by an engine that looked like the Toonerville Trolley. There was a lot of hustle and bustle as troops piled on. I was about to follow them when I passed a British major in battle dress. We nodded courteously to each other and I proceeded on, praying silently that he hadn't really noticed me in the dark, when suddenly he came running back and grabbed me by the arm.

"Who are you?" he asked, astonished. "What on earth are you doing here?"

I told him who and what, and he shook his head, uncomprehending.

"Tell me that again," he said.

I told him. He could not get over seeing me here. He kept shaking his head. The only thing he could say was "Most irregular. Most irregular."

Then, still holding my arm, he said I had better come with him to the British mission and get sorted out.

The British mission was in a small house in the middle of town and there was no one there except Major Randolph Churchill, son of Winston. I knew it was Randolph Churchill because I had seen his picture in magazines. He looked like his father, although not as beefy. The major turned me over to him and left, repeating again that this was all most irregular, and Churchill interrogated me. When he discovered I had written for *The New Yorker*, he became very friendly. He was a big fan of the magazine and had once met Harold Ross, whom he thought odd. He offered me a stiff drink and complimented me on getting the first interview with Tito. The two reporters and photographers from the pool were still waiting to come in, having been assured they would have the exclusive story. I had certainly put it over on everyone. He offered me another drink. He thought what I had done was hilarious. On the other hand, I should consider myself under arrest. He said this with regret, assuring me he had the utmost admiration for my exploit. By this time we were both a little drunk. He said I should just stay in my farmhouse while he informed Allied Force Headquarters in Algiers and they told him what to do with me. Naturally I was not to see Tito again without permission.

I wove my way back to the farmhouse and found the lieutenant waiting anxiously with several other partisan officers. They had been worried about me and wanted to be sure I was all right. I told them what had happened and they said if I wished, they would spirit me out of Drvar and then anywhere else I wanted to go. I said I had better stay where I was. I think they were disappointed. They had the guerrilla's love of subterfuge. I spent the next few days waiting to see what would happen. Then I was summoned back to the British mission. Churchill and the major were there. They said I had been ordered back to Algiers. Headquarters was upset at what I had done. In fact, as Churchill put it, Headquarters was roundly pissed off. The article I had written on the island had gotten to *Yank* and been printed, and so firsthand news about Tito and the partisans was already out. The civilian press was irate since they had been promised an exclusive. The four American and British reporters and photographers selected from the pool were therefore being sent in at once, while I was to be got the hell out of there. Churchill was still very friendly and offered me his personal apologies and another stiff drink. He said to get my things and return by eight that evening. I went back to the farmhouse and said reluctant good-byes to Srdjan and everyone else. Someone opened a bottle of wine and we toasted one another and the war and Tito and a federal Yugoslavia. Then we all embraced, which took awhile, and I returned to the British mission.

Churchill was still there, by this time very drunk but still cordial. He, too, was going back to Italy, although for reasons of his own. A partisan soldier drove us to a darkened landing strip in the valley and we waited silently for about an hour. The night was cold and I kept shivering. I hoped it was dark enough so no one would notice; I did not want anyone to think it might be from fear. Also waiting were about twenty wounded partisans who were going to a British hospital for treatment. A few were on stretchers. There was the noise of a plane, dim lights came on to illuminate a bumpy dirt runway, and a British transport plane descended through a cleft in the mountains and landed. We waited until the passengers came off. There were partisans returning from hospital and there were the four men from the press pool. I had briefly met the American correspondent in Cairo and we nodded hello, but he did not seem overjoyed to see me. I thought he should thank me for not being dropped in by parachute. Then the wounded were placed on the plane and then Churchill was poured on and then I climbed in and we took off into the night.

The flight was short and uneventful, and when we landed in Bari, a British captain was waiting for me. He, too, was very friendly. His name was Malcolm and he said he was my arresting officer and would be escorting me to Algiers, but he made it sound as though he were simply taking me on a guided tour. He said the British were not turning me over to the SBS here in Bari—the normal procedure—because they didn't want to see me terrorized. Major Koch was in a rage at what I had done, and Malcolm thought he might seriously do me harm. A court-martial was the least he promised. I liked Malcolm. He took me to a house in Bari and showed me to a tiny attic room and said he would come for me in the morning. I immediately phoned Dedijer at partisan headquarters. He had heard what had happened to me and, like the partisans back in Drvar, offered to help. He said he could get a couple of other partisans and easily break me out of where I was and I could spend the rest of the war in Yugoslavia with them. I was touched by the offer. It had a definite appeal. But I declined with effusive thanks, not wishing to hurt his feelings. He sounded disappointed.

The next morning Malcolm called for me, asking solicitously whether I had slept well, and we flew to Algiers. An American captain was waiting for me at the airport. He was not friendly. He accepted me from Malcolm with minimum grace. I shook hands with Malcolm, who watched sadly as I was led away. I think he expected chains. The captain put me in the back of a jeep while he sat in front with a driver, and we drove to Allied Force Headquarters in silence. If he meant to intimidate me, he was succeeding. I was starting to get worried. I had not just disobeyed any old order; I had meddled in affairs of state. A court-martial was not out of the question. My one consoling thought was that maybe, by forcing public acknowledgment of Tito, I had changed the course of the war or even shortened it, but a demented grandiosity was no match for reasonable fear.

When we got to headquarters, the captain led me brusquely inside, sat me down in a small waiting room and disappeared into an office. He came out in a few minutes and motioned for me to enter. He stayed outside, which was a relief. Sitting at a desk was a one-star general. He was not friendly, either. On the other hand, he was not unfriendly. He looked severely neutral. He told me to sit down and looked at me for a long moment, as though to match what he saw before him to the historic misdeed that had been done. Then he pointed out that I had caused a lot of people a lot of trouble besides going what could fairly be called AWOL, breaching regulations and disobeying a direct order. He said the SBS in Bari wanted me fried. He wanted to know exactly what I had done, where I had gone, how I had gotten there and what I had seen. He wanted to know about Tito. Unlike Churchill, he was not impressed that I had written for *The New Yorker.* I gave him a full report, trying for a modest sincerity. When I finished, he nodded and said he was going to have to think about this for a while before deciding what to do with me. He wasn't sure what the punishment should be. Meanwhile, I could go back to Naples and resume my authorized reporting. I asked if I could write up my interview with Tito. He said I could write it, but *Yank* would not be allowed to publish it until the pool reporters had returned and published their account. They had been promised the first Tito interview, and so far as the civilian world was concerned, that's how it was going to seem.

I returned to Naples, angry about being denied my scoop and apprehensive about the looming punishment. But a reporter from *The New York Times* wrote a story about what I had done and the *Times* printed it on the front page and the army evidently thought it would look bad if it punished me any further, so nothing happened except that I lost my exclusive. I heard that the day after I left Drvar, the Germans had dropped two paratroop battalions into the valley. Tito and his staff had escaped, but there were many casualties. The English photographer had been killed. I felt sad and lucky.

Our troops in Italy were still slowly pushing their way north, but we had tried to outflank the German line by landing a hundred thousand troops on the beach at Anzio, a town below Rome. The attack had stalled and there was an uneasy, bloody stalemate. I caught a ride on a landing craft and went to Anzio. It was bloody all right. I did a story about a field hospital and watched a stream of bodies coming in. A nurse was writing the names and addresses of the dead into a register and one of them had lived down the block from me in Brooklyn. The name wasn't familiar, but the odds were good that he had gone, like me, to P.S. 161. I tried to fit the name to a face in class or playing ball in the schoolyard. The ages couldn't have been that different.

Then *Yank* offered me a choice. The second front was about to open in France and I could cover the invasion, or I had enough time overseas that I could go home. The choice was no choice. I returned to Naples as quickly as I could and waited for a flight home. The wait seemed endless, although it was no more than a few days and I got to see *You Were Never Lovelier* once again, this time with Italian subtitles. I spent the time walking around the city, caught up in its ferocious energy, marveling at how you could get anything you wanted on the black market, from clothing to food to guns, all stolen from Allied supplies with the complicity of Allied soldiers. You could even order an item and it would be delivered. There was the sense that not to take part in this cheerful corruption would be impolite.

Finally, I was promised a seat on a transport plane going to New York. The night before I was supposed to leave, there was an air raid. I lay in bed in the *Stars and Stripes* apartment in the Galleria, listening grimly to the bombs crash around the harbor. It seemed unfair, a last, desperate attempt by the enemy to get me. I could hear people outside in the hall hurrying down to the bomb shelter. I resolved not to move. I was warm and comfortable and going home the next day. Rushing down to huddle in a cellar with strangers lacked dignity. Also, there was no way a bomb was going to hit me on my last night in Naples. It would be too much like the movies. I lay there relaxed, unafraid, waiting for the planes to unload and leave, and then, as though propelled, I was throwing on my pants, pulling on my boots, grabbing a shirt and dashing for the bomb shelter. Full of shame and exhilaration, thoroughly despising myself, I fled to safety. To be killed the night before going home would have been unforgivable.

3

I stand in a sunny yellow-bright room, looking at a crib in a corner. Standing in the crib, holding on to the railing, is a little girl. Her hair is blond and she has slanty eyes, the kind I had as a child, the kind she had in the infant picture I saw in Sicily. Only then her hair was black. She looks at me gravely; she has never seen me before. I smile at her, a tentative smile, unsure of its reception. She does not smile back and I become anxious. I feel I have lost valuable time and want it made up quickly. A truck rattles by outside and she turns her head to listen. Suddenly she lets go of the railing and sits down with a thump. Her expression of delighted surprise makes me laugh. She looks at me through the bars of the crib. She smiles. I am home.

THE SECOND front opened without me. Yugoslavia was moved to the back pages, but everyone knew about the partisans now. I was pleased with what I had done. My aunt Sara, now working as a secretary at Communist Party headquarters, called and asked if I would meet with some highly placed Party functionaries who wanted information about Tito and his movement. They came to my apartment, two friendly men named Dennis and Landy, and listened politely as I told them what I knew, which was no more than what I had already written. They asked intelligent questions, refused a drink and left with thanks. Dennis later became head of the Party and went to jail under the Smith Act. Landy wrote a book called *Marxism and the Democratic Tradition* which tried to place communism within a tradition of American democracy. For this he was attacked as a bourgeois revisionist and driven into Party disgrace. But that came later.

My apartment was in Greenwich Village and I would take the Fifth Avenue bus to get back and forth from *Yank*. I would wait for a double-decker so I could sit on top. It was almost summer when I came home, and the bus tops were open and, when the traffic was light, there was the sense of sailing through the city. I could not get enough of New York. The best ride was on the Third Avenue El. From the Battery to 125th Street it cut through Wall Street and the financial district, through Chinatown and the Bowery; past flophouses and factories, low brick buildings with dirty windows through which you could dimly see men and women working hunched over tables; past bars and candy stores and shoemakers and the railway flats that rose above them with old iron fire escapes and lines of washing; past the Upper East Side where you could look down tree-lined side streets with rows of elegant town houses.

You felt you were slicing through the city from top to bottom. You rode close enough to windows so that you could see the people inside, sometimes close enough that you felt you could touch them. Sometimes you caught them, or they caught you, looking straight back at you and the moment froze as if a flash had gone off, leaving both sides a little startled. You could see people working and eating or listening to the radio; you could see them happy or sad or violent or loving. It was like the opening of a Warner Bros. movie, a city for conquest, full of public enemies and marked women. I ate it all up. It was my city, my America, as my grandmother would say. I was back where I really belonged. Once I saw a couple making love in a bedroom, but the slow-moving train still moved too fast for more than an impression of tumbling naked bodies. I felt no shame at my voyeurism, only regret I hadn't seen more. After all, why had they left the shades up?

The work on *Yank* was peaceful and routine. The staff was a disparate group, but we liked one another and would often socialize in the evenings, a keg of beer and cold cuts in someone's apartment or once in a while at a "Beefsteak," that New York institution where for five dollars a head you could hire a hall and sit at a long table with your friends and consume all the sliced sirloin you could hold, washed down by pitchers of beer. My work was mostly rewriting and editing stories from overseas. There was the occasional visit to army bases to report on how we were training our troops. I also wrote feature pieces on topics such as having lunch at the White House with Mrs. Roosevelt. She was softer-looking than in her pictures, but with a hint of steel beneath the polite, attentive surface. The food was bland and tasteless. I was reprimanded by some higher-up in Washington for writing jokingly about this, and forced to send a letter of apology. Mrs. Roosevelt wrote a charming and gracious letter in reply, saying she agreed about the food; eating was not important to her, although she realized it was to others.

But *Yank* was unique in the army in that we were permitted a wide range of expression. There were no blacks on our staff and only one woman, but we covered discrimination issues and ugly matters of segregation and tried as best we could to represent the enlisted man's point of view. We tried to write the truth and, surprisingly, we were often allowed to print it. We had the nature of the war on our side, an antifascist war, a just war. Everyone believed in it. We had been treacherously attacked; now we were fighting not only to survive but to defeat the forces of unambiguous evil. In this we had brave and gallant allies, not least among them the Soviet Union. No matter the different system; that was an internal affair. The enemy of our enemy was our friend. I was free to write glowingly about this, which I did at every opportunity.

On days off I took my daughter to Washington Square Park and pushed her on the swings and watched her play soberly in the sandbox. The war was far away—except when I was in a car that was going slowly. Then I would find my feet pressed hard against the floor and my body tense, willing the car to go faster, faster, faster as I waited for the fire from a German cannon zeroed in on us. I was back in Sicily, racing through that exposed area along the coast, certain that any minute I was going to be blown apart. My friend and colleague Justin Gray had it worse, but then he had been shot at more. Loud noises did it for him. Justin had fought bloody battles while with the Rangers in Italy, and the backfire from a car would catapult him out of wherever he was. Once he was in my apartment when a truck backfired outside; he leaped straight up out of his chair and nearly hit the ceiling. Justin was an anomaly on *Yank* in that he had no aspirations to be a writer. He had enlisted while at Harvard getting a master's degree in Asian studies, so naturally the army sent him to England in an engineer company.

The army was segregated in those days, and bigotry was the norm. Unfortunately for Justin, his outfit was stationed across a road from an all-Negro regiment. He immediately got into trouble by refusing to go on guard under an order that said any black soldier trying to cross that road should be shot on sight. Justin had not been court-martialed for this disobedience, but his life was made miserable. When the company got to North Africa, he applied for transfer to the Rangers, a high-risk commando group that needed volunteers because of its high casualty rate. They did not care what Justin had done. He fought as a rifleman through North Africa and Sicily and into Italy and took the time to write about this and send his articles to *Yank*. They were simply written and chillingly authentic. *Yank* printed them and then had Justin transferred back to New York. He turned out to be a modest, nervous intellectual with a shy integrity who managed to be diffident and stubborn at the same time. When he had calmed down a bit, the magazine sent him off to the Pacific, where he disappeared. We later heard rumors about some footloose noncom who was advising some inexperienced general how to run his island campaign against the entrenched Japanese. It was, of course, Justin.

I went to the movies as often as I could. A few films were now coming out in glorious Technicolor, but these seemed paradoxically pallid beside black-and-white. This had nothing to do with their content. Their shadows had no mystery. In fact, they had no shadows. Color had diminished them; they had lost the quality of dream. Movies were going in the wrong direction, from silent to sound, from black-and-white to color. It should have been the other way around, it should have become simpler rather than more complex. But the temptation was irresistible. As with any scientific discovery, if it could be done, it would be done. Possibility was all. Talkies had interrupted my grandmother's repose and driven her from the theater, but they had also aborted an increasing subtlety of form. Movies were now propelled as much by speech as by images, and the honest unreality of black-and-white had given way to the false reality of color. The symbiosis between audience and movie became edgier and less trusting.

You had to be careful not to miss what was being said. I liked the tough, colloquial talk of gangster movies and the verbal wit of the screwball comedies and the songs and dances of the musicals. But I felt something precious had been lost. Maybe it was only my childhood. I caught up to *You Were Never Lovelier* on a triple feature on Forty-second Street, sandwiched between Roy Rogers and Boston Blackie. I had gone just for the one but, out of courtesy, stayed for all three. They spoke and sang and snarled and whinnied at me, all still in glorious black-and-white.

The war in Europe ebbed and flowed, but mostly flowed, along with the necessary blood. President Roosevelt died. Or it was said he had died; it was not a death I immediately accepted. It meant facing a void, like the death of a parent. I had never really known any other president. There was a dim memory of my father voting for Herbert Hoover instead of Al Smith, but Franklin D. Roosevelt had been my president. I had grown up under Roosevelt. He was that mellifluous, comforting voice on the radio, the handsome, patrician face in the newsreels. He had gotten us out of the Depression and guided us through the war. Whatever my disagreements with him, whatever flipflops I had made following the Party line, Roosevelt had always been there. He was part of my life.

I was not the only one who felt this way. You could see the loss on faces in the street or on the subways. We did not realize then that an era had also passed, that what the future held was the assault on the idea of beneficent government. I searched out *The Grapes of Wrath*, playing in a revival house. The Joad family was heroic, but the movie had another hero as well: the government. Hospitable camps for migrants, protective agents to feed them and help them get work and see that they were not cheated, supportive officials to protect them against bigoted hoodlums: the government helped. It was there for its neediest citizens. You took for granted that it cared. You knew he cared. It was why so many babies, particularly among the poor, were named Franklin or Roosevelt or even Delano.

And just as suddenly, the war in Europe was over. Germany surrendered. Hitler killed himself. American and Russian troops met at the Elbe River and hugged and kissed and exchanged souvenirs. The full horror of the concentration camps became known. People began to use the word *Holocaust*. It was not a new word, of course, not even a new idea. The practice had been around forever. It was a specialty of the house. But now it had an added, twentieth-century meaning. And there were pictures to confirm the unbelievable stories. What had been done could not be denied. I hated the Germans. They deserved everything they were getting now. I would happily have seen the country razed and I exulted in its destruction.

The war continued against Japan, but we were winning that, too, and it was only a matter of time before we invaded that country and finished it off. My new assignment was to cover the invasion and I prepared to embark for the Pacific, although this time with circumscribed orders. But the army instituted a points program for discharge, based on length of service, and I had enough points. I never got to the Pacific. Instead, along with a friend from the *Stars and Stripes* who had sheltered me in Naples, and another long-serving *Yank* writer, a former NYU track star who had been known in his running days as the Violent Violet, I was discharged.

It came as a shock. I had no experience as an adult civilian. True, I had written for *The New Yorker*, but that had been as either student or soldier. Now I had a wife and a child, no job, and an old blue serge suit that no longer fit. Even my old shoes didn't fit. My feet had broadened. My mother was upset at this, since she had carefully preserved my shoes over the years, stuffed with paper. I suggested she bronze them. I bought a new pair at Thom McAn and another blue suit and a white shirt and a striped red-and-black tie at Rogers Peet. The army had given us a little pin to show we had served honorably and I put that in the lapel. My image in the mirror was strange to me. Who was this masked man? I kept trying to convince myself I was glad to be out. But I wasn't; I was nervous and scared, unprepared for marriage, fatherhood and the uncertainties of civilian life. The uniform had been armor against all this. The army had taken care of me. *Yank* had been a haven where I had been able to write and be approved. Perhaps I would have felt differently if I had been in longtime combat like my friend Justin or stationed in a hellhole like the Aleutians or the Persian Gulf or on some miserable, malarial island, but I had had an exciting, satisfying war. It was not what war was supposed to be, but it had been mine. And some secret part of me, looking at this uncomfortable stranger in the mirror, didn't want it to stop.

Instead, I took a vacation. Gasoline could be obtained only with ration coupons, but my rowdy Uncle Nat got me some on the black market and I borrowed a car and went off with wife and child to a beach in Maine. There, coming out of the freezing water to lie on the hot, gritty sand, I opened a newspaper and learned about this new bomb we had dropped on Japan. It sounded great. We dropped another one and that was even better. After all, we had been trying to kill as many Japanese as we could before they could kill us, and while we had killed an inordinate number of civilians this time, it did not seem much different from what we had done in Dresden or Berlin or any of the other cities when we had been killing Germans. It meant we might not have to invade Japan. Many American lives would be saved. I felt no guilt. A bomb was a bomb. That it was an atom bomb was meaningless to me, a scientific illiterate. It was not even a case of the end justifying the means. I did not understand that dropping this bomb was different from dropping any other kind of bomb. It did not occur to me that maybe I was morally illiterate as well. All this meant was that the war would be over soon and then there would be no necessity for any kind of bomb.

The war did end soon. Japan surrendered. The war, everyone's war, the war of the whole world, was really over. It was finally over. I was not only a civilian but a civilian in peacetime. Even the idea of peace was new. It had been something that would certainly come. There had never been any doubt about that; its arrival was as inevitable as victory. It was like growing up, something that would happen in the future. Now it was here, the expected guest who turns out not to be entirely welcome. For the past nine years I had lived with war or the expectation of war. My life had been conditioned by war. War had shaped my thoughts, my actions, my dreams, my hopes and my politics. War had treated me kindly, given me purpose, shielded me from ambiguity and choice because this war had been different from World War One, my war of *The Big Parade* and *All Quiet on the Western Front*. This one had truly pitted the forces of light against the forces of darkness. I had seen for myself what the fascist Ustachi and the German SS had done in Yugoslavia, seen the mutilated bodies of their victims and listened with horror and rage as numb villagers testified to atrocities no longer unspeakable. I had also seen the courage and idealism of the partisans and the bravery of ordinary Americans. War had shown me what people were capable of, the extremes of behavior, the best and the worst. War was a terrible, murderous confusion that I had profited from.

The New Yorker had a job for me, though. When I went to

pay my respects to Ross, he assumed I had returned to work for the magazine and gave me an office and a small drawing account. What I wrote was left up to me. I went there every morning and dutifully pretended to write. In the afternoons I would go for a walk and try unsuccessfully to avoid the temptation of the movies. Justin Gray came over and we went to see *The Westerner* with Gary Cooper. The next day I went back and saw it again by myself. The next day I saw it again. My excuse was that I wanted to study a long early scene between Cooper and Walter Brennan, a model of movie acting that naturally required frequent viewing. The real reason was that the alternative was sitting in my office and staring at a blank sheet of paper. Civilian life had paralyzed me. I had difficulty writing my name, let alone anything more demanding. *The New Yorker* was friendly and supportive. Harold Ross took me to lunch and talked about his hometown of Aspen, Colorado, and how friends from there were trying to interest him in making it into a ski resort, an idea he found hilariously improbable.

Other staff writers, all older and wiser than I, also took me to lunch. Many of them had been newspaper reporters and they liked to drink. I did, too, but not at lunch, although it was tempting to use it as an excuse to go back and lie down. Their talk was keen and witty, but their eyes had the faraway look of drinkers, fixed on some invisible watering hole in the distance. Still, they always heard what you were saying. Sober, they were talented professionals, proud of their craft, not easily fooled. They looked on the world with a cold eye. None of them confused reporting with public relations. They rarely put themselves into their stories. They treated words with respect. They believed in the word. Drunk, they became mean and sloppy and belligerent.

One in particular, a lapsed Catholic, liked to sit in bars and assault convivial clergymen, regardless of denomination. He had an uncanny eye for picking out men of the cloth, even when they were dressed like anyone else. Another would sit on the porch of his farmhouse, a bottle in one hand and a pistol in the other, and shoot at anyone who crossed his property. Most of the time he missed, which only irritated him further. A third backed his car out of his garage and ran over his child. My editor was William Shawn, gnomish and soft-spoken and brilliant, and we would sit with long periods of shy silence between us, waiting to discuss what subjects I might write about. He was patient and kind, but my head held my creativity in a punishing vise.

I looked forward to the weekends, when I played softball or touch football with friends in Central Park. Then there would be the magic release of sport, the sweaty pleasure as we raced around the field, the freedom to dare without consequence. We took the games seriously, especially Irwin Shaw. He would come wearing parts of his old football uniform and shoes with cleats. The rest of us wore old clothes and sneakers. A few wore camouflage suits from their army days. One time Irwin arrived with a large and thoughtful heavyweight boxer named Lou Nova whose shared distinction with other heavyweights was having been knocked out by Joe Louis. His manager said Nova had been done in by too much thinking. Nova was an amiable, peace-loving man, but when he lined up with Irwin to run interference, the opposing team stepped aside politely and let the two of them rumble down the field unhindered. Once I managed to block Irwin, who outweighed me by sixty pounds, and he just stared at me astonished, as John Cheever ran cackling past with the ball. Another time, playing softball, I won a game in the bottom of the ninth with a single past the shortstop. It was possibly the most satisfying moment of my postwar life.

My other friends at *Yank* had also been discharged by now. A few went on to graduate school, but most got jobs on newspapers and magazines, and sometimes we would meet again for lunch or a drink and talk about this and that, careful not to talk too much about the war. It was too soon for nostalgia. We were still friends, but there was no longer the war to hold us together. We had split along the fault lines of normalcy. Differences held in check by mutual purpose, some political, some of taste or lifestyle, now surfaced and divided us, not seriously for the most part but enough for regret, as if you were on a boat leaving a port where you had been happy and were now watching the buildings, the people, the land itself recede into an irretrievable past. I was drifting, unsure how I wanted to live. Secretly I wanted to go to Hollywood and write movies, but inertia and snobbery held me back, and anyway, no one was asking me.

A year after my discharge I joined the Communist Party. The move was natural; I had been there in my heart for some time and what I had seen in the war had only solidified this. The Communists had led the antifascist fight. They had led the fight against racism and colonialism. They had dared and sacrificed the most. They had a moral position, believing in what Rosa Luxemburg had called "the highest idealism in the interests of the whole." And they not only had a vision of a better, more humane world, they knew the way to get there. The example was the Soviet Union, even if the ideals transcended any particular state.

I was assigned to the Cultural Section and, within that, to a branch of people in the media. About ten of us met every couple of weeks, usually in someone's living room. We were all urban, middle-class intellectuals shaped by the Depression and the war. About half of us were Jews, which did not seem to me disproportionate. This was where Jews belonged, wherever there was a struggle for human rights. This was what being a Jew meant. There was also one young black writer and one very beautiful woman with pale skin and cheekbones that went up to her eyes. She was said to be a famous model, but no one knew for sure because no one had the courage to approach her. She seemed too out of place. She seldom spoke, but when she did, it was in simple declarative sentences, startling in a group lost without the conditional phrase. Usually she just sat with a regal, unbending posture that must have come from years of training with books on the head. She seemed unaware that every time the discussion became too boring (much of the time), all the men and most of the women sneaked looks at her. Everyone wondered what she was doing there. Our normal speculation about members revolved around which one was the FBI plant. J. Edgar Hoover had already announced his stepped-up war against the Reds and we took for granted that we were being followed, spied upon and infiltrated. But this woman was too beautiful for the FBI. She belonged with the CIA, sent abroad to compromise Soviet diplomats.

Our meetings mostly concerned such subjects as the entertainment unions, how we could help actors or writers or musicians, how we could mobilize them for political purposes. Also on the agenda were racial and sex discrimination, veterans' rights, poverty, unemployment, the issues of the day. There were talks on Marxism-Leninism. There was the study of the *Short History of the Soviet Union.* There was our own Party's history to study and take comfort in: American Communists had led the struggle for the unemployed during the Depression, had helped form the CIO, had led fights for Negro rights all over the country. It was something to be proud of. We were serious and dedicated and concerned about what we perceived as social injustice. We would develop, or be handed, a Party line and try to implement it. But as whom? There was the question of openness about being Communists. In a union meeting, for example, should we speak as Party members or not? No one had to declare whether he or she was Democrat or Republican. It was still legal to be a Communist, although Party leaders were being prosecuted under the Smith Act for allegedly advocating force and violence to overthrow the government. The main evidence against them consisted of selective quotes from Marx and Lenin. We were a legal secret society, a powerless sect with grand ideas. Nothing we did that I knew about was even remotely treasonous, let alone revolutionary.

But it was not simply a matter of being open in a public meeting; it was telling the world who you were. And what could happen then? There were any number of reasons for my opting not to declare myself openly a member of the Party. Legal was not the same as accepted. America was not Europe, where you could be a Communist without stigma, even with honor. Friendship with the Soviet Union had been an aberration, a brief consequence of the war. In America the history of socialism was a history of persecution. As a Communist you would be ostracized, certainly marginalized; you could lose your job. You would be condemned to the fringe. Your usefulness to the cause would be diminished. You told your friends—that was something else again; that was voluntary—but you had no obligation to reveal yourself because your enemies demanded it. The reasons for secrecy were all legitimate. There was also the part of myself that simply feared being refused entry into the ranks of the accepted. I had scorned my father's bourgeois hopes for me but could not totally forsake them.

Discussion of foreign events was simpler: Whatever line the Soviet Union took, we followed. It seemed only right. The

Russians had suffered more than anyone (thirty million dead in the war) and they "Knew the Way." We questioned what was happening there, but always within the context of their suffering, their terrible struggle to build the first socialist state in a world that had tried from the beginning to destroy them. This was not always easy. We could not explain the increasing news of Soviet anti-Semitism that way. It did not explain the so-called Doctors' Plot, Jewish doctors imprisoned for supposedly plotting to kill Stalin. If that wasn't anti-Semitism, what was? The Party was concerned and made official queries, demanding an explanation. The Russian answer was that there was no anti-Semitism in the Soviet Union. How could there be? The Soviet Constitution forbade it.

Treason trials had also begun in the Communist countries of Eastern Europe and the people on trial, like the old Bolsheviks executed in the thirties, had also been loyal and devoted Communists. Many had fought bravely in Spain and in World War Two. Some had been captured by the Nazis and tortured. It was inconceivable that they all could be traitors. Here, too, was the rank smell of anti-Semitism. Something was happening there that frightened and confused us. Again, we asked questions and got familiar answers: Fascist intelligence services had penetrated everywhere; some who had been loyal had become disloyal; others had been hidden traitors all along. The answers provoked hot debate in our branch. Some argued that even with its imperfections we still had to defend the Soviet Union. Others said that these were not just imperfections; they were, if true, mortal wounds. I thought the trials smacked of frame-up but felt I had not enough evidence to be sure.

Trying vainly to find some firm ground to stand on, our branch pressed the Party leaders for clarification. Everything was slippery. Dissatisfied, a few left the Party, but most of us stayed. The heart could always find reasons. For me the ties were still too personal and too strong. I had not become a Communist only because of the Soviet Union. Capitalism had not stopped being red in tooth and claw. The people I had known, respected and admired most, wanted most to be like, had been Communists. I felt I could not desert them; I wanted still to belong where they were. I still believed in the cause. Facing the growing attacks from the outside, I dug in my heels. It became a matter of pride and defiance, of identity, the image I had of myself. I would not join the band of ex-Communists, welcomed into a club I wanted no part of, full of people I could not stand, too many of whom were in it only for their own profit. I would not give the bastards the satisfaction of leaving.

But to call our particular meetings subversive was non-sense. Our little group, and all the other Communists I knew, believed in this America we had organized to change. We obeyed its laws. We cherished its values. True, we were still riding a patriotic high from the war, but that was only confirmation of our basic beliefs. There were no contradictions here, no dissonance between supporting Russia and being a good American. And we believed ourselves good Americans. There was nothing else we wanted to be.

The major dissonance for me was between the Party and art. A left-wing novelist and Hollywood screenwriter, Albert Maltz, wrote an article in the *New Masses* criticizing the concept of "art as a weapon." He condemned the vulgarization of art that lay behind most left-wing thinking. He defended James T. Farrell, a novelist of the thirties who was also that most treacherous of apostates, a Trotskyite.

"Writers must be judged by their work, not by the committees they join," Maltz wrote.

This was heresy. He might as well have attacked Stalin. The Party fell on him like the wolf on the fold, led by six articles in the *New Masses* by its literary critic, Samuel Sillen. These were followed by a statement in a report by the party chairman, Eugene Dennis, to the National Committee, condemning the indulgence of the *New Masses* editors toward a "bourgeois-intellectual and semi-Trotskyist article." After more bombardment Maltz recanted, modifying his remarks. We had debated all this in our branch as well as at larger meetings of the Cultural Section called for this purpose. I had spoken at these, siding with Maltz, as did most of my friends, but after the Party's ukase, discussion was ended. This was called democratic centralism. Irwin Shaw asked me how I could take orders from such idiots. I said these idiots were not all the Party was about.

The Party was also not just about America. There was Yugoslavia, for example, symbol of how a socialist pluralism could work. I was often invited to speak about Tito and his new government. I accepted eagerly. It was the first time I had ever spoken to an audience and felt I knew more than they did. Vladimir Dedijer came to New York with another high-ranking Yugoslav official and prepared to tour Slavic communities in the Midwest. They were worried about the pallid American food they would have to eat on the train, so I saw them off with nourishing loaves of black bread, tomatoes, onions and a couple of large salamis. They were grateful and Dedijer told me he had just heard that a street in Belgrade had been named after me. My breaking the story had been valuable to the Yugoslavs, making Tito known to the world and preventing the Allies from putting them on the back burner. Dedijer didn't tell me, though, what neighborhood my street was in.

My other political concentration was on veterans' affairs.

There was much talk about which veterans' organization to join. The American Legion was the largest one in the country. Others were the Veterans of Foreign Wars, started after World War One, and two new ones, American Veterans of World War Two and the American Veterans Committee. The AVC had a good liberal agenda and attracted intellectuals. But the Legion was where the action was, where you went for a beer, a house, a job or advice about benefits. This was especially true in the smaller towns and cities. The Legion was part of local and national politics. It had a powerful grassroots base. It was where you made connections. It had clout. It was also segregated, reactionary and nothing I would ever dream of joining. But most veterans who joined anything were joining the Legion. If you were concerned about veterans' rights, this was the place to affect. This was where you could have real leverage. A group of us met with the Party functionary responsible for veterans' affairs. He was a smart, quiet World War Two veteran named John Gates who had also fought with the Abraham Lincoln Battalion on the Loyalist side in Spain. We all agreed that you went where the masses went.

So a group of us from *Yank* and *Stars and Stripes* formed the Duncan-Paris Post of the American Legion. We named it after Greg Duncan, a *Stars and Stripes* writer, and Pete Paris, a *Yank* photographer. Both had been killed while on frontline assignments. As Commander we elected Marion Hargrove. The Legion was delighted to get us. They had never had anyone like us before. Our ilk had either not joined anything or gone into the AVC. We had also reached beyond writers to include actors, directors and other veterans from the entertainment world. Some joined as a joke, seeing risible possibilities for raising a little hell. Most saw it as a chance for doing some good.

The heads of the Legion were very impressed. We had actors whose voices and faces they knew, writers whose work they had read. We had connections of our own. We could raise money. They were impressed by our induction ceremony, held at the regal Hotel Pierre. Among our speakers was a senator whom the Legion had been wooing for some time without success. We had gotten him with a phone call. There was also a warm message from General Omar Bradley, head of the Veterans Administration, delivered by one of his aides. The Legion brass was even more impressed when we held a housing rally that filled a New York armory and got most of the city's congressmen to attend, along with Lucille Ball and Gene Kelly. We also got the front page of *The New York Times* for that event.

Our grasp seemed entirely adequate to our reach. Meetings were serious and well attended, although the comics tended to get out of hand. They would take the floor and do numbers at any opportunity. One member was an actor who had been attached to Army Intelligence and he told me jovially that one of his assignments had been to check up on me periodically in case I was passing secrets to the Russians. I said I had had no secrets to pass. He said the army knew that but liked keeping an eye on people like me. He hoped I wasn't bothered by his telling me this. I said I wasn't bothered. I knew there was a file on me and assumed there would be some kind of checking up.

My friend Justin Gray, uninterested in going back to school, even found a job organizing for the Legion. He had the same success there as he had had advising generals how to run their war in the Pacific. The Legion felt as if it had struck gold, and after a dizzying success as an organizer Justin was transferred to the national headquarters in Indianapolis and appointed Assistant Director of the National Americanism

Commission in charge of Subversive Activities (*sic*). This was slightly more than we had bargained for. It was one thing to form a Legion post, quite another to have a friend in the job of investigating you. There was a certain frisson in having a spy in the very belly of the beast, but like me with military secrets, Justin had nothing much to spy on. Occasionally he phoned in the middle of the night and whispered that he had found a file on one of our friends and destroyed it. His closest call came when he was sent to check on who was attending some radical rally in town and saw Howard Fast, a prominent leftist writer, arriving as one of the speakers. Fast was another friend and, seeing Justin, started toward him with a wide smile of greeting. Justin turned and fled. Later he told his Legion comrades it was a sudden call of nature. In the Legion, the members called one another comrade, without irony.

But darker forces were tracking us. A columnist for the *New York World-Telegram* denounced the Duncan-Paris Post as a Communist front. He named several of our members, including me, as agents of a Communist conspiracy to infiltrate the American Legion. We answered with a scornful letter to the editor on Red-baiting, but Justin and I also felt an obligation to Marion Hargrove. He was a decent man whose politics were far from radical, and we didn't want him to think he was being duped in any way. We told him we were both Communists. The knowledge did not surprise or shock him. He thanked us in his polite southern way and we went on as before. Then the New York Department of the Legion suspended us. No reason was given; we were included in a list of other posts suspended for inactivity or lack of membership. Neither applied to us, but Winston Churchill had recently made his Iron Curtain speech and the anti-Communist bandwagon had started to roll.

We decided to appeal to the annual National Convention, which was about to open in San Francisco. Money was raised from the working members, and Hargrove and an actor named Arthur O'Connell and I flew out. Justin was there in his official capacity and we took the Presidential Suite in the Fairmont Hotel and immediately held a press conference. It was a great success; knowing the needs of a free press, we had provided a lavish buffet and plenty of scotch. The local papers praised our post and criticized the Legion. We knew we had them beat. As with our housing conference, we had laid on the glamour and celebrity, and it had worked. We knew America.

The next day there was a summit conference between us and three older delegates selected by the Legion. They all looked a little like the actor Guy Kibbee, who played kindly, avuncular roles in movies. They looked friendly and harmless. One was the Republican boss of Iowa, another had been governor of either North or South Dakota, and the third owned most of Arizona. They were very kind to us. They drank our scotch and ate the leftover shrimp. They told stories of World War One and we lied about our war. Then, in their kindly, avuncular way, they told us we were out of the Legion, there was no way of getting back in, and if we tried we would be extremely sorry. There was no further discussion. There was nothing to discuss. They treated us like children. When they left, I thought they were going to pat us on the head.

We hired a lawyer and took the Legion to court, but they won. They knew America better than we did. They knew who made the rules and they knew who enforced them. The post dissolved. I went to Hollywood on a ten-week contract, stayed six months and then came home.

But I had seen how movies were made. I had been initiated

into the mystery, participated in the sacred process. This did
nothing to diminish the illusion. The magic remained. Knowing how it was done only enhanced the appreciation. Making
a movie was like building a cathedral, the hard and skillful
work of many hands. Then you looked at it when it was finished and, if you were blessed, you saw Chartres. If not, you
saw St. Patrick's on Fifth Avenue. It was still a cathedral.
Even as an acolyte I could still enter that dark, embracing
cave and feel mysteriously freed. That was still the same.

The movies were changing, though, as they always did, although maybe only the emphasis changed. Glorious war had
given way to dubious peace, usually shown on screen by
beautiful women betraying vulnerable men. It was as if the
worst fear of the soldier had now safely burst forth: not fear
of the enemy, of being killed or wounded, but of the woman
back home and what she might be doing with her freedom.
Jane Greer did it to Robert Mitchum, Ava Gardner to Burt
Lancaster, Doris Dowling to Alan Ladd. Treachery and dis-
appointment were in the air. Even if the woman remained
loyal, love came to a bad end. Yvonne de Carlo stayed true to
her man (Lancaster again), but Dan Duryea killed them both
anyway. We had won the war, but for what?

Perhaps it was a presentiment. The disturbance was political. Truman proclaimed his doctrine: The United States
would defend "free peoples" anywhere in the world. He instituted a loyalty oath for civil servants. We had "lost" China
to the Communists and someone had to pay for this; the result was a witch-hunt in the State Department. The attorney
general drew up a list of subversive organizations and belonging to them meant serious trouble. Richard Nixon was
elected to Congress on a fervent program of anticommunism.
He had no other issue, but it didn't seem to matter. The Soviet
Union had once again become the enemy. The Russians were

heartless, ruthless, godless and insatiable. We were no longer buddies.

It was happening too fast; it lacked sense. The war had been good to us. Our cities had not been bombed. Our economy was booming. The war had taken us out of the Depression. It had enriched us while impoverishing everyone else. We were the strongest, most powerful, most secure country in the world. We were the only ones with the atom bomb. Still, the government and the press were telling us that we were being threatened from the outside and subverted from within. Congressional hearings were called to validate this and received wide publicity. As always happens, what drew the headlines were the accusations, not the denials, and they had their desired effect, which was to create a climate of fear and suspicion.

I was part of the subversion. The organizations I belonged to were on the attorney general's list. People were starting to lose their jobs for being on that list, for associating with others on that list. Speech was now punishable. You did not have to do anything; you needed only to advocate. The Bill of Rights had suddenly become no protection. And yet, unreasonably, I still felt protected. It was not because of any illusions about freedom of speech or assembly; I knew how power worked when it wanted its way. Laws could be twisted or simply ignored. The evidence was mounting; loyalty oaths were extended to unions, teachers, librarians, scientists, doctors, artists. I felt schizoid in my response, watching this growing attack on decency and reason, the damage it was starting to do, yet feeling I would somehow remain untouched. Perhaps it was simply denial. Or thought being father to the wish. Or stupidity. I thought I was safe because I was as American as anyone else. I was that Yankee Doodle Dandy.

Then came Peekskill.

Paul Robeson tried to give an outdoor concert in a field outside this small city about an hour north of New York. The sponsor was a theatrical agency called People's Artists and the proceeds were to go to the Civil Rights Congress, a left-wing organization devoted to fighting discrimination. Robeson was Promethean: singer, actor, social activist, twice an All-American at Rutgers, a huge star in everything he tried. During the Spanish Civil War, he had gone to Spain to sing for the Loyalists. He was a friend of the Soviet Union and had had his son educated there for a while. He was not a Communist but would not distance himself from Communists. He was admired, even venerated, by both Negroes and whites, although there were those, of course, who hated him just as fiercely for his color and his politics. He had given three previous concerts in the Peekskill area without incident and this one was eagerly awaited.

People got there early, many coming on buses chartered for the occasion. About a hundred women and children were waiting for him when they were attacked by several hundred men and boys from the surrounding area. This crowd carried rocks, clubs and brass knuckles. They yelled that they were going to lynch Robeson. They cursed the nigger bastards and the Jew bastards. They burned a cross on a nearby hill. They also burned a display of books and pamphlets on civil rights. No police were in sight; there were only three FBI agents, who watched without interfering until several of the defenders were seriously hurt, and then offered to drive the wounded to a hospital.

The police came after a while and restored order. No one was arrested. The organizers of the concert were blamed for causing trouble. The following week a protest rally was held at Harlem's Golden Gate Ballroom. The crowd overflowed into the street and afterward marched down Lenox Avenue. Another Robeson concert was scheduled at a picnic grounds that had once been a Peekskill country club. More than ten thousand people came to that concert and a defense perimeter was set up around the field and manned by volunteers from the fur workers' union, the teachers' union, the catchall District 65 and veterans who had fought in World War Two and for the Loyalists in Spain.

I drove up with friends and linked arms on the defense line and watched jeering men parade up and down the road in front of us. Among them were delegations from the American Legion and Veterans of Foreign Wars. I wondered how many of them had read what I had written in *Yank,* how many like them I had admired and written about, what we had in common now. They looked familiar, some even wore their old uniforms, but which ones had burned the cross? What had it taken to get them to beat up women and children, a few drinks fueling the menace of Reds? They had fought and won a war against hatred and bigotry—to become this? I watched them parade, trying to match these hate-filled faces with those I had known. They carried banners denouncing communism and called us the usual names. But there were local and county police this time and state troopers and reporters and photographers, so they made no move beyond invective. They would not have, anyway, even if the police had not been there. On this sort of mission they had no stomach for a fight where they, too, could get hurt.

The day was warm and sunny, and people had brought picnic lunches and listened to the concert as they ate. If you looked at the stage and not out at the road, it was easy to think you were at just another hootenanny. Pete Seeger sang and there were other folk singers, and then Paul Robeson sang and it was no longer possible to think this one was like any other. Our guards reported that two men with high-powered rifles had been seen on the hills overlooking the grounds, so when Robeson stood up to sing, a dozen young men, white and black, formed a wall around him. But he was taller than any of his protection and I thought what a good target he made, what an easy head shot. He sang spirituals and he sang "Water Boy" and "Warsaw Ghetto" and his own militant version of "Old Man River." He had changed the words so it wasn't "get a little drunk and land in jail" but "show a little grit." His voice was not what it had been, but no one cared. He was who he was, a towering, enormously impressive man. He believed what we believed and he had risked his career and, at times, his life for those beliefs. He had size. The audience didn't want him to stop.

Then the concert was over and everyone started to leave. The mood was relaxed and relieved. It had been a fine concert and there had been no trouble. But the police had cordoned off the exits so that there was only one way out, a narrow country road that wound between hillocks of scrub grass. State troopers lined this road as the cars leaving the concert crept along, bumper to bumper. You could not go any faster than two or three miles an hour. Waiting for us were the marchers. They stood on the grass above the police and they had rocks, and as the cars slowly passed, they screamed their abuse and threw those rocks and the police did not stop them. The troopers did not even turn around to look at them. They concentrated on the cars, banging on them with their clubs, yelling at the drivers to move along when there was no possible way to go any faster. A rock crashed through the window of a car ahead of us and a woman screamed and I leaned out and called to a trooper, pointing to some men behind him getting ready to throw more rocks.

"Move, you son of a bitch," he yelled at me, smashing my car's fender with his club. "Move!"

There was no way to move, no way to avoid the assault. The air was filled with rage and terror. Sounds overlapped: the cries of the wounded and the crashing of glass, the banging of rocks against cars, the oaths of the police as they smashed fenders and, over all, the hate-filled words spewing from the gleeful, twisted faces of the rock throwers.

"Nigger bastards! Red bastards! Jew bastards!" Niggerjewcommiekikebastards, the words running together in one long shriek of vomitous racial abuse. I slid down in my seat, everyone except the driver doing the same, but there was no safety anywhere. We were not even free to fight back. Neither was anyone else in the long line of cars. The cops were there to protect the attackers, not us. But the police were not really there for protection at all. They were there for assault. They were the infantry in this attack, guarding the front line so that the artillery behind them was free to fire.

We got through finally and headed back to the city, picking broken glass out of our hair. I don't know how many concertgoers were hurt. About 150 were treated at various hospitals. Most of the injuries were cuts and bruises, but there were also broken arms and fractured skulls. Cars had been attacked even after they had left the area. It did not seem to matter where they were coming from so long as they contained blacks. Two busloads of black students returning from a visit to the Roosevelt Library at Hyde Park were stoned as they drove through Peekskill. All I could think of was that there would have been no riot if it were not for the police. It took me awhile to digest that simple fact. Maybe it was its simplicity. This had been a riot sanctioned and supported by legitimate authority. It had not mattered how much of an American I thought I was. I had been on the wrong side.

The riot was condemned, of course, by the ACLU and the NAACP and liberal newspapers and magazines like the *Nation*. There were demands for hearings, which were rejected by Governor Thomas Dewey. He announced that after investigation by the Westchester County district attorney, it was clear that "Communist groups obviously did provoke this incident." No further statement had to be made; notice had been served. The promise was in the sanctioned attack and the implied justification: Communist groups were to blame and Communist groups were whoever we said they were. They were the people we were against. In the case of Peekskill they were organizations openly supported by the Communists, but in other cases they could be just about anyone, which made them difficult to trap. They were slippery and sly; they used Aesopian language to conceal their real intentions; they were expert in deceit. And so we had our own experts to tell us who they were, and informers to back up the experts, and it did not matter if the informers had to be paid to inform or were caught lying or otherwise discredited; what mattered in this new climate were the accusations.   .

So when the blacklist came to me, I was no longer in denial. On the other hand, I did not believe that fascism had come to America or was even on its way. What had happened at Peekskill was still isolated behavior. We were not a desperate country calling for a savior or the extermination of the other. True, many in the Party thought otherwise. There were rumors of government concentration camps already being set up for radicals when the time came. It had been done for Japanese Americans in World War Two. Detention camps were now sanctioned under the National Security Act. The U.S. Department of Justice had what it called a "Security Index File of individuals to be apprehended and detained in connection with the Detention of Communists Program." The program was known as DETCOM. The Party leadership prepared to go underground.

I continued to write for television, also underground. But

operating under a pseudonym presented problems, like working for *Danger*. Russell had told Lumet, who immediately agreed that they should continue hiring me as Paul Bauman. But there was a catch: Bauman could not be used too often since that would draw attention to him. This brought up the matter of making a living. Working occasionally for only one half-hour television show was not going to pay the rent. I now had an apartment of my own and alimony and child support to pay. I tried for work on other shows, which brought up other problems. Bauman didn't yet have enough credits to get assignments. He needed an agent. Even if he wrote scripts on speculation, he needed an agent to submit them if he wanted them read by anyone in power. I called my agent at the William Morris office. He told me to wear a tie and took me to lunch at an expensive restaurant. This was a clear sign of bad news. He had always picked fine restaurants for a client's lunch, but not that fine. He waited until his second martini before telling me that he could no longer be my agent. Like Russell, he had received orders from above and, upon pain of dismissal, he was not to handle anyone blacklisted, no matter what name he or she put on a script. He said he hated the whole lousy business. I believed him. I hated it even more than he did. I was also worried, scared, anxious and in a rage, a condition not entirely natural to me. Usually it was my ulcer that had to tell me I was angry. Now I didn't need its lacerating help. I was suddenly furious at what was being done to me, even though I accepted without question that if you took a stand, you had to be prepared to pay the price. The agent saw my face change and quickly offered to lend me money. He said he would always be there if I needed anything. He was a kind man, wishing me well.

But in a business where agents were essential I was suddenly agentless. I went to see the few producers I knew besides Russell. They were all sympathetic. None of them liked or wanted the blacklist. They just wouldn't chance giving me work. Their fear was understandable. They could lose their jobs, be banned from the industry. The industry's fear was less understandable. It had the power to fight what it claimed to abhor. But it is difficult to overestimate either the cowardice or the cupidity of large corporations. A man named Laurence Johnson, who owned three supermarkets in Syracuse, New York, urged his customers not to buy products that sponsored shows with Communist talent. He also named those shows, using as authority *Counterattack*, a publication put out by Aware, Inc., a business that accumulated names of alleged Communists or their sympathizers and then cleared them for a fee. Either suspects would come to them or Aware would write to them or to their employers, pointing out the trouble they were in and offering to help. The networks then began sending Johnson names to be cleared by him. The gesture seemed at best redundant. Unlike the movie studios, however, which stressed their patriotism as a reason for refusing work, the networks simply denied there was such a thing as a blacklist. The results were the same.

The sponsor of *Danger* was Ammident toothpaste and the head of the company was a genial, kindhearted man named Mel Block. He liked everyone connected with *Danger*. The ratings were good and the show sold toothpaste. Then he received a visit from Johnson, who said that *Danger* was a Communist-influenced program. It was written by writers and acted by actors who Johnson knew for a fact were Reds. He had been told by experts. Johnson told Block that he had put a sign under the Ammident display in his stores. It said, "Would you buy this toothpaste if you knew the money was going to the Communist Party?" Under the sign were two boxes marked Yes and No. A handy pencil and pad hung

My parents, Louis and Hannah Bernstein, during World War I.

In Marseilles, when I was sixteen. My "year of study" abroad included only an occasional appearance in the classroom; most of my time was spent bicycling and discovering politics.

With Irwin Shaw in Cairo in 1943. Often we would sit back to back at our respective typewriters, I for *Yank* and *The New Yorker*, Irwin writing a play.

My contacts with the left in America helped me become the first journalist granted an interview by Tito after he had emerged as Yugoslavia's leader. I traveled in Yugoslavia in a partisan uniform to avoid being found by the OSS.

Television was already with us as the war wound down. Here I'm interviewed about Yugoslavia after returning to the States.

Walking in New Orleans with Elia Kazan in 1948. I was there to discuss a play I was writing for him.

At that time, Kazan was directing *Panic in the Streets*, in which I found myself (second from right) drafted as an extra. (Richard Widmark and Jack Palance were the stars.)

On that same visit, I met the Greek actor Alexis Minotis (right) and the wildly talented Zero Mostel (left). During his years on the blacklist, Zero's anger and frustration were sometimes frightening.

Producer Charles Russell (left) and director Sidney Lumet on the set of *Danger,* a popular half-hour mystery show for which I wrote in the early days of television. Clearly Russell and Lumet ran considerable risks in employing me.

The writer and director Abe Polonsky (right) didn't want to overthrow the government—just CBS. He and I, along with the writer Arnold Manoff (left), formed a sort of cooperative—sharing whatever work came our way.

1949-50

TITLE: Studio One: **The Storm**
NETWORK: CBS
SPONSOR: Westinghouse
DATE: 10/17/49 (Monday)
HOUR: 10:00-11:00 P.M.

PRODUCER: Worthington Miner
DIRECTOR: Yul Brynner
WRITER: McNight Malmar
ADAPTOR: Worthington Miner

CAST: Marsha Hunt, John Rodney, Dean Haren

First produced in 1948 with Margaret Sullivan, and unfortunately not kinescoped, this show was repeated the following year. Although essentially naive in both subject and technique, Marsha Hunt's performance and a perennially hardy suspense story make it an excellent example of television's primitive period.

1951-52

TITLE: Danger: **The Paper Box Kid**
NETWORK: CBS
SPONSOR: Ammident
DATE: 6/3/52 (Tuesday)
HOUR: 10:00-10:30 P.M.

PRODUCER: Charles Russell
DIRECTOR: Sidney Lumet
BASED ON A STORY BY: Mark Hellinger
MUSIC: Tony Mottola

CAST: Martin Ritt, Grant Richards, Joe Mantell

The half-hour television play picked up where the "two-reeler" and the one-act play left off. This example shows its possibilities in the hands of an adventurous director and actor. Where it may fail on a literal realistic plane, it more than succeeds on an emotional, almost expressionistic level.

TITLE: Philco Playhouse: **The Rich Boy**
NETWORK: NBC
SPONSOR: Philco
DATE: 2/10/52 (Sunday)
HOUR: 9:00-10:00 P.M.

PRODUCER: Fred Coe
DIRECTOR: Delbert Mann
WRITER: Walter Bernstein
BASED ON A STORY BY: F. Scott Fitzgerald

CAST: Grace Kelly, Gene Lyons, Phyllis Kirk, Tom Pedi, Robert Pastene

In its continuous and desperate search for material, television naturally turned again and again to adaptations, ranging from Henry James and William Faulkner to Zane Grey and Jack London. After struggling more or less unsuccessfully with the novel, it discovered that the short story was its proper milieu. W. Somerset Maugham, Arthur Conan Doyle and, as in this example, F. Scott Fitzgerald, enjoyed considerable success.

1952-53

TITLE: You Are There: **The Death of Socrates**
NETWORK: CBS
SPONSOR: Prudential Insurance Co.
DATE: 5/3/53 (Sunday)
HOUR: 6:00-6:30 P.M.

EXECUTIVE PRODUCER: William Dozier
PRODUCER: Charles Russell
DIRECTOR: Sidney Lumet
WRITER: Kate Nickerson
SET DESIGNER: Bob Markel

CAST: Walter Kronkite (Narrator), E. G. Marshall, Barry Jones, Paul Newman, Jim Gregory, Philip Bourneuf, Robert Culp, Richard Kiley, John Baragrey

"You Are There" was one of radio's most original concepts. Transferred to television, it lost none of its excitement, and gained enormously in its ability to re-create history with respect to authenticity, and for educating and entertaining equally well. This particular episode illustrates its power to dramatize material that in another form might be academic or dry.

TITLE: Goodyear Playhouse: **Marty**
NETWOR[K]
SPONSO[R]
DATE:
HOUR:

PRODUC[ER]
DIRECTO[R]

This poster from a Museum of Modern Art Film Library show demonstrates one network solution: if it couldn't use my name, or my front was suspect, a writing credit would simply be omitted.

My dear friend the director Marty Ritt (left) chatting with Richard Harris and Samantha Eggar during the filming of *The Molly Maguires*. I'm clutching my script, while the great cinematographer James Wong Howe (far right) looks on.

The Front—Woody Allen acted, I wrote, Marty Ritt directed. During this period, the mid-seventies, if any film on the blacklist was to be made, it had to be made as a comedy.

The author as the typical screenwriter watching a scene he has written.

nearby and the consumer was asked to indicate his preference: Buy or not buy. The patriotic winner by a large margin, he told Block, was a resounding No. Johnson was certain that Block would understand the significance of this. Block assured him he would clean house at once. Actors and writers would be screened to Johnson's satisfaction.

This extended even to Sidney Lumet. *Counterattack* ran an article claiming Lumet had been not only an associate of known Communists but a former member of that left-wing theater organization, the Group Theater. That Lumet was twelve years old at the time made no difference. The fact that he was not now and had never been a Communist did make a difference but had to be substantiated. *Counterattack* claimed there was evidence to the contrary. Block called Lumet and asked if he would come to his apartment to meet with Victor Riesel and Harvey Matusow. Riesel was a columnist for the Hearst press who moonlighted as a clearance center for blacklisted people who wanted to come clean. Matusow had been a member of the Communist Party when he contacted the FBI with an eye to possible advancement. They hired him for $70 a month to stay in the Party and report to them. He was quickly exposed and kicked out, leaving him free to testify before any committee that would have him. He testified before HUAC, before Senator McCarthy's committee and at various trials for the Justice Department. In all, he named 216 people as Communists. He claimed the Sunday section of *The New York Times* employed 125 members of the Communist Party. He said that *Time* and *Life* magazines had only 76 Communists, but these were "hard core." He was considered a star witness with impeccable credentials.

Two years later, Matusow repented. He confessed publicly that he had lied about those people he had named. He named

other government informers as liars. He wrote a letter to
Henry Luce, publisher of *Time*, saying he didn't really know
of any Communists working for the magazine. He was sorry
for what he had done. The Justice Department retaliated by
indicting him for perjury and sending him to jail.

Matusow was riding high, though, when Lumet arrived at
Block's apartment on Park Avenue. He was there with Riesel
and the worried host. They were looking at a photograph in
the monthly American Legion magazine. It was a picture of a
Communist Party meeting. They looked at Lumet when he
entered, looked again at the picture and then Matusow
turned back to Lumet.

"Don't get your balls in an uproar," he said genially.
"You're not the one."

"What about his wife?" Riesel asked, hoping for the best.
"Maybe she's there."

She wasn't in the picture, either. They had been told that a
couple in the photograph were Lumet and his wife; this had
been *Counterattack*'s evidence. Now they knew better, but no
one apologized to Lumet for bringing him there. Block was
relieved and offered him a drink. Riesel left without a word.
Matusow slapped him on the back and wanted him to know
there was nothing personal. Lumet was free now to work; he
should go out and celebrate. In fact, Matusow would even
give him a lift home.

But Paul Bauman was in another kind of trouble. A CBS
producer named Worthington Minor asked Russell where he
could contact this new writer. Minor had seen and liked his
work and wanted to hire him for a prestigious show he produced called *Studio One*. Russell was forced to be inventive.
He told Minor that Bauman was peculiar, even for a writer.
He lived alone on a mountaintop in Colorado and shunned
personal encounters. He had no telephone and mailed in his

scripts. Minor insisted. Russell grew desperate. Bauman was ill with a rare tropical disease. He had gone to Switzerland for a cure. In any case, he was unavailable. Minor became testy. He said nobody went to Switzerland for a tropical disease. He accused Russell of wanting Bauman all to himself. This was serious. Blacklisting a writer was one thing, hogging him quite another. Russell and Minor had been friendly colleagues. Now they became enemies.

I felt sorry for Russell, who was rather enjoying himself. He felt he was lying in a good cause. Russell was not a natural liar and it pleased him to be able to lie without guilt. He had no sympathy for Minor, who was, after all, a competitor of sorts. There were other writers out there and he thought Minor would soon forget about Bauman. My problem was paying the rent. I was no longer on staff at *The New Yorker*, although I had left with the understanding that I would continue to write for it. But the atmosphere had changed there, too. It had become murky. Shawn was unfailingly polite, but assignments that had been habitual were not now forthcoming. I began to feel I was slowly being pushed off a cliff. The FBI paid its first call, asking about Bill Remington, and then it came again, two different men, equally polite, asking about me. This time I was prepared. I was not about to talk to them about anything. Talking would only increase the file they had on me. It would implicate me further and possibly be used against my friends. The FBI was always after two things in its interrogation: what it could find out about you and anything else it could glean from what you may unwittingly have told its agents. I said I had nothing to say and the men left as politely as they had come.

Russell's pleasure at orchestrating Paul Bauman did not last very long. The networks were nervous and suspicious, and they soon decided that blacklisted writers were not playing fair. They were undoubtedly hiding behind pseudonyms. The networks would be blamed if this were discovered. They could even be accused of being a party to the subterfuge since some network executives had made impulsive statements about the iniquity of a blacklist. Frank Stanton, the president of CBS, said a blacklist was not only un-American but illegal. It was nothing his network would ever be a party to. On the other hand, there was no point asking for trouble. Sponsors might be less high-minded. Congressional committees could come calling. CBS producers were told that writers must show their faces in order to be employed. A live body had to accompany each script.

Suddenly the blacklist had achieved for the writer what he had previously only aspired to: He was considered necessary. Scripts had always been reluctantly acknowledged as necessary; after all, you really couldn't have a show without them. This didn't mean once the script was in hand that you needed the writer. But now the writer was needed: for conferences, rehearsals, publicity, even the shooting itself, although what writers could do once a live show went on the air was problematical since it could not then be stopped. But a name alone was no longer acceptable.

"Someone has to go in as Paul Bauman," Russell said to me.

I said that was impossible.

"You could hire an actor," Russell said. "Actors will do anything for a part."

It was not possible. I could find no way of getting someone to appear as someone else who didn't exist. Bauman would have to go. Still, it was nice to be needed. For years writers had fought unsuccessfully for the right to be included in those matters affecting their work. Now our presence was required, even demanded. But there was a contradiction to be resolved

here, at least for those of us blacklisted. We were both
wanted and unwanted at the same time. Invited in while being thrown out. Simultaneously heaped with praise and
dumped on with calumny. And in the same body. The answer
turned out to be simple, if schizoid. What the networks always sought were shows that seemed different but were actually the same. We would simply carry on the tradition. I
would be two people, the same but different.

I buried Paul Bauman with sorrow. He had been good to
me, although I never did get to like the name. Russell told
Worthington Minor that Bauman's tropical disease had
proved fatal. He had died of brain fever in a Swiss hospital.
Russell had really wanted Bauman to commit suicide by
jumping off an Alp when he learned his illness was terminal.
As a producer he thought this kind of death more dramatic
than a bland expiration between sheets. He also thought it
more appropriate for a writer. I thought it a little too exotic.
Credibility was not the issue, of course—Minor did not believe Russell any more than he had before. But the unhappy
deed was done.

Now I had to find a live body that could show up. He did
not have to be in the business. Anyone could write a television script and send it in. He did not even have to be a writer,
although that would certainly help. He could be a salesman
or a dentist. Writing scripts was what people now did in their
spare time, the way they used to do embroidery or collect
stamps. It seemed easy. They constantly saw bad movies in
theaters and stupid shows on television and thought anyone
could do better than that. The assumption was not entirely
unreasonable. As fronts, though, they had to be intelligent,
articulate and fast on their feet. They would be claiming as
their own scripts I had written and they might have to answer
story questions. A certain amount of stalling was normal; a

writer did not always have the answer on the spot; but there was even artfulness in that. You had to be able to pretend you knew what you were stalling about.

And there was the matter of trust. We had to trust each other. In particular, he had to trust me. I could not be black-listed any more than I was, but whatever life a front had apart from me could be severely hurt if it were known what he was doing. So there had to be a very good reason why a front was doing this.

While I was searching for this elusive individual, I still had to find work. The blacklist had not yet extended to maga-zines, although it was on its way, and I was lucky to get a few assignments. I wrote mainly about sports, interviewing fight-ers and fight trainers and jockeys and jockeys' wives and baseball umpires. The subjects were safe and took me into a world whose politics were too parochial to be damaging. I wrote for *Argosy* and *Life* and *Sports Illustrated* and did a three-part article for *Collier's* on the fighter Rocky Graziano. At the time Graziano was under suspension for failing to re-port a bribe offer and the *Collier's* piece helped get him rein-stated and we became friends. Rocky was very polite outside the ring and anxious to please. Like many fighters, he had a surprisingly soft handshake. We would meet in a saloon on Second Avenue called Fox's Corners and sometimes Graziano's good friend Jake La Motta would join us and we would drink and talk away the afternoons. La Motta would then leave to find some dubious action, but Graziano had been warned to stay out of trouble if he wanted to fight again and he would climb sadly into his car and head home to Brooklyn.

Other times we met in a bar owned by the father of a styl-ish lightweight named Billy Graham. When a fighter is deemed stylish, it usually means that he does not pack a punch that can upend an opponent, and that was true of Graham. Before the war I had seen him knock someone out at Sunnyside Gardens, in Queens, and I mentioned that to him when we met. He was still puzzled over how it had happened. Graham was a delight to watch in the ring. He came to work like a master craftsman who knew exactly how to get the job done. His tools were his hands and his feet and his head. He told me once that he felt totally safe in a bout. He knew no one could really hurt him. He was good enough to beat another very good fighter, Kid Gavilan, for the lightweight title; at least everyone but the judges saw it that way. They gave the decision to Gavilan, who was as shocked as everyone else. Graham just stood in his corner and tried to hold back the tears, his face contorted at the effort, while the crowd howled its disapproval. His battle against showing what he felt as weakness was as hard as the one against Gavilan and finally he lost that one, too. He closed his eyes when the tears started rolling down and his trainer slipped his robe around him and the crowd continued to howl and throw paper cups and programs and even chairs into the ring.

Graziano had been a bad boy in his youth and frequently ducked out of training to find less strenuous pursuits. He could always be found on a street corner, hanging out with his friends. He got homesick easily. Drafted into the army, he had been sent to San Francisco and immediately went AWOL. He was picked up the next day in his old neighborhood. It never occurred to him to hide. All he wanted was familiarity. As a fighter Graziano got away with a lack of conditioning because most of his fights didn't last long enough for him to get tired. He was the opposite of Billy Graham: He did not box very well, but he was a knockout artist. The fans loved him.

When the Boxing Commission allowed him to fight again,

Graziano was quickly booked for a main event at Yankee Stadium against a good club fighter named Charley Fusari. He behaved himself in training, working hard with his sparring partners, keeping curfew. When fight night came, he was in the best condition of his life. In the fight itself he was terrible. Possibly it was ring rust. Always before there had been a wild animal ferocity about Graziano when he fought. Now he seemed tamed. Fusari jabbed him for nine rounds and made him look foolish. In the tenth round he caught up to Fusari and, in a flurry of desperation, knocked him out. The crowd went wild; Rocky had not disappointed them.

I went to see him afterward in his dressing room. The room was packed with reporters and photographers and jubilant well-wishers. The smell of sweat and money was in the air. Rocky was back, the gate attraction. He sat on a table, still in his trunks, and saw me standing in the doorway and beckoned me over. I pushed my way through the crowd and he slid off the table and drew me aside. He did not look like a man who had just snatched victory from the jaws of defeat. There was no satisfaction on his face, only a kind of bewilderment. He knew what had happened, but he could not really understand it.

"I was good," he kept saying. "I trained. I stood home at night."

He had done what they had wanted him to do and what he had never been able to do before. He had been a good boy. He had conformed. And in the process, he had lost what had made him successful. He had lost his ferocity, his killer instinct. He could still punch, but a lot of fighters can punch. Few could match that power with Graziano's savagery. It was what made him popular, what the crowd came to see. It had been his ticket out of the streets. Now it was gone. He had been domesticated. At that moment he felt he had made a very bad trade. He had given away something integral to him and he did not know what could take its place. Later I wondered, without evidence, whether the fight had been fixed, if Fusari had gone into the tank. A Fusari victory would have made no one happy, especially not the people who controlled boxing in those days. There was no money to be made from Fusari. He was a dull, competent fighter who could not, as they say, draw flies. Graziano need not have known.

I also interviewed the great Sugar Ray Robinson. I had seen him fight numerous times. He was the best fighter I ever saw. He could box and he could hit and he fought with arrogant grace, totally exposed, because there was no caution in how he fought. He fought like a true artist, daringly. So he could be hit and even knocked down, but then he would always get up and either knock out the other man or coolly go on to win the decision. No one wanted to fight him. He was a natural welterweight at 147 pounds, but he was forced to fight middleweights who weighed 160. He won those fights, too, until he met Jake La Motta, who was so good that nobody wanted to fight him, either. Robinson gave away 15 pounds and beat him. Then La Motta beat Robinson, the first time Sugar Ray ever lost. Then Robinson beat La Motta again.

In that fight Robinson leaned against the ropes in a late round and put one arm on the top rope and dropped the other arm to his side and just let La Motta swing at him. Robinson ducked and bobbed and weaved and didn't throw a punch. He was not hurt; he was showing off. Or maybe he was just showing La Motta the difference between talent and genius. Or proving something to himself. It seemed to go on forever. You wanted it to stop because it was too dangerous, La Motta was too good to be held off this long, but you also wanted it to go on because you were seeing greatness. The crowd, which had a love-hate relationship with Robinson (it even took his refusal to sit down between rounds as disdain for it), started to boo. Then, as La Motta swung fruitlessly at a target he thought he had finally cornered, the booing turned to reluctant applause and then finally the whole arena was cheering and only then did Robinson spin off the ropes and resume punching.

Interviewing Robinson was another kind of fight. He lied to me as he had lied to La Motta: Here I am, I offer myself to you, hit me. He was pleasant, articulate and hostile without ever being personal. His smile made it plain that he did not care whether I believed him or not. Most of the time I didn't. But he invited me to ride with him some nights in his pink Cadillac, driving slowly through the Harlem streets, stopping to chat and sign autographs and occasionally make a date with a girl. Once he was to present an award at Sunnyside Gardens and asked me along. He drove a hundred miles an hour across the Triborough Bridge and I thought we would never get there alive. After he presented the award, we stayed to watch the main event, a bout between a black journeyman heavyweight named George Parker and a recent white hope who had been a bomber pilot in the late war. About halfway through the first round Robinson began to laugh.

"Georgie's doing business," he said, chuckling.

The fight had seemed on the level to me, even exciting, but now I could see that the terrible blows absorbed by Georgie were being taken on his arms and shoulders while the crowd cheered wildly for the handsome ex-pilot throwing this other kind of bomb. Finally, Georgie sank to the canvas after a stupefying blow to the forearm and was counted out. A satisfied buzz ran through the crowd; they were certain this new hope was real. But Robinson was critical of the performance. "Georgie needs lessons," he said with professional disapproval.

But Robinson was not mobbed up and refused to give away pieces of himself and he had a big mouth when it came to racial matters and was known to have spoken well about Paul Robeson and so he was not getting any shots at a title. This wore on him to the point where he went to the columnist Walter Winchell and asked for help. Winchell had influence. He was friendly with J. Edgar Hoover and also various luminaries on the other side of the law, some of whom were interested in boxing not only for love of the sport. The fugitive head of Murder, Inc., the notorious Louis "Lepke" Buchalter, would surrender only to Winchell rather than to the police, who he thought, not without reason, would shoot him down like a dog. Soon after his pilgrimage to Winchell, Robinson was allowed to fight Tommy Bell for the vacant welterweight title. Bell knocked him down, but Robinson got up, as usual, and won the decision and was finally a crowned champion. Now, when he spoke publicly, it was often about God, and if he mentioned Robeson at all, it was critically.

I was blacklisted in 1950. In the previous year the leaders of the Communist Party had been convicted under the Smith Act. This was more criminal nonsense. The Party never advocated force and violence. Anyone trying to overthrow the government would have been immediately expelled. It only made most of us more defensive. Some of those convicted went to prison; others skipped bail and went underground. The irony was that the Party had justified the Smith Act when it had been used during the war against the Socialist Workers Party, a Trotskyist group protesting the war.

It was a dishonorable year all around. By 1950 the CIO had begun expelling its left-wing unions. The McCarran Act was passed, enabling the president to order, during "internal security emergencies," the roundup and imprisonment of "dangerous Americans." Definitions were not included. What was meant by "emergency" or "dangerous" was not specified. Alger Hiss, a high-ranking State Department official, was convicted of perjury on the testimony of a witness whom psychiatrists called a psychopath, President Truman announced we were going to build a hydrogen bomb, and the Korean War started.

Also in that year Senator Joseph McCarthy told a meeting of Republican women in Wheeling, West Virginia, that he had in his hand a list of 205 Communists in the State Department. He had no proof of this; he did not have a list; he had nothing in his hand except air. But in the climate of the day his accusation made immediate headlines. The next day, meeting a friendly reporter, McCarthy held up a rolled newspaper as if it were a club.

"You know what I've got here?" he said, grinning. "A sockful of shit."

He had indeed. The air turned smelly and poisonous. Both the Senate and the House of Representatives now had committees in full cry, hunting down Reds, pinkos and other affronts to the social order. A pliant press decried their methods but supported their aims, and rarely questioned their right to prosecute for political association. I began to accept that phone calls to people I knew at the networks would probably not be returned. When they were, I was surprised. Most of the time they weren't. Even though I no longer worked for *Danger,* I occasionally met Russell at a bar near Grand Central Station, where the show was shot. CBS executives, advertising agency executives, actors and production people also met there, and we had had friendly drinks together. Now some of them moved away when I came in or turned their backs, trying to make the movement natural or imperceptible. They were nice people who did not want to hurt my feelings. Not all did that, of course, not actors or costume designers or art directors; the fear seemed restricted to executives. It was one of their perks.

Still, even a few of those would make a point of coming to our table or joining us at the bar. They would tell me they hated what was going on. Everyone hated what was going on. Some offered to loan me money. In the coming days that was to be a frequent pattern: commiseration, frustrated anger at what was happening and the offer of a loan. They were all sorry they could not help me find a job. They were all sincere. They did what they felt they could. One evening, as I was about to leave, the bartender handed me an envelope. He said it was from one of the advertising executives. We had drunk together; he liked to swap stories about the war. He was one of the men who nodded now when I caught his eye and then turned away. In the envelope was a hundred-dollar bill. I left it there and wrote "thank you" on the envelope and handed it back to the bartender.

Job loss for political association was not, of course, restricted to the entertainment business. That was only a kind of loss leader. Newspapers liked hearings involving show business because the names were sometimes familiar, or at least the shows or movies the names went with, and congressional committees liked them because they gave them publicity. But the real effect was intimidation. The content of movies and television, like that of newspapers, was always controlled by the people who owned them. They did not like anyone telling them whom they could hire. They wanted the largest talent pool available. They did not take seriously the idea that Communists had infiltrated the media; they knew better. What they did take seriously was the government. Federal regulations could hurt them. Federal prosecution could damage them badly. They did not want to cross the powerful Hoover and his FBI and they did not want to be investigated

by any congressional committee. They wanted to be left alone
to make money. If a condition of that was a blacklist, the
price was trifling.

Patriotism was the touchstone here. Whose side were you
on, were you really on, since true subversives assumed many
guises. Marxist scripture was not all the devil could quote; he
also knew the Bill of Rights. He could sing "America the
Beautiful" and make you think he believed it. We were in a
cold war with the Russians and a suddenly hot one with their
Asian—what? Cohorts? Minions? Stooges? All those words
were used, as if neither the North Koreans nor the Chinese
had identities of their own. Being Communists, they were
simply tools of a Soviet conspiracy. Being Asian, they were
faceless. They were hordes. The Korean War was not discuss-
able in any rational way. Probably no war is when it is going
on. Either you accepted this one as unprovoked aggression or
you were soon a pariah. I was already a pariah, but I found
myself quarreling with supportive friends like Irwin Shaw or
a gentle man named Gus Lobrano, an editor at *The New
Yorker* with whom I regularly played squash. We had disagreed before on things, but there was an intolerance now—
on both our parts—that turned the argument bitter and
created a distance between us.

I chose to consider my intolerance defensive. After all, I
was the one being punished for having exercised my rights as
an American. I had a good excuse to feel sorry for myself, although I felt sorrier for the actors and directors. They had to
show their faces to work, whereas writers could hide behind
pseudonyms or fronts. My problem was staying afloat until I
found a front. The magazine assignments were drying up as
the climate worsened. Rent had to be paid. I lived in an old
sea captain's house in Chelsea and my landlord was an ec-
centric Englishman who lived in the West Indies. He had be-

come rich by inventing a valve for difficult liquids with the intriguing name of the Saunders Stopcock. He belonged to a sect called British Israelites. He was not around very much, but he was friendly when he came and liked to visit with the tenants. When I would tell him he would have to wait awhile for the rent, he would urge me to buy the house instead. He was willing to sell at a more than reasonable price.

"That way, dear boy," he would say, "you would not have to pay any rent."

I pointed out in turn that I did not have enough money to pay the rent, let alone buy the house. He failed to understand why that should be an impediment. He thought less of me for thinking so. He had never paid any rent, he told me, any more than he had ever paid income tax. The trick there was never to declare any income in the first place; then they've got nothing to get you on.

I needed money and had no skill besides writing, unless an encyclopedic memory for old movies could be called a skill. It was certainly not a marketable one. I briefly considered doing what John Maynard Keynes had done: Get up early, loll in bed while doping out the stock market, make some money with a phone call and then go off to my real work. A friend of mine was actually doing this and he said it was a snap. The requirements were simple. They were the same as being a movie director. You had to be normally intelligent and you had to do a little homework. Given that, you could beat the odds. It sounded great, certainly easier than writing a script. My qualifications were obvious: I was reasonably intelligent, an expert loller, hated homework but could do it if cornered, and I got up early, anyway. I couldn't wait to get started. Unfortunately I soon discovered that you had to have money to make money. That took care of the stock market.

I invested in other kinds of lotteries. The Irish Sweepstakes seemed promising, but my horse ran next to last. For a while I believed there was not a raffle I would not win. I bought raffle tickets for cookies, mink coats, trips to Florida and automobiles. I figured if I won something I didn't need, I could sell it and then have money to play the stock market. I lived each day in a manic, totally unreal hope. Every time the phone rang, I thought it was either my winning ticket or the FBI. The times were pushing me off center. At night, when I couldn't sleep, I would go out and wander around the city, much as I had done as an adolescent. Unconsciously I longed for a time of promise and safety. Some nights I would ride the subway out to Coney Island and walk along the deserted boardwalk and look out at the dark, quiet sea, where, on Tuesday nights through my childhood summers, brilliant soaring fireworks were shot off from a barge while thousands of people packed the sands to watch and I sat high above them, awestruck, on my father's shoulders.

Then I found a front, by accident. I was visiting my reluctant agent when one of his working clients came into the room. His name was Paul Monash, and he was an established writer of television dramas. The agent, eager to be of assistance so long as he was not involved, told Monash about my predicament and Monash immediately offered to help. We had not known each other before. He did not know me even as much as Russell had when he stuck his neck out for me. Monash was taking this big risk for a total stranger. I had no idea of his politics, whether we agreed or disagreed, or anything else about him except that he was a good writer. Now I knew that he had courage and class. I was very grateful. I wrote a *Danger* show for Russell and it was shown under Monash's name. It turned out that he had a show of his own on another program that same night, but no one noticed any difference in styles, only how prolific he was.

But Monash had his own work to do and could front only

this one time. He could not seem prolific to the point of suspicion. I had to find someone else. It was like trying to find an apartment. I asked everyone I knew. No one seemed willing or qualified. I bought more lottery tickets. Then a musician I knew suggested his girlfriend. He said she had always wanted to be a writer and he had often seen her reading books. The woman's name was Rita and my friend said she was smart and articulate and crazy enough to do this. Lunacy was not high on my list of qualifications, but I agreed to meet her at his apartment.

Rita turned out to be a tall, skinny blond woman with a mind of her own. She did not like to be contradicted. She was sensitive to slights. She had an interesting way of showing this. My friend lived on the tenth floor and, when piqued, Rita would open a window and climb out on a ledge and sit there until unpiqued, legs dangling over the side, blond hair flying in the wind. The first time this happened, I reached to pull her back, but my friend restrained me. He said it was best to leave her alone. He was confident no harm would come to her. He had a theory that people as batty as Rita only destroyed others.

Rita agreed to front for me. She saw it as a chance to break into the writing game. She asked for 20 percent of whatever I got and was annoyed when I told her it wouldn't be what I normally got. Payment was based on credits and she had none. Rita, the unknown writer, would be starting at minimum. She was ready to go out on the ledge again at that one but was persuaded to stay in the room when I offered 25. I told Russell, who was pleased although he thought 25 percent steep just for a name. I told him what agents always told me when I complained about what they took, that 25 percent of something is better than 100 percent of nothing. She was doing me a big favor.

I wrote a *Danger* script that Russell bought under Rita's

name. He told CBS it was one of the many unsolicited manuscripts he received. No one questioned this. Rita cashed the check that came in her name and mailed 75 percent of it to me. The problem now became taxes. The income had to be declared, but as what? On the face of it she was paying me for services rendered, but I didn't know what to say if asked what services. A friend suggested sexual favors, reasoning that the IRS would believe anything so long as the tax was paid. This was tempting, but not subject to close scrutiny. Being her collaborator was out, since my name was not on the script and it would seem odd to be a researcher who took three-quarters of the fee. I also had to be not only legal but scrupulous. All the blacklisted people were convinced by then that along with other forms of surveillance, the FBI was inspecting our tax returns. Finally, I just banked the money and decided to declare it simply as income and worry about its provenance when the time came.

The arrangement worked perfectly. I would rendezvous with Russell at some anonymous bar and give him the script with Rita's name on it. We would have further clandestine meetings about rewrites. There was no need for Rita to appear, so long as everyone knew she was a real person and could be produced if necessary. The sponsor, the advertising agency and the network all were pleased at discovering this new writer. Rita was pleased at seeing her name on the screen. By now I was used to seeing someone else's name on my work. It no longer gave me a pang. Whatever grief or anger I may have felt was masked by the demands of survival. I took comfort from the fact that I was outwitting the bastards who were blacklisting me, that I was not being destroyed, that at least Russell and Lumet knew who wrote those scripts. I valued their appreciation.

After a couple of scripts Russell expressed his pleasure by

raising Rita's fee. She thought this was only fair. Her shows had been well received and she believed she deserved more money. She asked what would her friends think if they knew how little she was getting. Her friends were seeing her differently now, as a person of substance. The only one who treated her the same was her boyfriend, who knew the truth. This rankled. She wanted more respect and she was getting it now from other men. She was thinking of dumping him but thought he might retaliate by telling everyone she was only a front. I assured her he was too honorable for that. But they were not getting along. She was spending too much time out on the ledge. For the first time she worried about falling off. I thought that was a good sign. Maybe this all meant that she would take better care of herself. I was getting to like Rita and hated myself for the despicable, if fleeting, thought that if she did fall off, I would have to start looking for a front all over again.

Happily Rita did not fall, but she did call one day and asked if she could come to see me. She was in tears when she arrived. She said she could no longer be my front. Her analyst had said it was bad for her. She had a weak enough ego as it was and this was only making it worse. She had told him it was making her happy, but he said it was a false happiness and not to be trusted. If she wanted to get well, she would have to be herself all the time, however miserable. Indeed, if she were not miserable, how could she know when she was getting well? He acknowledged that her fear now of going out on the ledge was a good sign, but, like all good signs, it was deceptive.

By the time she finished telling me this, her tears were gone and she was starting to get angry. She was not angry at the analyst. She was angry at me. I was the cause of her false happiness. I had taken her into the promised land only so that she could be kicked out. She had even lost her fearlessness on the ledge. What would her friends say? What could she tell them to explain her falling star? I offered suggestions. The one she liked best was that she had suffered a mammoth writer's block. Even the best writers got that. Her friends all knew she was in therapy and whatever was surfacing there had caused this unfortunate dysfunction. She didn't know how long it would last. She was working on it, but her analyst had given no guarantees. Perhaps she would have to give up writing altogether as the price of mental health. Sometimes being an artist exacted too high a toll. Rita found this consoling; it appealed to her sense of drama. She thought of herself now as a tragic heroine.

I was back to beating the bushes. The only consolation was that I was not alone in this. The Un-American Activities Committee was in full swing across the country and the McCarthy Committee was not far behind. They claimed to be on a Red hunt, but the net was cast wider than that. They were really after the New Deal and the welfare state and pantywaist liberals and the civil rights movement and militant unions and the traitors in the State Department who had "lost" China to the Communists and anyone who did not support the cold war. Those who did not cooperate with them lost their jobs. It was as simple as that. It was bipartisan. The Democrats had started this race with the Internal Security Act, calling for the registration of "Communist organizations," excluding from entry into the United States anyone affiliated with any organization advocating totalitarianism, and setting up detention camps for Communists should there be invasion, insurrection or just national emergency. They then passed the baton to the happily accepting Republicans. With a few exceptions, the press performed its usual function of not questioning real power. Schools and school boards, professional organizations, corporations and even libraries all went along. *The Wizard of Oz* was taken off the shelves of a Minnesota public library because it was deemed a socialist tract. Actually it *was* a socialist tract. L. Frank Baum intended the Wizard to stand for William Jennings Bryan and the yellow brick road for the gold standard. *Huckleberry Finn* was also banned in some libraries. The bigot's eye is unerring; it finds only the best. Dalton Trumbo, the blacklisted screenwriter, wrote a pamphlet calling this period the Time of the Toad. It was worse than that. It was the time of the adder.

Most of the people in *Red Channels* refused to clear themselves by confessing error or giving names. They became immediately unemployed. Some were able to leave the country. I applied several times for a passport but was turned down for reasons of state. We found ourselves drawing closer together. Before, we might assemble for politics or fund-raising; now we went to one another's houses simply for comfort. Plates of food would be set out, and horror stories exchanged. Surprisingly we laughed a lot. No matter how horrendous the story, we could usually find some dark humor in it. Maybe it was because many of us were Jewish. We specialized in the hilarity of doom. New friendships were formed and quickly became precious. If someone were in particular need, money would be pooled and given. We helped one another without thought of repayment or consequence and did not think this unusual. I came to depend on these gatherings. In a way I could not explain, I was becoming more free. The feeling was strange and even disquieting; it did not correspond to the facts of the case. Yet some generous part of me was being liberated. I began to realize how used I had become to the anxiety of competition, how much I had taken it for granted. Here it was gone, replaced by the pleasure of cooperation.

On rare occasions, serendipity struck. A blacklisted actor

named Lawrence gave up and left to live on some arid land he had inherited in Oklahoma. Lawrence was a good-natured man who had played violent character parts, quite in contrast to his own genial personality. He had a good-natured wife and three well-behaved children. We hated to see them leave. Lawrence had no idea what he would do in Oklahoma, but at least he would not have to worry about rent. He figured he could get some kind of job. His land was useless for growing anything, but there were small towns nearby and he was handy with tools. He did not have enough money for train fare, so we gave him a party and took up a collection. Everyone wept as we saw the Lawrence family off at Penn Station. Six months later we received a check for the money we had given him, plus five thousand dollars to spread among those in need. In desperation he had leased some of his useless land to a speculator who had then struck oil. Lawrence figured he was now a millionaire.

The FBI had settled into regular visits. At first the agents came to my apartment, two different men each time, wearing neatly pressed dark suits and snap-brim hats. The clothing made them look both oddly alike and mismatched, as though they were unrelated but from the same orphanage. They would introduce themselves, show their badges and say they would like to talk to me. I would answer that I had nothing to say and close the door. They would go away. They never insisted, never threatened. But then they began accosting me on the street or outside a store or a theater when the performance was over, or on a subway platform or even once when I got off a bus. They would do this about once or twice a month. The object was to let me know that they always knew where I was. It seemed a great waste of the taxpayer's money. I knew they knew, just as I knew they were tapping my phone. That is, I didn't really know, but I took it for granted.

I did know that they inspected my garbage, because the janitor told me. He was the younger brother of a well-known actor and our landlord had given him the ground-floor apartment rent-free in return for custodial duties. He was an agreeable young man still trying to make up his mind what he wanted to be when he grew up. Being a janitor in a small building with nondemanding tenants was a congenial way station. But he loved his brother and all other actors and considered me part of the fraternity. He said the FBI was interested in the letters I received and the magazines I read. The agents also asked him to describe the people who visited me. I wondered what they could glean from the descriptions. My friends looked as harmless as rabbits. At best, they had a wary, hangdog look. But in a paranoid age even rabbits were not above suspicion. There was danger in being excessively harmless, like being prematurely antifascist.

I was not the only one they were doing this to, of course, and they did no harm to me except increase my level of suspicion. I worked at home; I had no employer they could intimidate. But some of my friends had found other jobs, outside the entertainment industry, and they were more vulnerable. One blacklisted actor was working as a cashier in a meat market when the usual pair of FBI agents visited his boss and asked if he knew the kind of man who was working for him. The boss then fired my friend, although with apologies and a package of lamb chops to take home to his family. Other times the FBI agents simply asked an employer if they could speak to his worker; the visit alone created a climate of fear. Once in a while the employer resisted, but not often. The implied threat was that it would be known he was sheltering Communists and that could be bad for business.

On the whole the visits accomplished their purpose. I was starting to look around when I left my house, looking over my shoulder when I walked down the street, bracing myself for the inevitable encounter. Even expecting it, I was startled when it came, and there would be the sudden sour taste of fear for a moment and then a shaming wave of anger, not at them but at myself for being afraid. I could never get really angry at them. They were only doing their job, like delivering milk. The only time I got mad was when one of the agents was named Cohen. Then it suddenly became personal. It was no longer just a job, it was a betrayal. Jews were not supposed to be in the FBI, chasing down other Jews, or anyone else for that matter. They had not survived this much persecution to become persecutors. I had loved Cagney in *G Men,* but my feelings about the FBI had evolved since then. I asked Cohen what he was doing there. They had stopped me as I was about to get on a bus and the bus driver held the door open until I signaled he could go ahead. The passengers watched curiously through the windows as the bus pulled away. The heavy smell of its exhaust hung in the air. The street was quiet and I felt good. Here was something I could attack. Special Agent Cohen stood stolidly in front of me, his partner beside him. I asked him again. What was a Jew doing in the FBI? I said he should be ashamed. He didn't answer, his turn not to talk.

As usual, movies provided succor. I even started going in the afternoon and felt again the guilty pleasure of coming out of a movie into daylight. When I had exhausted the first-run theaters, I would troll Forty-second Street for the B movies or the revivals, finding comfort in the familiar. The prints were worn and grainy, and the old, broken-down theaters smelled of urine and lost hope, but none of that mattered. You could find on the screen what you needed. I even found *You Were Never Lovelier* in a print where the sound was always a few beats behind the action. It bothered everyone except me; I already had a perfect print in my head.

The new movies were different. They were becoming glossier. They were also becoming emptier. Psychology was in, social criticism was out (unless it was criticism of communism, but that was not so much social as religious). People were bad because they were bad. Occasionally they were bad because their parents had not loved them enough, although they could also turn rotten if their parents had loved them too much. Whether it was Raymond Massey refusing parental love to James Dean in *East of Eden* or Margaret Wycherly dandling a crazed and murderous James Cagney on her knee in *White Heat*, parents were a handy excuse for truant behavior. It was easier to blame it on Mom and Dad than on some kind of system. It was also more fun.

Sexual betrayal was still a big theme, as it had always been, but now, if a woman betrayed a man, she might be doing it for the Russians. The studios embraced anticommunism with the same calculated fervor they had recently reserved for Stalin. Hot or cold, a war was a war. There were good guys and bad guys. All the studios needed was to be told who was who. The government told them that. None of these movies was successful. They had all the moralizing of the World War Two movies, but none of their skill. They had titles like *The Iron Curtain, The Red Menace, The Red Nightmare, I Was a Communist for the FBI, I Married a Communist*. They presented a gullible America on the verge of being taken over by ruthless Communists even though most of these seemed to be either seriously stupid or alarmingly out of shape.

We were always being betrayed by our good impulses. Innocence would be our downfall. Women were a trap, unless they were suffering wives or patriotic mothers like Helen Hayes in *My Son John*. Her problem was her son, played by Robert Walker, who had become a Communist because of too much intellect. Learning had corrupted him. She blamed herself for not being more aware; he had always been too studious. He was not like his two athletic brothers, serving bravely in Korea. A canny public stayed away in large numbers. The studios, equally canny, had anticipated this and kept the budgets of these pictures very low. They considered them loss leaders, necessary to get Congress off their backs so they could get on with the real business of making pictures that made money.

My life seemed to move in ever-decreasing circles. Few of my friends dropped away, but the list of acquaintances diminished. I appeared contaminated and they did not want to risk infection. They avoided me, not calling as they had in the past, not responding to my calls, being nervously distant if we met in public places. No one was overtly insulting. I had become armored against this early on, but I worried about the effect on my two small children. I saw them on weekends and one Sunday I took my seven-year-old daughter to the Rockefeller Center skating rink. I was lacing on her skates when a producer I knew passed by with his daughter. I opened my mouth to say hello, but he hurried past, averting his eyes. My daughter looked puzzled; he had been to our house and she knew both him and his child. But she handled it her own way. She skated swiftly out onto the ice, took a few practice turns and then skated back to where I watched from the railing, flanked by other parents.

"Daddy!" she called out in her loudest voice. "Do you believe in God?"

Conversations stopped. Heads turned. Even a few skaters braked to a stop and turned to us. The tinny waltz over the loudspeaker system seemed suddenly muted. The silence was enormous.

"Well?" she demanded.

It was not exactly the question I had expected. It was worse. Being a Communist in America was bad enough; being an atheist as well was excessive. She knew perfectly well she was putting me on a spot. But what she wanted to know was crucial. She had not been told about the blacklist. Her weekend life with me had remained the same. She took for granted that I was around the house a lot while other fathers went off to work. She had asked me once what I did and seemed satisfied with the answer. But now she wanted an answer to a different kind of question.

I was unsure what to tell her. It was easy enough to say no, I didn't believe in God. That would only risk the disapproval of all the other parents. That didn't bother me; I was at home with disapproval. But I felt the question was not really about God. It was about me. She was asking me every child's question: Who are you? She knew something was wrong and I realized in that moment that I had been wrong in not telling her what was happening to me. My excuse was that she was too young, it would only frighten and confuse her. But what was frightening and confusing was *not* being told. She had sensed there was trouble but had been abandoned to uncertainty. She was left where it was scariest, in the dark. It did not matter now whether her question was about God or the producer or anything else. She wanted to know where I stood. God now, the blacklist later.

"No," I said. "I don't."

She nodded firmly. "Laura's daddy doesn't, either," she said, and skated off.

Parents sidled away from me, throwing me looks. I watched my daughter skate, blond hair flying in the wind, more secure than I on the slippery ice.

Exclusion from polite society had other costs. Not so much for my children: They were lucky, they went to a liberal private school that gave scholarships to children from blacklisted families. The teachers were sympathetic and the atmosphere was supportive. "Red diaper" children were not ostracized or called names or sneeringly told that their parents were traitors, as was the case in some other schools. But we developed a siege mentality, the dark side of the nurturing friendships. We were defensive, we protected one another, and that meant protecting what we believed in. And that meant not examining too closely what we might otherwise have been challenging. Not our basic beliefs: We were secure in those. Capitalism rested on domination and exploitation. Socialism offered a way out of this, a world free of racism and war. But we did not challenge the Soviet Union, the country of "already existing socialism." Perhaps, given normalcy, we still might not have challenged. We questioned among ourselves in our branch, questioned Party leaders who came to explain, but we believed. We were not quite stupid enough to believe the Soviet Union was perfect, but we believed that with all its faults it still stood for a better world. It had fought and suffered beyond human reason trying to create that world. Now evil had been defeated. Hope was still alive. America was not a fascist country. I might be jailed for being a Red, but I would not be killed for being a Jew. Russia was strong and committed to peace. My feelings about the Soviet Union were firm, derived from Stalingrad, where the war was won, not from the gulag, where socialism was lost. I knew little about the gulag and wanted to know less, fearful of its meaning, distrusting the sources of this terrible information.

The new treason trials in Eastern Europe had seemed incredible with its news that once again staunch Communists had turned out to be traitors. The split between Tito and Stalin, when the Yugoslavs insisted on taking their own road to socialism, was also hard to understand. The Soviet Union might not be infallible, but the CPSU was still the party of parties. The Russians led; others followed, more or less willingly. And yet I had been with the Yugoslavs and seen their commitment. How could this indivisible movement be divided? Of the Yugoslavs I knew, half went one way and half the other, confounding me further. Vladimir Dedijer remained loyal to Tito. Pavo Lukin, the dedicated Marxist with whom I had taken long walks on the island of Vis, left for Czechoslovakia. The structure had begun to show cracks, but I plastered them over with belief in the rightness of the cause and the reassuring knowledge that at least I knew my enemy. He was right there in my face. The United States had started the cold war, needed it for imperial purpose, needed the terror of a blacklist to make that war seem necessary. Political persecution was becoming an acceptable norm. The law was being twisted in the name of anticommunism; government informers perjured themselves without fear of consequence.

It was easier to follow the trials of my fellow Dartmouth alumnus William Remington. He had been working for the government until Elizabeth Bentley accused him of spying. Although he denied this under oath, a federal loyalty board dismissed him. He sued for reinstatement and won. He sued Bentley for libel and won that, too. The government persisted. A federal grand jury in New York indicted Remington for perjury. The foreman of that jury was helping Bentley write her memoirs, the federal prosecutor of the case had once been Bentley's lawyer in a civil suit; none of this was deemed prejudicial. Remington was tried and convicted. The conviction was overturned on appeal. The government tried him again, circumventing double jeopardy by claiming he had lied during his trial. This time he was convicted and sent to jail, where he died, as the Justice Department stated, getting in the way of a nonpolitical robbery.

In Party meetings and later in private we talked about the European trials and the splits, the disturbing signs of Soviet anti-Semitism. We debated fiercely but came to no conclusions. We could not afford the vulnerability of doubt. Part of this was being hostage to ideology. Most of it was being under attack. We felt too threatened and wanted no splits among ourselves. With so few resources, a united front was necessary. We also had little information and were unclear about what was happening. We trusted neither the bourgeois press nor, increasingly, the official Party pronouncements. We trusted one another. That was the important part. We had come to depend on one another and that dependence had become precious. We always knew there were informers among us, spies planted by the FBI, but they were irrelevant. They would do what they were paid to do. Our security lay in friendship and they had no access to our hearts.

Zero Mostel had become a friend and I often visited him at his painting studio. Zero had been trained as a painter and during the Depression the WPA had given him work lecturing in museums. He had drifted into performing when he found his audience laughing instead of taking notes. But he always continued to paint. He considered himself a painter first and an actor only as an unfortunate necessity. He looked down on his performing and pretended not to take it seriously. His real name was Sam; a press agent decided it should be Zero so he could be advertised as someone who had made something out of nothing.

Zero had been a hit as a nightclub comic, famous in particular for a parody of a racist senator, and had also acted in movies. The movies could not really contain him. Zero was large and loud, and everything about him—his expressions, his gestures, his movements—was too big for the screen. He had large, limpid eyes and a face startling in its mobility. His performing heroes were Chaplin and the French actor Raimu, and he combined elements of both, the grace of Chaplin and the heavy, sad honesty of the Frenchman. In close-up Zero was too much to absorb and he was best on the stage, where he could be seen in all his delicate bulk. He had a fat man's lightness of step. Cast properly, with a director he could respect, he was mesmerizing. In life he was gross and sensitive, artistic and coarse, a highly cultivated man who went out of his way to persuade you he was nothing of the kind. On the other hand, if you could get him talking about art, his voice would drop along with the obscenities and it was no longer all about him, it was about what he passionately loved and believed in. Once he phoned me excitedly and told me to meet him at a certain art dealer's. When I got there, he was standing in front of a small Daumier oil painting called *The Audience*.

"What do you think?" he said.

I said carefully that I thought it was beautiful. I had had experience with Zero when I had thought something not beautiful and he had bellowed at me without mercy, usually in front of large crowds. But I did think this one beautiful.

"We can buy it for only five thousand dollars," he said.

I knew how he felt. It was how I had felt when my landlord offered to sell me his building. It was a great buy. You were a fool to let a chance like this slip away. You could even resell it at a considerable profit, although I would not have dared suggest that to Zero. We stood and looked at the painting for a long time. The longer we looked, the more beautiful it seemed. It made no sense not to buy it. Owning a Daumier; why not? Buying it was reasonable. It was everything else that was unreasonable: the blacklist, that we could not work at our trade, the fact that we didn't have a hundred dollars between us, let alone five thousand. Zero knew when he called me that we couldn't afford the painting. He didn't even believe in the individual hoarding of art; he thought it should all be in public museums. But there was a gesture to be made, a small moment to be seized when we could believe we were like people who did have money. After all, we had been like that once. We kept up the pretense, carefully appraising the picture, until finally Zero let out a long sigh and thanked the art dealer and we turned around and went home.

Since *Panic in the Streets*, Zero had acted in a few more movies and then had been called before the House Committee on Un-American Activities. He had been an uncooperative witness, refusing to give names. This had gotten him blacklisted in nightclubs as well as movie studios. Now he lived precariously, performing in small country hotels and appearing in occasional off-Broadway plays. Once in a while he sold a painting, usually to a friend. He proclaimed loudly that if he didn't have to support his wife and two children, he would happily do nothing but paint for the rest of his life. Zero did everything loudly and he was matched by his wife, an earthy ex-Rockette named Kate with a voice as loud as his. Their elder son was the same age as mine and I often brought my son over to play with him. The boys hated each other on sight but played together dutifully while Zero and Kate yelled at each other in the kitchen. My son wanted to know why they were always mad at each other and I tried to explain that they weren't really mad, some people just talked to each other that way. My answer made no more sense to him than it did to me. But in their own particular context of love and anxiety it was how Zero and Kate communicated. The anger was peripheral. They were two emotional people, easily aroused, and in those days there was a lot to be aroused about.

Zero's studio was a walk-up in an old brownstone in the flower district. The door was always open and friends were always dropping in. Zero would insult them as a matter of course when they came in the door, but his most extravagant curses were reserved for an actor named Philip Loeb. He knew Loeb was suffering and it was an attempt to cheer him up. Zero loved Loeb, a short, sweet, sad-eyed man who had been in many Broadway plays and also for many years in a radio soap opera called *The Rise of the Goldbergs*. He played Mr. Goldberg. He had also been very active in Equity, the actors' union, too active for *Red Channels*, which had listed him among its other subversives. This had gotten him fired from *The Goldbergs* and he had not since then been able to find other work, even off-Broadway. Loeb was the sole support of a seriously disturbed son whom he kept in a private mental home and he was constantly afraid he would be unable to keep up the payments and his son would be moved to a state hospital for the insane. For a while, after Loeb had lost his apartment, he lived with Zero and Kate. Once or twice they found him shouting out the window at pedestrians below. Zero could never cheer him up, no matter how hard he tried. I never saw Loeb smile, even when Zero was at his hilarious best. He gave the impression he could not be touched. Finally, one day, he checked into a hotel and made sure he took enough pills to kill himself.

Not all of Zero's visitors were blacklisted, though. Some were well-heeled businessmen who would take us to lunch at one of the dairy restaurants on Broadway. There Zero was still a star and he would sail in like an overloaded Jewish galleon, kissing the cashier and insulting the waiters in Yiddish, and they would insult him back and bring him extra portions. Everything about him was outsized. He needed to be outrageous. He would board a subway pretending to be blind and then get up and courteously give his seat to an old lady. In a restaurant he would start buttering a slice of bread and continue buttering up his arm. Once in Lindy's he became a barber and "shaved" his friend the actor Sam Jaffe with whipped cream from his strawberry shortcake. It was as if only his painting had held him back, as if leaving his studio had released some demonic urge to call attention to himself, to stop traffic.

My life revolved around those friendships. They were almost entirely with other blacklisted people; we had circled the wagons and it was dangerous to go outside the perimeter. In the morning I tried to write—speculative scripts or articles or the occasional short story, but they were desultory, lacking conviction. I seemed to need a validation I could not produce from myself alone. The days were aimless, as they had been when I was waiting to be drafted. I felt suspended; my real life was somewhere else, on hold, waiting to be resurrected when the country came to its senses. Finally, I had to admit that I was depressed, a recognition that only added to the depression. To be unhappy was normal; to be depressed was weak. A conspiracy was afoot to make me feel unworthy and I was giving it credence. I was letting down the side. I went into therapy, careful to choose a Marxist psychiatrist; the Party warned us against non-Marxist psychiatrists on the theory that we might divulge some of those secrets we didn't have. He was a caring man, but we were not a good fit. He offered solace, but I could get that at the movies. Meanwhile, money was running short and I could not find a front. The few who were willing were too implausible for the part or ill equipped to perform in a meeting or wanted too much of a cut. Self-pity was a constant threat, lurking around the corner like the FBI.

Then—just when the landlord, giving up on me, sternly issued an ultimatum: Either buy the house or pay the rent—I found a front.

His name was Leo and he was a friend of a friend. I never knew what he did for a living; all my friend said was that Leo gambled. He lived cheaply and had no telephone. But he had a system to beat the roulette table, and like most gamblers with systems, it both kept him poor and went along with a story. Leo's story was that once his system had worked, had fulfilled its glorious promise. This was in Florida before the war, when gambling was legal. Leo had saved some money and hitchhiked down and found a congenial casino. In a week he had doubled his money; in another week he had tripled it. He moved off the beach into a hotel. He bought a car. He found a girlfriend. He kept winning. He even sent money home to his aged parents.

Then, one night, the manager of the casino took him into his office and advised him to quit while he was ahead. The advice made Leo feel even grander. He thought the manager was worried that he might break the bank. The man assured him otherwise. He didn't mind Leo's winning all that money; it was a good come-on for the other suckers. No, he had been watching Leo and thought he was a nice young man, and he didn't want him to go home broke. He thought Leo lacked the resolve to stick to his system when it started to lose, as all systems eventually do before, if they are any good, they start winning again. It becomes a question of character. The manager told Leo sadly that he didn't think Leo had matured enough to have that character.

Naturally Leo resented this. He continued to play. He went home broke. The manager paid for his train ticket and drove him to the station. I became the beneficiary. Leo had since been hard at work developing his character and thought that fronting for me could be a step in that direction. I didn't disabuse him. He also thought maybe he might learn the television business, which he saw as another kind of gambling. He wanted no money for what he did. Character was formed by principle. I liked him a lot. There was a certain elegance about Leo. He had a saturnine look and a dry wit, and he hid a generous nature behind a mocking view of life. He was disappointed that he was given no opportunity to meet with high-level executives; he would have relished the con. But the only work I had was for Charles Russell on *Danger* and I needed only to give Russell my script with Leo's name on it. As with Rita, there was no reason for him to appear; Russell and Lumet could testify that he existed. I did several scripts this way. The pattern of payment was the same as with Rita. Since Leo had no previous credits, Russell could at first pay only the minimum, but after a few scripts he felt free to pay more. I was able to pay my rent, thus being saved from having to buy the house that eventually would have made me rich.

Unfortunately Leo lasted only a little longer than Rita. The problem was not an analyst. Leo disdained psychotherapy, which he had tried once to cure himself of compulsive womanizing but quickly abandoned when he thought it might also cure him of gambling. In terms of priorities that was no contest. Women were a hobby; gambling was his life. Leo's primary problem was his aged parents. They wanted more money. They saw his name on the screen and figured he was in the chips. Leo had been giving them the small amount he could afford, but now they accused him of being a cheapskate. They hinted about new furniture, the necessity of going to Florida for their health. He sent them to a doctor who pronounced their health perfect. They told Leo the doctor was a quack, and told his other relatives that Leo was an ungrateful son. Leo loved his parents, or thought he did, but they were driving him crazy.

His friends were also making his life miserable. They, too, wanted money but were content only to borrow it. They didn't believe Leo when he said he had nothing to lend. They asked why he continued to live in the same cruddy apartment. They accused him of being a miser and spoke sadly of how he had changed. Leo's life became intolerable. He could not tell them the truth; he could only make feeble excuses no one believed. He became desperate to make some money he could spread around and so rehabilitate his name. The only way he knew how to accomplish that was to raise the stakes in his gambling. This led to disaster as desperation overcame good sense. Leo had been making a modest living as a skilled poker player and cautious bettor on sporting events. Now he began to bet wildly and play hunches. His cunning deserted him. Anxiety corrupted his skill. His small stake began to diminish and Leo grew even more desperate.

Still, he would not take any money from me. I could not shake his stubborn integrity. His principles remained firm even though his newly developed character was flushing him down the toilet. I did not know how to help him. I offered to lend him money, but he felt that was no answer. For one thing, I couldn't lend him enough to make a difference. He began to drink, which only increased his losses. His elegance deserted him. He grew careless in his dress and his wit became sour. Unlike Rita, however, Leo did not turn on me. He blamed himself, sensing a pattern in his life, gold always turning to dross. We discussed it at length and I finally told Leo he had to stop being a front, it was killing him. He could take comfort in knowing he was a man of moral purpose betrayed by circumstance. Leo wanted to continue. He had grown to hate the blacklist. There was a certain purity about his hate; it came directly from the streets, uncontaminated by politics. In Leo's circles of hell, politicians placed only slightly above stool pigeons and he thought rightly that the blacklist depended on a synergy of both.

I lost touch with Leo after that. Our mutual friend said he

had gone out of town, which could have meant anywhere there was gambling. I hoped he would recover. Meanwhile, I took up the hunt again, without success. People were scared. They had good reason. Witch-hunting also extended to anyone helping the witch. And the truth was that I was the witch. Everything about me in *Red Channels* was true. No one had publicly named me as a Communist, but I knew that somewhere, in an FBI file, a committee record, there was a dossier on me. I was a threat, a menace, someone to avoid. I carried contagion. What I could promise a front did not equal the infection he or she risked. I spent hours on the telephone, following leads. My phone bill grew as my prospects diminished. Even the magazine assignments dried up. Editors who had once hired me were apologetic or simply unavailable. I fled to the movies but eventually had to come out of the comforting theater and go home or to a bar, which also eventually closed. There were friends, of course, but they had their own troubles. Blacklisted people were banished from professions they had spent their lives practicing. Doctors lost hospital privileges. Lawyers were fired from firms and became salesmen, teachers went back to school and became therapists; they were the lucky ones. Most took any job they could get, selling door to door or driving a taxi. There was no shame in the work, only anger and despair.

Except that sometimes there was also shame. Zero called me one day because I had access to a car and asked if I would drive him upstate to the Concord Hotel in the Borscht Belt, that cluster of Jewish vacation hotels in the Catskills. The social director of the Concord had offered him a one-night stand performing his act. Zero's fee when he had previously played there had been three thousand dollars and now he was being offered only five hundred, but he was philosophical about it. His rent was overdue; it was better than nothing. I picked him up on a sunny afternoon and we drove across the glittering Hudson and up toward the low-lying mountains. My childhood summers had been spent at these hotels and I had awed memories of vast plates of food disappearing at an impressive rate. Zero was in an expansive mood at the thought of having a little money in his pocket. He warned me about the women I would meet at the hotel. They were not interested in a good time, they were interested in finding husbands. He insisted on stopping at a certain roadside inn for lunch, and when I asked why, he said he had been there once and in the rest room had spoken casually to a man urinating next to him. He had asked the man if he knew that Marc Chagall, the famous painter, lived nearby and was sometimes seen eating here.

"*Ich bin Chagall*," the man said, zipping up his fly and walking out.

Since then Zero had stopped there every chance he had in the hope of meeting Chagall again, but the only painters he met were abstract expressionists on their way to mountain hideaways. Chagall had never appeared again, either to eat or to relieve himself.

When we got to the Concord, we were greeted by the manager, who ignored me and fell all over Zero. He proclaimed loudly that Zero was the greatest comic of the age. He said how lucky the Concord was to have him perform again. The guests crowded around Zero, asking for his autograph. He obliged cheerfully, rolling his eyes suggestively at the women, offering them the key to his room, making them laugh. It was nice to see Zero in the limelight again and the good feelings lasted until we reached the manager's office and he told Zero that instead of five hundred dollars for the night's performance, his fee would be three hundred.

There was no discussion. There was nothing to discuss.

The manager did not even bother to explain; he just shrugged. Times are tough all over, the shrug said. What are you going to do about it? He knew he had Zero over a barrel. He knew Zero's position, his plight, his need for money. I think he really believed what he had said about Zero. The Concord was lucky to get Zero again. At five hundred he was a bargain. At three hundred he was a steal.

We checked into our room and then took a long walk. Neither of us spoke much. Once we paused on top of a hill and looked out across other hills turning purple as the sun went down and Zero talked quietly about Renaissance landscape painting. Then we went back to the hotel and he changed into the baggy blue suit he wore for his act. We were supposed to go first to the vast dining room, where they had set out dinner for us in the kitchen, but Zero never ate before a show and I had no appetite. We walked around a little more and then went to the theater. The house was already full; there must have been at least fifteen hundred people waiting expectantly. I stood in the wings and watched Zero do his act.

He was a smash. The audience loved him. He did all their favorite numbers and everything he did got a laugh. And all the laughter did was feed his rage. He took no satisfaction from it, no vindication of his talent. Instead, their approval became a kind of taunt, a reminder of the money and fame he had once commanded. It was another insult and all he could do was insult them back, roaring obscenities at them, cursing them in Yiddish. They roared with laughter, refusing to be insulted. They thought it was part of the act. Zero was in a fury he could not mitigate or expunge or get off on. They would not allow him his anger. He cut the act short, but they called him back for encores until he would not come out anymore and they began reluctantly to file out. The manager stood beaming in the back of the theater, accepting congratulations.

I mopped Zero's face with a towel and we went back to the kitchen and a waiter brought food and a full bottle of whiskey. I picked at the food and watched Zero drink most of the bottle. Then he stood up and said he wanted to find the manager. But I called the waiter and together we harried him back to our room and laid him on the bed and I took off his shoes and he fell asleep. In the morning I woke before him and went to the manager's office and collected the three hundred. I was afraid if Zero went, he might kill the man. The manager was still beaming. He said to tell Zero he would let him know when he had another spot. He thought maybe in six or seven months. Then we drove back to New York.

Zero never talked about that time. If anyone brought it up, knowing he had performed again at the Concord, he changed the subject. In 1952, though, he found work on Broadway. Elia Kazan was directing a play by George Tabori called *Flight into Egypt* and offered Zero a part. The play opened in March. There were no protests. Zero was not a big enough star to protest about. In April Kazan testified as a friendly witness before the House Committee on Un-American Activities. Zero remained in the play, avoiding Kazan.

I hunted fruitlessly for a front. A pair of blacklisted actors started an acting school and decided they should include a scriptwriting class and hired me to teach. The course was three hours once a week for eight weeks. The pay was minimal but welcome. I had about twenty students and at the first class they listened raptly as I talked for the whole three hours. I thought I was brilliant. So did the class; they left glowing and eager to return. Going home on the subway, I sat in superior silence, basking in the brilliance I had unleashed. Suddenly I felt a cold chill. I had read that this sort of chill runs down the spine. This one ran all over me. I realized that in those three hours I had revealed everything I knew about

scriptwriting. There were still seven weeks to go, and I had
nothing left to say. The course would be a disaster. I was
right; it was. I had no teaching experience and no ability to
get anyone else to talk. By the end of the eight weeks I had six
students left. I was not asked back.

But one of the students was a friend of my sister's and
knew about my problems, and one day she said that she had
been talking about me with her old college roommate. The
roommate's name was Shirley and she was married to an as-
piring actor, and while he had not yet had a success or even a
part anywhere, she had learned a bit about show business.
She had said she might not mind fronting for me. Shirley
seemed to have all the qualifications and we met and she
agreed. When I asked her about her reasons, she only smiled
and said it might be fun.

I sold two scripts under Shirley's name. One was to Russell
and the other was to my former agent, who had quit the
agency business to become a television producer. He was now
producing an hour dramatic show called the *Westinghouse
Summer Theatre*. My script was a light romantic comedy and
he called me after the first rehearsal to tell me how well it was
playing and how the cast was pleased to be performing a play
written by a woman. They wanted to meet the author, but he
had told them she was too shy to meet actors. Shirley was
also pleased and asked if possibly her husband, Glen, might
have a part in the *Danger* show I was then writing. She was
modest in her request.

"It doesn't have to be the lead," she said tactfully. "Any old
part will do."

She confessed that the real reason she was fronting for me
was to get a foot in the door for her husband. She had not
told me that because she thought I would have turned her
down as insufficiently noble. I assured her that nobility was

not an issue. I then arranged for Glen to come in and read for Lumet. To our surprise, he turned out to be right for the part and Lumet hired him. I was happy that I could do something for Shirley, who had also refused to take any money, and even happier when Glen turned out to be good enough so that his agent got him an immediate job in a Hollywood movie. I was less happy when Shirley told me they were moving to Los Angeles. She was sorry she couldn't front for me anymore but wanted me to know they both were grateful. She wished me luck. I smiled benevolently as I felt any generous impulse wither in the face of malign self-interest. I was sorry I had helped him get that part. Why couldn't he have turned out to be lousy? What was I smiling about?

I was smiling because I was a hypocrite. I was smiling because I was not a hypocrite, I was a good person and really wished her well. I was smiling because I knew I was not really a good person, but it was important that no one else thought so. I smiled because I would be ashamed of myself if I did not smile. Because not to smile at this nice woman who had helped me, whatever her motive, and now wanted to live her own life would violate what I pretended to be. Because if I didn't smile, there was a scream gathering inside me that might slip its tether and be very difficult to get back in. I smiled because smiling, whether I felt like it or not, was another barrier to throw up against the rage and despair and exclusion and, beyond all reason, the hovering sense of guilt. There was nothing to feel guilty about, but there it sat, the seductive logic of oppression. There must be something wrong with me, otherwise why would I be shunned? Of course, I knew why. Every visit by the FBI, every unanswered phone call, every time someone crossed the street to avoid me, every time I was told I was unemployable because my name was on a list—all this made perfect sense. These people saw me as a

threat. I was a threat. I was glad to be a threat. It was important to accept that there had been no mistake. I had not been
blacklisted for nothing.

Perhaps the guilt came from wanting acceptance too much.
Perhaps it came from internalizing the rejection. It could also
have been the guilt I'd always obligingly carried as part of my
heritage (what's the matter, you didn't like the other tie?).
Wherever it came from, it was a constant slithering presence,
there to remind me of my impurity. My parents disapproved
of my politics but were concerned about my predicament,
and one day my mother came to set me straight. She came
with a brisket of beef she had cooked especially for me. My
mother was a poor cook except for dishes that did not suffer
from being overdone. I offered her tea, which she refused, sitting nervously on the edge of a chair. She was not an educated
or articulate woman and so she had carefully prepared a
speech. America is a dog-eat-dog society. You have to look
out for number one. No one is going to do it for you, you
have to do it for yourself. Nothing is more important than being able to work, except maybe your family. Your life is being
ruined. You have to do something before it's too late. Where
is it written you have to destroy yourself for other people?

I said that I understood and could go back to work immediately. All I had to do was name a few names.

"How can you do that?" she said.

She was not so much indignant as puzzled. It was clear to
her that some things you just didn't do. For one, you didn't
become a stool pigeon. She saw no contradiction between
that position and the one she had previously held. America
was still America, where dog ate dog. She left, unconsoled.
But I found myself visiting my parents more often, usually on
weekends when I had my two children. I would take them
swimming in nearby Union Temple and my mother would

cook a brisket one time and a roast chicken the next and nobody talked politics.

But politics was everywhere. Politics made the world go
round. Politics was the name of the game. I was bludgeoned
by politics. But mine was a constricted politics, its limits determined by survival. It allowed too little space for unre-
stricted thought. Like a disease that attacks the immune
system, the blacklist opened the way to secondary infection.
It impaired judgment and weakened criticism, except of your
enemies. Party meetings were increasingly concerned not
with what was happening to the world or even to the Soviet
Union, but only with the CPUSA. Its leaders were going to
jail. It had no vision except staying alive. This only added to
its irrelevance. The paradox was that the cold war needed us
to be relevant. Relevant meant dangerous. We had to be dangerous so that what was being done to us (and the American
people) was justified. This was not easy to prove, since on the
face of it we seemed about as dangerous as the Salvation
Army. Therefore, informers were trotted out, perjuries overlooked, maleficent scenarios devised in which fiction was
made synonymous with fact and Red-baiting equated with
patriotism. If that did not fool the customers, there was always simple demonizing. The Soviet Union was the Great Sa-
tan; we were its American coven. We did the devil's work,
taking the place formerly occupied by witches, warlocks and
occasionally goats. The compensation was a certain importance. We might be negligible in fact, but we were mighty in
the eyes of the FBI.

Some blacklisted people died of politics. They died of the
insult to their hearts. A few, like Phil Loeb, took their own
lives. Others had their bodies damaged beyond repair. The
toll was greatest on actors. Ostracism hurt them almost as
much as poverty; an actor lived by being able to show his

face. Even when they found other work—teaching or selling or waiting on table—their lives were only marking time in a way different from mine. Writers could fulfill themselves in secret. Actors had to be out there. They had to be seen. If they were not, for many of them, they did not exist.

Of the people I knew, Mady Christians, the Mama of the hit show *I Remember Mama*, died of a cerebral hemorrhage. J. Edward Bromberg, prominent in the Group Theater and later as a Hollywood character actor, died of a heart attack in London, where he had gone to find work. John Garfield, the movie star, died of a heart attack. I had met Garfield shortly after the war, when he acted in a radio play I had written for the United Jewish Appeal. He was a friendly, unintellectual man who liked being a movie star. He was also a product of the New York streets who believed the worst thing you could be was a snitch. While he was never a Communist himself, most of his friends were of the left and that was where his sympathies lay. Hungering for a star who could get them on the front page, the Committee on Un-American Activities subpoenaed him. Trying to keep both his career and his honor, Garfield waffled. He denounced communism while professing not to know any Communists. He lent his name to a ghostwritten magazine article called "I Was a Sucker for a Left Hook." He was caught between John Garfield, the star, and Julius Garfinkel (his real name), the kid from the streets. He would debase himself, but he would not inform.

He moved to New York, ostensibly to find more rewarding parts in the theater but really to feel rooted again, to plant himself in earth less treacherous than Hollywood. He needed to find some kind of purchase; he was still a boy who needed his neighborhood. He played the title roles in *Peer Gynt* and a revival of *Golden Boy*, getting bad reviews for the first ("literal and casual," said the *Times*) and good ones for the second ("brilliant and satisfying," said the *Post*). He had been turned down for the lead part in *Golden Boy* when it was first performed by the Group Theater in 1937. The director, Harold Clurman, thought he lacked "the inner torment" for the part and gave him a lesser, comic role. He had the torment now, whether he wanted it or not.

I saw Garfield briefly during this torturous time. His face was lined and drawn, and he was drinking. He had always had the face of a bar mitzvah boy gone just wrong enough to enhance his appeal. Now he seemed old without having grown into it. He still saw his friends, no matter their politics. He was loyal to what he still believed. As an actor he had been best at playing the rebel, the angry young man at odds with the system. Now the system had him by the throat. Dissatisfied with his testimony, the committee turned the matter over to the FBI, seeking grounds for a charge of perjury. Some of his lawyers advised cooperation, others resistance. Cooperation, of course, meant giving names. Resistance could possibly mean jail and certainly an end to his career. But Garfield found a way to preserve his honor, although at terminal cost. He thwarted them all by dying. His heart gave out on a visit to a woman friend to whom he had gone for solace.

We tried to counter death with conviviality. Parties took the place of the Party. I went dutifully to meetings, but Party work was defensive and uneasy questions about the Soviet Union were not being answered. What about the anti-Semitism? The gulag? It was better not to ask them at all. They ran the risk of sapping the will. I thought of it as a tactical evasion. There was enough truth I had to face without facing that one. And I did not feel defensive. I did not even feel defeated. My feelings were often an inchoate mixture of anger and anxiety, but when I was with other blacklisted people, I felt what I had felt in the war, a comradeship based on common purpose. This was a different war and I was not as sure we were going to win this one, but when we were together, I always felt that this was where I wanted to be. I did not want to be blacklisted or ostracized or without a career or on the edge of poverty and I certainly did not want to go to jail. I wanted to be able to work according to my ability. Under other circumstances I might not have picked these people for friends. Maybe I was simply making a virtue of necessity. But there was affection and support and even love in those gatherings, and acceptance in the world of commerce and competition did not usually bring any of those things. What I felt now was unjustified by my social condition. Bitterness and despair were more appropriate. But with these people the scream stayed dormant in my throat. What I felt was a kind of happiness.

We hung out at Downey's, an actors' saloon on Eighth Avenue, and often at the Russian Tea Room, where the owner, a warmhearted enthusiast named Sidney Kaye, made us welcome. On fortunate weekends some of us might be invited to one of the left-wing hotels in the Catskills, where we would earn our keep by giving lectures on everything from acting to politics. Many in the audience were old-time socialists, still passionate in their beliefs, and they would ask fierce, partisan questions. They knew nothing about acting, but there wasn't anything they could not make political. Argument was as nourishing to them as blintzes. But these were cheery affairs; the passion was without malice and afterward we would all sit around and argue some more and, as the night wore down, sing revolutionary ballads, stirring or sad, depending on the time of night.

The only place where I didn't want company was in the movies. That was strictly between me and what was on the screen. My surrender there was total and too intimate to be shared. Secrets might be revealed. In any case, who would want to go to the movies with someone who embraced with equal delirium both *Bride of the Gorilla* and *Singing in the Rain?* Not that I was without critical distance. Clearly, one was better than the other. Or maybe not so clearly. Love drew no distinction on the basis of quality. *Singing in the Rain* was a work of art, a film masterpiece. *Bride of the Gorilla* was not even scary. On the other hand, it had Raymond Burr turning into a gorilla. And it was a movie.

Still, it was not safe to go outside my closed circle. There were more pressing dangers than the unanswered questions at Party meetings. While the cultural climate turned blandly inoffensive, the political climate kept turning mean and intolerant. There seemed no bottom to its meanness. The House Committee on Un-American Activities was minor-league bigotry; Senator Joseph McCarthy was big-time show business. Television, the new arbiter of discourse, loved him. He combined two elements that had always brought shows high ratings: he was a gangster in a soap opera. He lay over the country like one of those disease-ridden blankets that white settlers had given the Indians. He sickened the body politic. The few voices against him were weak and ineffectual. McCarthy went his brutal, demagogic way, swinging his sockful of shit, doing the necessary dirty footwork of the cold war. The trade unions were stripped of their most militant leaders, the universities of their most liberal teachers, the government of its bravest civil servants. Unreason ruled the land.

In that outside world it was not easy to believe in the perfectibility of man. I tried my best, looking abroad. Good things were happening in Africa, an invincible anticolonialist movement led by men like Nkrumah and Kenyatta and Nyerere. China was now safely Communist and would soon be on its way to peace and justice. A rumor swept the Party

that the Soviet Union was going to make bread free. It was
not true, of course, but we clung to it as proof that any society providing the staff of life free to all its citizens must be
on its way to something good. Lenin had said that a society
could be judged on how it treated its children and I seized
on articles that described all the benefits Russian children
had.

The global outlook, however, was not getting us anywhere
at home. We had to find our own way to survive. This
brought up another question: the quality of survival. There
were fighters who had gone fifteen rounds with Joe Louis
without throwing a punch, just by holding on. They had not
won, of course, but the strategy had kept their senses intact. I
found it wanting. For us, just to make a living was a kind of
victory, but it was at best only a mote in the eye of someone
determined to destroy us. I wanted to blacken that eye. I was
a counterpuncher, anyway, most at home when the opponent
was coming at me. Tony from Brooklyn had trained me like
that on the rolling deck of the SS *Bantam*. His advice had
been succinct and to the point: bob and weave and throw the
hook. Hit him on top of the chin and then go down and hit
him where he won't appreciate it, in the *labonz*.

It was good advice. I had a friend named Sam Moore, a
comedy writer who had been president of the Radio Writers
Guild until he was blacklisted. Together we started publishing an occasional four-page newsletter called *Facts About
Blacklist*. We concentrated on the networks and advertising
agencies since they consistently denied there was any such
thing as a blacklist. Our object was to reveal what they were
doing and how they were lying about it. We raised a little
money from contributions and spread the word we were interested in information. The response was gratifying. We
were not quite as isolated as we thought. We had underesti-

mated how many others loathed the blacklist and were willing to testify against it, if only in secret.

Producers afraid to speak publicly talked willingly to us in private. We met clandestinely in bars or on street corners, and they gave us names, dates and places. Executives gave us details such as CBS's meeting with Johnson from Syracuse to go over cast lists for him to approve. They gave us copies of letters from advertising agencies or sponsors such as the Borden Company authorizing the blacklisting of actors and writers. We used my apartment as the editorial department, friends coming with sandwiches, making coffee, helping to sift through our stories to make sure what was verifiable. There was a lift to those evenings, a warm, happy atmosphere; we were fighting back, however minimally. Volunteers helped with our printing and distribution, leaving copies in offices and restaurants and union halls. People called to congratulate us, although many didn't want to leave their names. It was like being part of an underground.

Then, once again through the friend of a friend, I found a front. He was a talented writer named Howard who was making a name for himself writing television dramas. He was also writing plays and keeping up with the scientific literature because he was undecided whether to get the Nobel Prize for literature or for physics. He was serious about this. He would speak about it speculatively, weighing the comparative advantages. He had had no scientific training, at least so far as physics went, but felt that was no hindrance. It might even be an asset, freeing his mind for higher thought. I was in awe of his ego. He had a maniac's assurance, although in all other respects he seemed reasonably sane. He also had a generous heart. He loaned me his name for a *Danger* show and also for a frivolous comedy for a half-hour series my ex-agent was producing. I wrote them both too quickly, my mind on a more pressing matter of personal romance. Howard said nothing after the first show, but after the second he called and invited me to take a walk in Central Park. We walked in silence for a while and then he said sadly that my two shows were not very good. I could only agree. I apologized and said I hoped I had not hurt his reputation. But he was not worried about his reputation.

"I'm worried about you," he said.

He was worried about my psyche. He believed all this was doing me harm. I had written badly not through being temporarily deranged by lust but because I knew unconsciously that I had to write up to Howard's standard. Knowing that I couldn't, I had acted (also unconsciously) to prove the point. He thought this must only continue if he fronted for me. He did not want me to be hurt any further by having to write badly.

"Maybe I'll write better next time," I suggested.

He didn't think so. The hurdle was too great. He was sorry, he should have realized what would happen. I was not, after all, Eugene O'Neill or even Arthur Miller, each of whom, I gathered, might come up to Howard's standard.

"But it's your reputation that will be hurt," I pointed out. "It's your name on the script, not mine."

He shook his head. People in the business would know they were not his scripts; they were simply not good enough. They would think, knowing his liberal politics, that he had done exactly what he was doing: lent his name to a blacklisted writer. What they would not know was the identity of that writer. In fact, Howard's reputation would improve since everyone admired someone who outwitted the blacklist, especially if he took risks. By not fronting for me, he was actually making a sacrifice. He advised me to find a front on my own level or below. That way I would be unencumbered by comparison, free to write as best I could. He was kind about all this, trying not to hurt my feelings. I thanked him for what he had done while thinking seriously of burying an ax in his head.

But Howard was sincere in his hatred of the blacklist. One time he needed to do research for a project that entailed a knowledge of manual labor. A blacklisted actor friend was then working as a ditch digger in Westchester and got Howard a temporary job on his shift. By coincidence they found themselves digging in front of the mansion of a prominent TV producer. This so outraged Howard that he began yelling at the man's house, denouncing the owner for living like this while blacklisted writers like himself were reduced to digging ditches. It took awhile for his friend to calm Howard down to the point where he would accept that he was not, in fact, blacklisted. Later Howard went to Hollywood and became a successful TV and movie writer, although the Nobel Prize eluded him.

The contributions ran out and *Facts About Blacklist* folded after a few issues. We did not charge for it and there was not enough money or staff to keep it going. The blacklist still raged. We had not changed anything, but it had made me feel better about myself. The compensation was increased time for movies. More foreign films were coming in, the best ones from Italy and Japan, like *Umberto D* and *Ikiru*. They had a different understanding of life than American films, a sense of the tragic that Americans rarely saw in their own movies, where tragedy meant Clark Gable going to the electric chair. They went deeper and saw more. We just went for the jugular—though that did have its own rewards. I also went more often to the track with Marty Ritt. He had started teaching a private acting class but had carefully scheduled that at night so he could spend days at the track. The working class had not responded as hoped to the *Daily Worker*'s racing column, or perhaps it had been considered a capitalist tool. In any event it had been canceled, so I had to fly blind with my two-dollar bets. I usually chose horses by their names or their colors, whichever appealed to me most. I didn't do as well as Marty, but I didn't lose any more than most of the other horse players.

Then, Abraham Polonsky and Arnold Manoff came to New York.

I sit in Steinberg's Dairy Restaurant on upper Broadway, eating lunch with two other blacklisted writers. We meet here regularly to share what underground work we can find. We always have the same waiter, whose name is Max. He serves us with friendly suspicion. We look like bums but throw around big numbers. We are discussing prices for scripts, how to pay our various fronts, how to make sure the proper taxes are paid. The references are veiled for security's sake. Finally, this day, Max serves us with a broad, satisfied smile. He has figured out what we do. We are in the wholesale fruit business. He stands over us in triumph, balancing plates of herring, bowls of mushroom and barley soup.

BOTH Arnold Manoff and Abraham Polonsky were blacklisted screenwriters. I had met them in Hollywood when I first went there and had become especially friendly with Manoff. We often had dinner together, and on Thursday nights we went to the fights downtown at the Olympic Auditorium. Manoff was a handsome man with prematurely gray hair and large liquid brown eyes of the kind that used to be called bedroom eyes. Women liked him; men

were not so sure. He had the air of a licentious rabbi. His
manner was slow and deliberate, but he had an uncanny per-
ception of people and an often disconcerting ability to see
what others didn't. An argument would come to a satisfying
end and then he would say something that would make you
realize there was another, deeper layer to the discussion. It
was a gift, like extrasharp eyesight, but it did not necessarily
endear him to people. He was unsure of himself socially, and
that led him to become manipulative. I liked him, though,
sensing a shyness and feeling a warmth he found otherwise
difficult to express.

Manoff had come to Hollywood after publishing a novel
called *Telegram from Heaven*, unusual in those times as being
written by a man but told in the first person by a woman. Before that he had won several short story contests, had had poetry published in small magazines, and was considered
promising. He had gone to Hollywood in the wartime left-
wing migration, but he did not take well to the easy life and
worked only enough to make a modest living. Then he had
adapted one of his short stories into a long one-act play called
All You Need Is One Good Break and it had been performed
with great success at the Actor's Lab. This brought around
theatrical producers and Manoff expanded the one act to
three and a producer brought it to Broadway. But what was
electrifying in forty-five minutes became flaccid in two and a
half hours and the play quickly failed. By then Manoff had
been named before the Un-American Activities Committee as
a Communist. He was blacklisted and decided to remain in
New York.

He looked me up and I tried to help him get work in television, but he had the same problems finding a front as I had.
We would meet regularly, though, if only to pass the time,
and after a few months he suggested we add a friend of his,

Abraham Polonsky. Manoff knew Polonsky had also left Hollywood for New York and needed help. Polonsky had been blacklisted just as his career was taking off. He had written the script for the very successful John Garfield picture *Body and Soul* and then had written and directed *Force of Evil*, also with Garfield. That one was critically, though not commercially, successful, and quickly achieved cult status as an urban allegory of corrupt capitalism. Then Polonsky had gone to France to write a novel. He finished it just in time to hear that the committee had a subpoena out for him. He could have stayed and worked in Europe as some other blacklisted people did, but he chose to return. He had a writer-director contract with Twentieth Century–Fox and Darryl Zanuck, the head of the studio, suggested he work at home until the whole thing blew over. He liked Polonsky and wanted no harm to come to him. He also needed his talent. But it didn't blow over and Polonsky testified as an unfriendly witness and Zanuck reluctantly fired him.

I was glad to meet Polonsky, whose work I had admired. He was a quick-witted intellectual with a sharp, quizzical, humorous face, a lively, inquiring mind and an impressive knowledge of literature and science. He loved to talk. He was interested in ideas. He was clever, funny and very smart. Before the war he had taught English at City College and during the war he had been overseas with the OSS. The Depression had not defeated him. Polonsky was the same generation as Manoff, but he did not carry the same haze of sadness. He was perky and gregarious. He had a devoted wife and a happy marriage. He was different from Manoff and me, uninterested in boxing and only academically interested in women. But the three of us hit it off.

We turned to Russell for help. I told him I had two blacklisted friends who badly needed rent money and introduced him to Manoff and Polonsky. Russell told them he was not interested in their private beliefs. He only wished to know if they wanted to overthrow the government. Polonsky assured him they just wanted to overthrow CBS. That was all right with Russell. He said he would take the chance of using them on *Danger*, even if it were just with pseudonyms. He thought he could get away with a few shows before the network caught up with him and demanded bodies. Manoff made up a name and Polonsky took his wife's maiden name and Russell bought several of the speculative shows they wrote. Unfortunately the shows were too good. As with Paul Bauman, other producers began asking Russell about his two new writers. So did Russell's bosses at CBS. The pseudonyms were interred with Bauman and we were back where we were before. But by now we had settled into permanency, lunching two or three times a week at Steinberg's to pool our scanty resources.

I looked forward to those lunches. They were not really about work. They were about friendship. We enjoyed being together. We confided in one another and needled one another and laughed a lot. We became friends. Polonsky had his family and was not available nights, but Manoff and I found prizefights to attend or went for dinner at the Hickory House on Fifty-second Street, where we could eat a decent steak for under five dollars and listen to quiet jazz played on a platform raised above the bar. Or else, if we were in particular need of nourishment, we would go down to the Lower East Side and eat at a restaurant called Berkowitz's, owned at any given time by married pairs of actors from the Yiddish theater.

Not too long ago that neighborhood had been alight with Yiddish theaters, playing everything from *Yidl with a Fiddle* to *King Lear*, but they had closed one by one as their Yiddish-speaking clientele disappeared. The actors had to look for civilian ways to exist and some of them went into the restaurant business. At least there you knew you could eat. But they were unhappy away from their craft and they would sell out as soon as any acting job popped up, no matter what the language. I liked Berkowitz's because the food was familiar and good and because it reminded me of another restaurant called Greenberg's Romanian Casino, the first restaurant I had been taken to as a child. I remembered sitting in a high chair. But there had been no music at Greenberg's, only bald old Mr. Greenberg himself, patrolling the aisle that separated the glass-topped rows of tables. Berkowitz's had a sad-looking violinist and a pianist who muttered to himself as he played. Occasionally the violinist left his partner and wandered among the tables as he played and you could see the concentration camp tattoo on his arm.

Often we were the only customers there. The place was slowly going downhill. It was not the kind of food—heavy, garlicky and fatty—that attracted the young, and the middle-aged had already started their exodus to the suburbs. The old people, those who had also patronized the theaters, were dying out or moving to Miami Beach. But we would come in and the drooping musicians would spring to attention and play us to our table with a lilting Viennese waltz and then the pickles would arrive and the sauerkraut and the bottle of seltzer, and we would settle down for an evening of solid contentment.

Once in a while actor friends of the owners would come in and sit in the back and drink glasses of tea and tell sad stories about the death of their theater. One night a taxi stopped outside and the driver came in. She was a husky woman in a leather jacket and she shook hands with the owners and then grabbed the microphone and belted out a song in Yiddish.

She had a voice that rattled the seltzer. Then she shook hands with everyone, including us, and strode out to her cab and drove off. She turned out to be the sister of a well-known television actor named Herschel Bernardi, an actress herself, driving a cab while at liberty.

Other times, during the day, we would take my car and the three of us would just drive around, perhaps stopping at Bill Reiber's on the Sawmill River Parkway for lunch or driving out to Coney Island for a hot dog and a beer at Nathan's and then taking a stroll along the boardwalk. At those times, when we were enveloped in food and drink and fellowship, the blacklist seemed far away. We talked about art and literature and people and politics and anything else that came to mind. The talk was casual, far-reaching and affectionate. It roamed freely, without restriction. There was nothing we did not question. We talked of the Party and its problems, testing our beliefs. They remained firm, but some were fraying around the edges. Weakened by attacks, its membership dropping, the Party was too defensive to have any viable program, or perhaps it had simply run out of ideas that made any sense. It had lost the connection to ordinary Americans it had had during the Depression and the war. Now, in the absence of a viable domestic program, the Soviet Union loomed over everything, dense and intractable, blocking the view. But the Party found no way of dealing with it that was either honest or intelligent. Mostly, looking around the room at the sparsely attended meetings, I speculated on which one of us was the FBI plant.

It was Manoff who realized that our threesome needed rules so far as work was concerned. The rules he suggested made immediate sense to Polonsky and me. They were simple. If one of us found work, that work belonged to him. He kept any money coming from that work; it was not shared. On the other hand, if he desired help with his script, the others were obligated to help. If anyone had the good luck to get more than one assignment, he was free to keep the extra work for himself. He could also bring that extra work to the group and we would decide on the basis of need who was to take that job. It would then be presented to the producer as the work of the one who got the assignment. Success rested on two assumptions: that the three of us were of equal ability and could successfully write what was required and that the producer would not notice any difference.

Success also required getting fronts. Manoff was the first one to succeed there. He found an actress friend. She had an unexpected stipulation, though. She insisted on using a pseudonym. She belonged to an illustrious family of actors from the Yiddish Art Theater who would regard her writing for television as far beneath her station. This was all right with Manoff so long as she was prepared to appear at any necessary meetings. She was; she just didn't want her real name on the demeaning screen. We broached this to Russell, who thought there would be no problem so long as he could produce someone who would swear to writing the script. He immediately gave Manoff a *Danger* assignment, which he fulfilled so well under his distaff pseudonym that a television critic called the show an especially fine example of what the new breed of women writers could do.

Polonsky was next. Through a family friend he met an advertising copywriter named Jeremy who volunteered to be his front. Jeremy wanted no money and had no ambition to be a television or movie writer; he simply wanted to help. That left it up to me. I was lucky for a while. Leo came back into my life. He was mysterious about where he had been, but there was the hint of high stakes south of the border. As usual, none of his winnings seemed to have stuck to him. He commented on my predicament with wry cynicism and then offhandedly allowed that he might be available for another bit of fronting. I pointed out that the risks were still the same. His aged parents would still come after him. He said it was all part of character-building. I insisted that this time he take money, which it was obvious he needed, but he accused me of trying to hurt his feelings. There were things you did for money and things you didn't.

"Besides," he said, "I need a few laughs."

He would do anything to conceal the goodness of his heart. But, again, his fronting lasted only a short time. The pressures built beyond his capacity to absorb them. We parted professional company with the same fond regret as before. This time, though, Leo stayed in town and got a square job and then moved back into the television game as the indispensable assistant to the producer of two very successful series. He married and settled down, but we kept in touch. I chased around for a replacement. A good friend came temporarily to the rescue. His name was Eliot and he had been a minor-league baseball player when the war came and finished his career. After the war he wrote a fine novel about a minor-league ballplayer and continued to write both fiction and nonfiction, mostly about sports. Eliot was God's angry man, perpetually at war with the world's injustice. He did not suffer fools gladly. He was capable of storming unannounced into an editor's office and terrorizing the place. At times it seemed as though anger was what fueled him and gave him purpose.

It also made his life difficult. He could not fathom the difference between demurral and argument. There was a certain purity about Eliot, no capacity to dissemble, and that didn't help, either. But he had survived both wartime service in the Aleutians and having Marlon Brando as a brother-in-law, and after that fronting for a friend was comic relief. I wrote a script for Russell under Eliot's name and then one for another half-hour dramatic program. My only concern was that the second script was for a producer who really was a fool and would require foolish script changes. Eliot had to go in as the writer to listen to this, and even though it was not his own script, his sense of injustice was boundless. It was a toss-up whether he would simply, if colorfully, denounce the producer for what he was (not just for what he was doing) or just hold him out the window until he saw the error of his ways. Fortunately Eliot did neither of these and the shows went on without incident, but he had his own writing to pursue and could not front for more than a few scripts.

With all this uncertainty I found that an unexpected feeling of comfort had entered my life. It came from our little group. We had established in fact what we had always extolled in theory, a kind of commune. We had not really planned it that way. We had come together for selfish economic reasons, simply to make a living. We knew that the group would not work under any share-the-wealth program. Each of us had to be free to pursue his own individual interest and reap whatever reward came with that. But something else had begun to happen. We found that we were operating on the subversive principle of "From each according to his ability, to each according to his need." Since we were each of similar ability, at least so far as television was concerned, that took care of itself. So did the question of need. No one took more than one job for himself. That became automatic, taken for granted, an unconscious basis of the group. If one of us had a job and found another, the second job was offered to the group as a matter of course and taken by whoever needed it the most at that moment, to pay rent or a doctor's bill or even alimony. The need was never questioned; we all were in need. One time Polonsky suddenly took sick and had to be hospitalized.

He had a script assignment when this happened, so Manoff and I wrote the script for him and sent him the money. The producer never knew the difference. There was no sense of charity or even obligation. We had simply discovered we were together not just to help ourselves but one another. It was what gave the group its moral and emotional base. It defined who we were. It was another liberation. It came as a surprise, except perhaps to Manoff, who always saw farther.

It was Manoff, too, who took the group to another level. He pointed out that trying to get assignments here and there was wasteful and time-consuming. We were already doing most of our work for *Danger*, but he was more ambitious than that. Because of the success of *Danger*, CBS was giving Russell and Lumet a new program to produce and direct, and it was Manoff's thought that we should do all the writing for that one. The idea had the arrogance of genius. Why should we work piecemeal when we could take over a whole show? What did it matter that we were blacklisted? A good offense was the best defense. It depended, of course, on Russell. He was enthusiastic. He was having the time of his life. We had shown that we could produce for him and we had become friends.

Russell was a shy and reclusive man. He had no close friends. He had come from an upstate uptight middle-class family in which no one spoke to anyone else unless absolutely necessary. His father came home from business every night and locked himself in his room and played the cello. At the first opportunity Russell had run away and joined the Civilian Conservation Corps. After a year spent planting trees and digging firebreaks, he left for the big city, where he worked first at a soda fountain in Grand Central Station and then as an usher at Radio City Music Hall. Then a girlfriend offered him a ride to Hollywood and he went.

We liked and admired Russell, liked him for his unpretentious generosity, admired him for his courage. He found us exotic. We included him in our insults, which he took accurately as a sign of affection. He came to lunch with us and took us to dinner in expensive restaurants. We appreciated his taste in all things, from scripts to clothes. Clothes looked good on Russell; he could have been an ad for the Ivy League. When we talked politics, he listened with polite disinterest, waiting patiently for the topic to change. He had no interests apart from his work. There was a secret girlfriend and the additional solace of carefully regulated drink; neither seemed appreciably to affect him. He looked forward to our meetings and they soon extended from the work to the social. Russell had been emotionally deprived all his life and in us he found some kind of improbably loving home. We grew very fond of him very fast.

The new show was called *You Are There*. It had originally been a radio program, taking a historical event and pretending it was occurring at the moment. Leading figures like Napoleon or Catherine the Great were interviewed by CBS reporters as though the event were happening now. For television, Russell's boss, William Dozier, had the idea to have the reporters dressed for the period, but Russell convinced him that the sight of Julius Caesar being interviewed by Mike Wallace in a toga was not quite what he had in mind. The audience might think it was Sid Caesar they were seeing. In the end a format was conceived in which the reporters were heard but not seen and the subject addressed the camera as though that were the reporter. The commentator who started and ended the show would be Walter Cronkite, rising star of CBS newsmen.

We embraced the idea as enthusiastically as Russell. Here was the chance not only to work but to have some fun. There was no need to make up stories with unhappy endings, as we had for *Danger*; history would provide more than enough. There might even be a few uplifting ones. We had millennia to choose from. Script conferences were held either at Steinberg's or in Russell's room in the Hotel Lombardy. We preferred the hotel since it had a fine restaurant downstairs and we could order room service. Russell had briefed Lumet on what he was going to do and Lumet had heartily agreed. We then set about choosing the subjects. Dozier had given Russell a few obligatory ones, such as the crash of the German dirigible *Hindenburg* and the killings of Jesse James and John Dillinger. We countered with the Boston Tea Party, the execution of Joan of Arc and the Salem witch trials. We were off and running, except that I still didn't have a front.

My younger brother came to the rescue. He suggested his childhood friend Leslie. I had known Leslie since he was ten years old and had always liked him. He had a sweet disposition. He and my brother had gone separate ways after high school but remained good friends. My brother was now a doctor and Leslie was a reporter for a civil service newspaper called *The Chief*. Leslie had been a naval officer during the war, considered brave but somewhat unreliable since he became instantly seasick upon boarding anything with a hull. He even got seasick on a sailboat while in training. This did not deter the navy when the war was over from sending him to Japan to take command of a landing craft and bring it back to the States. Leslie accomplished this by lying down as soon as the anchor was weighed and letting steadier hands take the helm. He was probably the only navy officer who ever sailed five thousand miles totally recumbent.

At first there was nothing for Leslie to do as a front except lend his name. Russell knew he could be displayed and that was all that mattered. To test the waters, I wrote a *Danger* show under his name and it went well, but his debut was overshadowed by Russell's being unexpectedly summoned to meet with Laurence Johnson, the supermarket owner from Syracuse. Present at the meeting were executives from CBS and the advertising agency that handled the *Danger* account. The subject was an actor named John Randolph whom Russell had just hired to do a *Danger* show. By now CBS was sending its cast lists to Johnson for his approval and this time he had flown to New York to express his particular disapproval. He wanted Russell to explain how he could have hired Randolph knowing he was a Communist. Russell said all he knew was that Randolph was a good actor, ideal for this part. He added that he was just doing his job. Johnson said he should do his job as an American. The CBS executive said Russell had been doing just that; hadn't he gotten rid of other Reds like Walter Bernstein? The agency executive pointed out that Randolph had a signed contract that had to be honored. In that case Johnson thought that the whole show should be canceled.

No one told Johnson this was none of his business. It had become his business by default. Everyone in the room accepted his right to determine who and what went on the air. They suggested Johnson bring his family down to watch rehearsals of the show. They would see what wonders talented, right-thinking Americans could perform. The effect was unreal unless it was your head on the block. Then it became real. Finally, Johnson accepted the fact that the show would have to go on with Randolph. But he would meet again with the show's sponsor to make sure this did not happen again.

The next day Dozier decided he wanted to meet Russell's new writer. We were certain this meant trouble. Leslie took it with aplomb. He said to leave it to him. He went into the meeting with Russell, who returned dazzled by Leslie's performance. Leslie had charmed Dozier into submission. He knew the Hollywood movies Dozier had produced and was warm with praise. He was sycophantic without being smarmy, a difficult act to bring off. By the end of the meeting Dozier was asking if Leslie thought the show he had just written, about an insurance investigator, might be the basis of a series. Leslie allowed that this was certainly possible. Dozier asked how he thought it could be done. Leslie said he would not insult Dozier by giving him opinions off the top of his head. He would go home and think about it and then give him details.

Nothing happened with the series idea, but we now had all the fronts in place. We began allocating the scripts for *You Are There*. Russell thought it would be wise to throw people off the scent by hiring someone legitimate for one of the early shows. He gave the Boston Tea Party to a good unblacklisted writer named Arnold Schulman. We accepted this with grace, recognizing the tactical need. Next, we had to deal with the show's concept, which meant more than its technique. What were we trying to do every week apart from putting historical figures on display? How were these people affecting history? What were the ideas animating them? What was making history move? The radio show had dealt with personalities, not ideas. No one at CBS had wanted anything else. Now they assumed the show could be transferred from one medium to another without any alteration besides the visual. Like most corporate enterprises, any problems would be handed down the chain of command until they came to someone competent to deal with them—in this case, Russell.

We discussed the problems at length. We did not have the luxury of radio, where you could go anywhere, simulate great crowds, tell the audience what was happening and let its imagination do the rest. We had to show what was happening. To make our stories dramatic, we felt we had to find and then dramatize the conflicts that characterized the periods we were dealing with. They could be momentous, as with Galileo, or just colorful, as with Dillinger. We still had to set protagonist against antagonist and each had to represent something beyond himself. Like any dramatic, journalistic or even academic work, it would be our interpretation of the facts, but we were not interested in propaganda. We had no message that came first, with the facts then selected to sell that message. We did have a purpose: We wanted to tell the truth about history so far as we could learn it through research, to show the reasons behind the event. Our agenda was to pick subjects that, if possible, had some bearing on what was happening in the world today.

You Are There went on Sunday nights at six-thirty, sponsored by the Prudential Insurance Company, intended at that hour for a young audience. Much to CBS's surprise, it also attracted adults. It quickly became successful. Cronkite's sign-off, written by Polonsky, even became famous: "What kind of a day was it? A day like all other days, filled with those events that alter and illuminate our times . . . and you were there!" Schools across the country asked for copies of the shows for their history classes. We found ourselves with a hit on our hands.

The position was curious. We could get no credit for the success and could not build on it, since that would give the fronts too much exposure. It meant nothing to our own careers because we had no careers. When the show began winning prizes and receiving awards, we could not appear to claim them. Russell could, but he was usually shunted aside by Dozier, who saw no reason why he shouldn't take the credit. None of this mattered. We were having too good a time. We were choosing subjects of controversy and importance: Galileo, Savonarola, John Milton, Cortez, Joan of Arc, Dreyfus, Benedict Arnold, Susan B. Anthony, Freud, Tom Paine, Socrates, Beethoven. We did the Scopes trial and the fall of Troy, the death of Cleopatra and the impeachment of Andrew Johnson. We roamed far and wide.

And history served us well. We had no need to invent conflicts to serve our purpose. They were there for the taking and we happily and conscientiously took them. In that shameful time of McCarthyite terror, of know-nothing attempts to deform and defile history, to kill any kind of dissent, we were able to do shows about civil liberties, civil rights, artistic freedom, the Bill of Rights. CBS let us do them, which caused some perplexity among its employees. Russell encountered Edward R. Murrow one day and Murrow pulled him aside, told him he watched *You Are There* every week and admired it and then, lowering his voice, asked Russell how he got away with it.

No one knew how, but he did, most likely because the show was successful or perhaps someone high up in CBS thought this was something worthwhile. But with Russell running interference, we fought a kind of guerrilla war against McCarthyism. We wrote and Russell produced and Lumet directed a dramatic program in which we tried our best to celebrate the human spirit, to show the forces that throughout history tried to stunt and oppress that spirit, to explain as clearly as we could its victories and its defeats. We never tried to shape history to prove a political point. What was important was the subject matter. Surprisingly there was little backlash, possibly because we were scrupulous in our research and Russell had taken the precaution of having distinguished history professors go over relevant scripts to confirm their accuracy. Only once was he called up before Dozier to justify a show and that was when the wife of the president of a Milwaukee brewing company wrote in indignation that we had slandered Marie Antoinette. We had made her too frivolous.

The success of the show also had ancillary benefits. We were able to give work to other blacklisted writers. While the three of us wrote almost all the shows, there were some we didn't have time for. Russell gave a few of these to unblacklisted writers, but kept a few for some blacklisted ones we suggested. There were also assignments for *Danger* until Russell and Lumet had to quit that show to devote their time to *You Are There*. If the other blacklisted writers had no fronts, we lent them ours. This arrangement worked because we could guarantee the scripts. In the rare event a script was not adequate, we rewrote it. The other writer still got the script fee.

Our little group became the axis of my life. I saw my two children on weekends and I had other friends, but the group was both work and play, an oasis in a desert of discouragement and fear. We were making enough money now to pay our expenses; we believed in what we were doing, believed it was of value, enjoyed one another's company. We criticized one another with ruthless abandon and accepted it as love. We felt ourselves lucky. There was even money for a small vacation. I went up to Maine for a few weeks and rented a cabin on a tidal creek off the ocean. The cabin had no heat, running water or electricity, but the enveloping forest was peaceful and quiet.

In fact, it was too quiet. After New York the stillness was abnormal. It was creepy. There had to be some crouching thing out there poised to eat me. The first night I awoke around midnight, having to go to the outhouse. Naturally I had no flashlight. The darkness was like a blanket over my head as I felt my way through bushes and into trees. My only consolation was that my blundering noise might scare away the wild animals that, if they were not helpless with laughter, were just waiting to pounce. I finally found the outhouse and sat down on the freezing board and, reaching out to steady myself, touched an enormous clammy hand. I think I screamed. I know I bolted out of there, pants around my ankles, and stumbled panic-stricken to the safety of the house. The next morning, armed with an oar, I crept back to the outhouse and slid the door open and saw what had scared me. It was a baseball glove.

The cabin was owned by an old Communist who owned another primitive cabin just across the creek. This came in handy when I received a telegram from an actor friend, Gary Merrill. We had been together, he as actor, I as publicist, in *This Is the Army*, when he introduced me to boilermakers. Gary liked to drink more than he liked to act, but he was a good actor who had scored a success on Broadway in *Born Yesterday* and had then gone to Hollywood with a contract at Twentieth Century–Fox. He had recently been in a movie called *All About Eve*, playing opposite Bette Davis. They had fallen in love and now they were married and on their honeymoon, driving East from California. The telegram asked if I could find them a place to stay for a week or two. They were both New Englanders and used to discomfort and any place would do so long as it was on water. I wired back that I had found the perfect place for them. The landlord was amenable and I rowed over to check out the other cabin. It was just like mine, with the same lack of amenities, but it also had a bookcase full of the collected works of Marx, Engels, Lenin and Stalin. I decided this was not exactly movie star reading, at least not in that day and age, and stuck the books in a closet and stacked firewood in front so they wouldn't be seen.

Gary and Bette arrived in a large Cadillac convertible

packed high with suitcases. They loved the cabin. Bette immediately sat down to make a shopping list. She seemed utterly familiar to me. It was as if I were finally meeting in person an old pen pal. After all, she had been part of my life since *Cabin in the Cotton*. I found myself searching her face for the scar from *Marked Woman*. She was smaller than I had imagined but formidable. Her manner was at the same time friendly and imperious. She was not stuck up, merely regal. She was a star. When she finished her list, she handed it to Gary and he and I went down to my boat and rowed across to the tiny village at the head of the creek. At the general store we bought most of what Bette had ordered. At the bottom of her list, after milk, bread and eggs, she had simply written "boat," but none was available for rental and Gary didn't think she wanted him actually to buy a boat, so we took our staples and rowed back to the cabin.

We had been gone about two hours. We came back to find Bette in an apron, feeding wood to the stove. On a table were the makings for martinis and a plate of canapés she had made. A fire burned in the fireplace. I had tidied up the cabin for their arrival, but she had swept it again and polished the few pieces of furniture. She had found doilies to put on the couch. Everything gleamed. And back in the bookcase were the collected works of Marx, Engels, Lenin and Stalin.

"Guess what I found!" she shouted at us. "The most wonderful books!"

It had been hard work for me, stacking the firewood in front of them, and just as hard for her getting them out again. I don't know whether she even read the books; it was more as if she had simply accepted the challenge of disinterring them. Bette's energy was boundless, fed by a constant inner fire that seemed fueled by some deep discontent, a dissatisfaction not only with her own life but with the way life was lived all around her. She was impatient with disorder and incompetence. She herself was enormously competent. Domesticity inspired her. She sewed and knitted and did embroidery; she was a good cook and ferocious cleaner. She disdained helping hands. She and Gary seemed to complement each other in some necessary way. Gary was passive and easygoing and a thinker; Bette was a doer. He dampened his fires with drink; liquor only aroused her. He sold his talent short, which infuriated her. He had no ambition, but he had an integrity she admired and respected. Gary acted on what he believed. Back in California he would often get up early on a Sunday morning and drive out into the countryside, stopping unannounced at churches to ask if he might speak to the congregation about the perils of the atom bomb. He was fearless in his liberalism. There was something very New England about both of them.

They stayed for two weeks, drinking a lot and fighting when they drank too much. We ate lobsters bought from the local fishermen and drank beer we kept cold in the creek. Once, awakened late at night, I heard loud, drunken voices from a boat on the water and asked Bette the next day if they were the ones. She was furious at me for thinking she would be that loud in public. She told me icily that she had better manners than that. Before they left, she got down on her hands and knees and scrubbed the cabin floor. They thanked me for the cabin and said they had had a swell honeymoon. Bette said if she and Gary could live like that all the time, they might even stay married. Later she wrote me a note asking if I would look for her eyebrow pencil that she might have left behind. I thought it a movie star indulgence, bothering about an eyebrow pencil you could pick up at the five-and-ten. But when I found it in a closet, it was pure gold.

The fact is, I was starting to be happy. There were still the middle-of-the-night flashes of panic and despair, the fear that this obscene, unfair time would never end. This was not a time to be happy, but there it was, this unexpected feeling of happiness. Naturally it filled me with guilt. What right had I to be happy? Given my heritage, the question had occupied me from birth, but it had added relevance now. Being happy while blacklisted seemed some failure of character, a superficiality or insensitivity, a want of feeling. Happiness at any time was suspect, but now? It was as though I were wearing an invisible gas mask that could protect me from the poisonous fumes that were felling honest people all around me. Guilt was appropriate. Happiness was unreasonable. I had no career; my mail was being opened and my phone tapped; FBI agents were constant visitors; the present was shaky and the future unpromising. Some of the blacklisted writers had slipped into a tolerant Mexico and a few others had gotten away to England and France, where the blacklist did not operate. Mainly they got away because their original names were different from their working ones and their FBI files were only on the latter. My decision was made for me because I couldn't get a passport, but I still wouldn't have wanted to leave. I could pay the rent and I was doing work that had some meaning. My friendships had become precious.

Stalin died.

Stalin died? How could he die, the great leader of the progressive forces of the world? He had been part of my adult life even longer than Roosevelt. The movie *Mission to Moscow* had made me cringe with its hearty adulation of Uncle Joe, but that was necessary wartime propaganda, as were the happy Russian peasants dancing in *North Star* and the other sunny views of the Soviet Union that Hollywood turned out in that ecumenical time. The CPUSA mourned Stalin's loss, unable to see it as release, an opportunity now to look past

the cult of personality to what really went on in Russia. The
Party saw Stalin only as the consolidator of the Revolution,
without blemish. My aunt Sara was inconsolable. I visited her
at Party headquarters, where she still worked as a secretary,
and her eyes were red from weeping. She was irritated that I
was not appropriately grief-stricken. But Stalin had been a
distant, vaguely avuncular figure and his death did not touch
me the way Roosevelt's had. The truth was that I was not that
interested in the Soviet Union. I did not know for sure what
was happening there, but I knew what was happening here.

There were Ethel and Julius Rosenberg, for example, executed for supposedly passing atomic secrets to the Russians. I
did not doubt that there were Americans, Party members,
who had given information to the Soviets. I had myself been
approached at a party by an affable secretary from the Soviet
Embassy. I was still in uniform and what he wanted to know
was trivial: what I thought about the morale of American
troops. He knew me as a friend of the Soviet Union and if I
would just write a few words on the subject . . . I declined as
politely as I could, feeling vaguely guilty afterward. Was I betraying the cause? It did not seem much for him to ask. The
Russians were allies; where was the harm? I had gone against
American policy in Yugoslavia, acting subversively in a time
of war. What was the difference now? Should I have told my
superior officer? (I didn't.) I was unclear, unhappy about the
choice I had made, thinking I had made it out of cowardice,
not conviction, but I had made it and knew, if necessary, I
would make it again.

But with the Rosenbergs I had no doubt they had been rail-
roaded, convicted on flimsy and corrupted evidence. Whatever they may have done, it had not been proved at the trial.
Certainly they did not deserve to die. The jury that convicted
them did not recommend a sentence. No American court had

ever sentenced a civilian to death for espionage, even in wartime. We had not been at war with Russia. Under law the Rosenbergs had not committed treason, even if they were guilty as charged, but an ignorant and ambitious judge treated them as though they had. His sentence-of-death speech insisted the Rosenbergs had given the Russians the atom bomb "long before our best scientists had predicted they would have it," and so caused the Communists to attack in Korea and kill thousands of Americans. None of the evidence had shown this to be remotely true. His stupidity was exceeded only by his venom. I felt the judge would not have been this murderous if he himself had not been Jewish, as were all the major participants in that trial. The accused, the chief witnesses against them, the prosecutor, the judge—it was a Jewish nightmare come true, as if they were all acting out some archaic, self-destructive ritual for the benefit of the goyim.

Many years later, evidence from KGB archives indicated that Julius Rosenberg, but not his wife, had been part of a spy ring smuggling secrets to the Russians. This did not mean that their trial had been fair or the sentence just. We may have been wrong about his spying, but not about the fact that the trial was corrupt, the evidence fabricated and the nightmare real.

But back then we raised money for the Rosenberg defense, organized meetings, wrote letters to an unreceptive press. On the night of their execution there was a huge rally in Union Square and I went with Marty and Adele Ritt. There had been other rallies around the world. Albert Einstein had protested the sentence. So had three thousand American clergymen. Even the militantly anti-Communist pope had appealed to President Eisenhower, asking him to temper justice with mercy. American embassies overseas had been flooded with letters urging clemency. None of it helped. We held hands and listened to impassioned speeches and then went back to my apartment and listened to the radio, hoping for a last-minute stay. When the news came that both Rosenbergs had been put to death, we cried. I had never seen Marty cry before; he was not given to tears. Even then he could not let anyone see him weep but went to the window and looked out with his back to us. I wept tears of sorrow and rage.

The sorrow was containable, the rage barely so. I didn't try to contain it. Anger was more useful than tears. It energized and cleansed, a visceral affirmation of my beliefs. It did not make me any happier, but I felt it made me stronger. Anger set traps, though, that you had to avoid. You had to be careful it didn't turn into bitterness. You had to be sure it didn't tempt you into justifying the unjustifiable, particularly in regard to the Soviet Union. We were increasingly unclear about the Soviet Union, how deep to go with our criticism, how much we really knew. We were afraid it might take us into the camp of the enemy. The enemy had enough ammunition without giving him more. Whatever went on in Russia, the fact in America was that the blacklisted people had been isolated, marginalized, rejected and criminalized. We were forced to live in a different world, a parallel universe with its own fields of force. We had our own citizenry, language, set of physical rules. Our chemistry was different. We had our own sly arithmetic; we could find fronts and make two become one.

We had exploding stars, like Zero, who could erupt at any minute. As I walked with him one afternoon, we saw the actor Lee Cobb coming toward us. He had been a cooperative witness before the committee, naming many friends of Zero, though not Zero himself. Seeing him, Zero began to inflate like a balloon. I watched him with interest, figuring one of two things would happen: he would burst or he would stran-

gle Cobb. But all Zero did was to start slowly shaking his
head, continuing to shake it even after we had passed the
frightened Cobb, who had instinctively raised his hands to
ward off the expected blow. I think Zero was shaking his
head at himself, not at Cobb, a warning not to explode. After
a while he stopped, but when I put my hand on his arm, the
muscles were twitching under the skin.

We had all the attributes of a true universe. We had galax-
ies scattered around the country. We had black holes into
which some of our people dropped. Unable to work at what
they knew, unwilling to inform so they could work again,
they exhausted their strength. They consumed their internal
resources and became sick and died or simply disappeared.
They moved where light could not reach them.

Finally, we were expanding like a universe. The House
committee had been joined by the McCarthy subcommittee
and they were joined by frightened employers and unions
stripped of their militants and obedient government agencies
intent on firing or jailing anyone suspected of Communist
advocacy or even liberal activity. Since this last covered a
spectrum ranging from the New Deal to what was called
"premature antifascism," the list grew exponentially. It had
constantly to be enlarged in order to keep the threat real.
There could be no such thing as a finite Red menace; evil cannot be seen as having boundaries. The impulse was religious
even if the need was secular. The blacklist was the result of a
politics grounded in fear and an economy dependent on military buildup. Based as it was on terror, falsehood and profit,
it needed constant justification. Otherwise, there was the risk
that like the physical universe, it might someday reach the
limits of its expansion and collapse upon itself.

Occasionally, though, it was possible to move from one
universe to the other. That was another benefit of living in

New York rather than a company town like Los Angeles. In Los Angeles you were in the entertainment business twenty-four hours a day. Everyone knew who you were and what you were doing. In New York you could leave your house and be anonymous. You could ride the subway and no one would suspect you were an alien. In the darkness of a movie house no one would know you were there at all. As always, the movies for me were comfort and escape, refuge and inspiration. As always, that same nameless weight dropped off when I handed the usher my ticket and, slowing down, taking my time now or, more precisely, taking back my time, pausing at the candy counter to make the familiar choice between gumdrops or chocolate-covered mints, then groping my way down the shadowy aisle, peering into the dark for an unobstructed seat, I entered a world in which I was finally safe. It did not matter how crowded or dirty or airless a movie theater was, I could breathe freely there.

It did matter, of course, what was on the screen. I had some standards, after all. The trouble was, I had no idea what they were. Once I was in the theater, they had no control over me. Movies disarmed me, defanged my critical faculties, left me happily helpless in their seductive grip. True, there were certain movies I knew were better than others. I could tell a hawk from a handsaw. I knew that *Torch Song* or *Abbott and Costello Meet Jekyll and Hyde* was really not as good as *Forbidden Games* or *The Earrings of Madame De . . .* But to see a heartless Joan Crawford reformed by the piano-playing love of blind Michael Wilding, to watch Lou Costello confront Boris Karloff—that was not to be taken lightly. That, too, was the real thing come along. The movies themselves were changing in perceptible ways. Women were becoming more benign; men felt safer with them now. It was the age of Audrey Hepburn, the safest woman of them all. Ava Gardner would have eaten her alive, with Burt Lancaster for dessert.

The success of *You Are There* inevitably led to its writers' being in demand. Once again Russell was asked about them by other producers. We warned him about literary excess— no writers disappearing into the Yukon—but this time he could answer truthfully: They were in thrall to his show and had no time for other work. We continued our guerrilla warfare and the show continued to win awards. The sponsor happily renewed. Russell was able to increase our fees. Even Dozier seemed to be on our side. After reading a script nominally by Jeremy, he handed it back to Russell, saying, "Tell Polonsky I thought he did a good job." If Dozier knew about the fronts and did nothing, we were home free. I felt we had drifted into a peaceful eddy of an otherwise raging river. We could paddle around in there and watch the less fortunate being swept along in the torrent. My children seemed to be safely in there with me. Their school, the Little Red Schoolhouse, was supportive. They had wonderful teachers, gentle, tough-minded women who did not so much protect them from the truth as with the truth. They offered pride in community. Much later, when my daughter was grown, I asked how she had felt about what was happening to me in those days. She said my enforced idleness had meant only that I was more available. The blacklist had not been as important to her as her parents' divorce. Whatever was happening had pleased her to the extent it had allowed her to see more of me. The politics were irrelevant.

I had money now to pick her up after school and deposit her for horseback riding lessons at a West Side riding academy. I took my son to Central Park and hit endless fungoes to him. I could pretend to be like any other father. He caught everything hit to him and threw it back to me on the fly. I had visions of a son of mine in center field for the Dodgers. He preferred the Yankees. I hated the Yankees. They were capitalism's team.

"How can you like the Yankees?" I would ask, worried.

"Because they win," he would explain, patiently.

His tone held the tolerance of a fond child for his dim-witted father. Why else would he like the Yankees? Because they lost? My boyhood Dodgers had always lost, which didn't make them less beloved. If anything, it added to their appeal. You could always dream they would get better, even as you watched Babe Herman back up against the right field fence and brace himself to catch a fly ball that then dropped twenty feet in front of him. My eight-year-old son couldn't see rooting for a loser. He thought maybe it was something people had done in the olden days.

Our complacency didn't last much longer. CBS decided to put *You Are There* on film. This was happening to many live shows and ordinarily would not have been a problem. But it was also moving the show to Hollywood and Russell was not going with it. CBS fired him. He found out from Dozier after the two of them had screened a print of "The Triumph of Alexander the Great," the final *You Are There* episode to be done in the East. As they waited for an elevator, Dozier told Russell that there was no need for him to go to the cutting room the next day, that the editor would handle anything that had to be done. He then told Russell that he, Dozier, would be going to Hollywood to produce *You Are There*. The elevator came, Dozier stepped in, turned back to Russell and told him he was fired. His services were no longer required by CBS. The elevator door closed, leaving Russell standing there. He went above Dozier for an explanation, but no one ever gave him one. He was told the subject was closed. Later a friend at the advertising agency handling the sponsor's account said he had asked Dozier why Russell had been fired and Dozier had said Russell was using blacklisted writers and if that got out, it would harm the sponsor's image.

We spent as much time as we could with Russell, who we believed was the true victim here. He had stuck his neck out when he had everything to lose. He had done it for himself, for his self-respect and for what he felt was right, but he had also done it for us. There was no way we could thank him enough or pay him back. All we could do was worry about him, about his future. It was clear that the television industry was moving to Hollywood and Russell would soon have to go there to work and we worried about him alone in that jungle. We were not sure he could survive without support. He would be defeated by his good taste and his lack of social skills and the simmering anger that lay beneath his drinking. He was a brave, fragile man who had never been nurtured and that lack was not going to be redressed by Hollywood. He and Lumet and the three of us had been lucky to have found one another at a particular time and now that time was over. There was no doubt that Lumet's talent would be rewarded with success, and we three believed that by now, by virtue of our group, we also would somehow survive, but we were not so sure about Russell.

A new strategy was needed. Since I had more contacts in the television world than either Abe or Arnie, I was deemed the outside man and sent off to see what work I could find. I realized that I had been spoiled by the time on *Danger* and *You Are There*. All I had to do then was write. Now I had to find producers and sell myself to them. Even when unblacklisted, I had never been very good at that. I had been known to mumble. Hostility was easier to project than confidence. Once, when pitching a story to a stone-faced producer, I found I had leaned so far forward in my chair that I was upside down, looking back through the rungs. Now I had to contend not only with my own anxiety but with theirs. The air was still poisonous. Senator McCarthy had gone a little too far in his hubris, had stupidly gone after the U.S. Army and been censured by the Senate, but what he had helped sow was still flourishing. The Korean War was over, but we had gained nothing except the unwelcome knowledge that now the Chinese were to be feared as much as the Russians. Anticommunism was still America's official religion and fear of excommunication was as widespread as ever.

I felt like a traveling salesman going door to door selling stolen jewelry. Word was out that the goods were real but hot to handle. Producers would still refuse to see me or would talk in whispers on the telephone (after I had assured them I was calling from a pay phone) or else meet me in a dark, secluded bar. They always insisted on paying for the drinks. None had any assignments. A few offered to look at a speculative script with the possibility of buying it, provided the front would make an appearance in the presence of witnesses. The front did not have to swear to anything, just show up. So far as they knew, they were dealing only with me.

The group decided we had no choice and each of us wrote a script for three different producers. As usual, we crossfertilized, helping one another with criticism and ideas. I presented all three as written by Leslie. Only one script raised a problem. The producer was my old agent from the Morris office and his show was going off the air soon and he was trying to get away with as much last-minute loot as he could. If certain products were shown or mentioned on his show, he stood to take home cases of scotch, articles of clothing or even a trip to Bermuda. The writer, of course, would get a small cut. This practice was strictly forbidden but often indulged. The only product I could fit in was Charlie the Tuna, the logo for a brand of tuna fish. I gave it as a nickname to a gangster. My reward was a case of tuna fish. The producer apologized and said there had not been enough scotch to go around after the director and the star had been paid off. But all three scripts were bought and Leslie showed up to charm each producer in turn. The script fees came to Leslie, who parceled them out according to who had written what. When the shows went on the air, no one noticed any difference in styles. No one commented on how fast Leslie could write, only on how versatile he was. Everyone wrote fast for live television.

Russell got an immediate job producing the New York segments of a dramatic show called *Stage Struck*. We celebrated being in business again, but it lasted only a short time. Few of the shows were done in New York; most came from Los Angeles. After a couple of months the producers moved everything to the West Coast. Russell's agent got him another job producing a series, but, as he feared, this was in Hollywood. We were happy he had found work and sad to see him leave. For a going-away present, we bought him an expensive clock that ran mysteriously on the atmosphere, and drove him to the airport. The only cheering news was that the Hollywood version of *You Are There* had been canceled. Dozier had no idea what had made the show a success; under his aegis it had settled for bland and safe subjects and the ratings had dropped through the floor. We bought champagne at the airport bar and drank to its demise. We felt it was the end of an era or, so far as we were concerned, the end of an aberration. We had had no business getting away with what we had. Now, quite properly, the blacklisted writers were back where they belonged, riding the rapids. But we had made a life raft by linking ourselves together and had no intention of going under. I got another job or two and then I met David Susskind.

I met Susskind through his partner, Al Levy, a friendly, generous man whom I had gotten to know from watching an ex-partner of his named Dick Dorso play tennis. Dorso was a handsome television producer, always immaculately groomed, even on the tennis court. You would not be surprised to see him wear an ascot under his polo shirt. His distinction as a tennis player was that he only played doubles and then only on one side of the court. His reasoning had been as meticulous as his clothes. He had taken up tennis too late to be as proficient in singles as he wished to be and he felt he didn't have enough time left to learn to play all-around doubles. But he could learn to play one side of the court and he chose the deuce court and took lessons on how to play that side and did, in fact, become quite good. Dorso had been one-third of a trio of talent agents who had discovered Doris Day in a trailer court. The other two were Levy and a man named Melcher, whom Miss Day later married. Dorso was married to a lady as handsome and well dressed as he was. Together they looked as if they had just stepped out of an ad for expensive scotch. He had no work for me but introduced me to Levy, who was partners with Susskind in a company called Talent Associates. They produced dramatic shows and series for television.

I knew Susskind was not afraid of the blacklist. When the news broke about *You Are There*'s going to Hollywood, he had called Russell, told him that he was sorry but that at least now he might get a shot at hiring Walter Bernstein. Susskind had an engaging brashness that too easily crossed the line into attack. He was a sensitive man who tried his best to be insensitive and usually succeeded. Where Levy was low-key, Susskind was hyper. He was in a hurry, on the make, anxious to interrupt. He had been an agent with MCA and still wore the black suit and white shirt that were that agency's uniform. It made him look like an eager undertaker. He wanted you to know he had gone to an Ivy League college. I found that I was always initially glad to see Susskind and that would last about a minute and a half, after which I would want to murder him. I was not alone in this. Susskind had an ability to get under your skin, whether by accident or design. He was everything Russell was not—crudely ambitious, devious and aggressive—but he wanted to do work that had class and, however reluctant its manifestation, he was not without taste.

Susskind hired me to adapt the Mark Twain story *The Prince and the Pauper.* Leslie did the fronting and the show went on with Christopher Plummer in the Errol Flynn part and Leslie won a Christopher Award. He wanted me to have it, but since it bore his name, we agreed it should stay on his mantelpiece. Leslie was also moving up in his real profession. He had recently been hired as the assistant press secretary to Mayor Wagner. He was willing to continue as a front, but now he had much more to lose. The risk was too great. We would not allow him to continue. So off I went, once again on the prowl for a front. Leo obliged for one show, and out of his genuine kindness, even Howard for another (I wrote better this time and did not shame him), but there was no one permanent. There never could be, of course. Permanency was an illusion. There were too many reasons why people could not remain fronts. Fronting made impossible demands on the person. It was unnatural, a violation of the ego. You had constantly to pretend to be what you were not. Polonsky always thought the fronts were saving our lives while we were destroying theirs. I thought he exaggerated, but not by much. None of these high-minded thoughts kept us from using whoever was agreeable.

Susskind gave me another book to adapt, *The Bridge of San Luis Rey* by Thornton Wilder, and told me not to worry, he would supply the front. She turned out to be a woman friend of his, a sometime actress named Ada. He assured me that Ada was trustworthy and very bright for an actress. I wrote the show and it went into rehearsal. At one point the director, a very talented man named Robert Mulligan, called and said I had to come right over; there were script changes to be discussed before he went any farther. At the rehearsal hall an assistant met me furtively at a side door and hustled me into a room next to the rehearsal hall. Mulligan was there and we talked and settled on the changes. Afterward I watched the rehearsal for a while, peering through a crack in the door. Ada was taking compliments from the actors. I thought she was behaving a little too grandly for a writer, but no one else seemed to mind. Susskind had said she had no writing ambitions, but the show received good notices and Ada was offered an assignment in Hollywood. By that time she was convinced she had really written *The Bridge of San Luis Rey.* She was now accepting compliments from a booth at the Russian Tea Room. She could not get to Hollywood fast enough. Unfortunately Ada did not do as well there since she had actually to write and Susskind received an angry letter from the producer, asking why he had not been warned and saying the least Susskind could now do was give him the name of the real writer.

There was by now, at least in the television business, a more or less general acceptance of the fact that blacklisted writers were getting work through fronts. One of the problems, though, was that no one quite knew who were the fronts and who were the writers. I would get compliments for shows I had not written. If I denied this, people would smile and wink at me; they knew. They had recognized my style. Or the little touches that gave me away. How I named my characters. How I liked unhappy endings. How I liked happy endings. They knew everything, but my secret was safe with them. They were content to be in the know.

I got credit for some excellent shows I had nothing to do with. My denials were taken as signs of a becoming modesty. There were certain advantages to this. It could take you far with attractive women who appreciated good writing. You had to choose, of course, between lust and honor, but that was no choice at all. People also had opinions about the names my presumed fronts were using. For some reason, they were bothered by the name of Paddy Chayefsky. I became resigned to someone always coming up to me after a Chayefsky show and asking why I used a name like that, it was so obviously a fake. They seemed offended; I was letting down the side. There was no use explaining that there was a real Paddy Chayefsky who was a very good writer all on his own. They knew.

I told Susskind about Manoff and Polonsky, and he was amenable to hiring both of them, but Harry Belafonte got Polonsky first. Belafonte hired him to write a movie script. The name on the script remained that of the writer who had done some preliminary work on it, so there was no need to find a front. The movie was called *Odds Against Tomorrow.* The other star was Robert Ryan and the director was Robert Wise and they all knew that Polonsky was the writer and were delighted to get him. Both Ryan and Belafonte were active liberals and Belafonte was also prominent in causes ranging from racial justice in America to colonialism in Africa. He spoke at civil rights meetings, walked in protest marches and, in general, put his money where his mouth was. When he was not doing that, he was touring the world and singing calypso songs to adoring audiences. He was very smart and brave and had the ego and talent to sustain all this. After that movie Polonsky continued to work for Belafonte on other projects and then he went briefly to Canada to work for the director Tyrone Guthrie on a movie of *Oedipus Rex.* Guthrie also didn't care about the blacklist.

But Manoff didn't last long with Susskind, who always thought Manoff was about to insult him. He was not wrong. In fact, most people wanted to insult Susskind or, more enthusiastically, to throttle him. In one way or another he was always asking for it. Manoff was not the throttling kind and wanted only to insult Susskind, whom he disliked for his lack of courtesy, but held his tongue because he needed the work. This didn't fool Susskind. He had the sensitivity of the perpetually aggrieved. The tension of waiting to be insulted proved too much to bear and he stopped giving Manoff work. This left Manoff free to insult him, and he did. Susskind was relieved, freed for more discourtesy, but Manoff was still unemployed. We had heard from Russell, though, who was busy with his new adventure show. He said he had some rewriting to be done. Since Polonsky and I were busy, Manoff took the job. We all were working again, with and without fronts.

Russell, however, was in trouble with his new show. The ratings were low and his bosses were demanding improvement. From what he said on the phone, we weren't clear whether he had personality or creative problems. The scripts he had sent were appropriately mediocre, not better or worse than anything else turned out by the networks. The lead actor was a stiff and maybe that was all there was to it. But we sensed that Russell needed more than long-distance script help. Polonsky was tied up, which left Manoff and me to go to Los Angeles and see what we could do. We all contributed an equal amount of money for the trip and the two of us flew to Hollywood. I had not been back for almost a decade, but little on the surface seemed changed. There was smog now and more traffic. You could still play tennis at night. The flowers still didn't smell. There was the same pervasive underlying anxiety. It was the same company town with perhaps a little more fear among movie people than there had been before. Television had arrived, oozing over the entertainment business like the Blob in the movie of the same name. No one knew who would escape alive.

Russell's troubles turned out to be mostly personal. He didn't like being in Hollywood and it showed. He was impatient with his writers and contemptuous of his bosses. He felt marooned and alone and he was drinking too much. Most of this could be solved by a few more points in the ratings. We applied ourselves to the scripts and did what we could, and while we were there, I heard that Ben Maddow was working openly again. He was at Twentieth Century–Fox, writing a movie for Elia Kazan. I found this hard to believe. It meant that he had given names. It was something I did not want to believe. I also did not understand it. Maddow had been working steadily since being blacklisted, mostly writing scripts for a writer-producer named Philip Yordan, who then placed his own name on them. He had written some very good ones, including the loopy western *Johnny Guitar*. Whatever he had done, he had not done because he was starving. Even if he had renounced his politics, had turned on what he previously believed, that still did not necessarily lead to informing.

I called Fox and found Maddow was there. He sounded pleased enough to hear from me and we made a date for breakfast the next morning. We met at a coffee shop and embraced. I found myself very glad to see him again and very apprehensive. We sat down and ordered two of the breakfast specials and then he said what I knew and feared he would say. He said it right away. He had testified in secret and named seven or eight or maybe ten people, he was not exactly sure how many, and now he was working again.

"Why did you do it?" I asked. "Why? You were working."

"I couldn't stand going into the screening room after the lights were out," he said.

It had nothing to do with money or politics or being afraid or not able to work. He simply could no longer stand living in the shadows. Something had broken in him. He said Yordan always wanted him to come to the first screening of a movie Maddow had written for him, so he could get both an audience reaction and Maddow's comments. Maddow said that he had done this for years. He would wait in an outside office until the screening room went dark, slip into a backseat to watch the film and then slip out before the lights came up. Then, one day, he could not do this anymore. He called the William Morris office and told his agent to get him out of jail. The agent arranged an executive session with a congressman who sat on the Un-American Committee. The session took no time at all. Maddow gave him names and was cleared. Most of the names he gave had been his friends, but he said to me that none of them had remained close. They had little in common now and he felt no special allegiance to them. He then said what informers often said: that they had all been named before, anyway, and so he had not really harmed them.

I felt there was something I should feel that I was not feeling. I should feel anger or contempt or disgust. Maddow had not been forced to do what he did. He had been working, being paid well, surviving the blacklist better than most. He had gone through the worst of it. But there are no gradations of betrayal. He had sold his friends so he could come out of the dark. Now he stood in the light and he could put his name on his work, but he had sold his name as well as his friends. All I could feel was sadness. He sat across from me, this pleasant, talented, witty, handsome man whom I had worked with and learned from, whom I had respected and enjoyed, who had been my friend, and I could feel him slipping away, receding, the friendship slowly fading as in a movie, irising out.

We didn't finish breakfast. I put some money down and

left. We both understood we would not see each other again. I don't know if he felt that as a loss; I did.

Manoff and I returned gloomily to New York, still worried about Russell and feeling there was only so much we could do to help him. Manoff had not been surprised at Maddow's informing; he had always felt something dark and elusive about him; but then nothing negative ever surprised Manoff. He had based a lifestyle on being negative. The position was a powerful one and often difficult to resist. It had a lot going for it. All you had to do was look around at the world. Now it was pulling me to believe that perhaps I, too, should not have been surprised at what Maddow had done. I should have been smarter or more aware, have sensed the betrayer in the friend. The thought was seductive, a way to make the past fit neatly into the present. You could control it that way. You could also end by distorting the truth of that time. It was a very slippery slope. The past had a stubborn habit of conditioning the present; you could not spring full-blown from your own head. To corrupt the past was to compromise the present. And what was true for Manoff was not true for me. Maddow had been my friend. I insisted on being surprised at what he had done, if only because it validated the friendship. At the same time I wondered if he had named me along with his other friends. I wanted to believe that he would not have met me for breakfast if he had. But then I suppose I didn't know him as well as I thought.

Back in New York the gloom lifted with news of another assignment. A woman named Hannah Weinstein had raised some money to produce an independent television series in England. She wanted to use blacklisted people and had called me to work on it. I had known Hannah when she was the executive director of the Committee for the Arts, Sciences and Professions, a liberal organization that was an offshoot of a similar organization formed to help reelect Franklin D. Roosevelt for the fourth time. The ASP had sponsored the Waldorf Peace Conference, among other antiwar, antibomb, pro–civil rights causes. The government considered it a Communist front. Hannah was not a Communist, but she was of the left and would work with anyone who believed what she did and was willing to put his beliefs on the line. Nobody gave her orders. She was a small, indomitable woman who had too much impatient drive to set policy but was wonderful at carrying it out. Hannah could get important people to give their names and their money to liberal causes and feel good doing it. Taking no for an answer simply did not occur to her. She was not above cutting a corner or two. The ASP was defunct, another victim of the times, and Hannah was on her own with three small children. She now had to make some money for herself. She had secured the rights to a series of British detective stories called *The Department of Queer Complaints,* had changed the name to *Colonel March of Scotland Yard* and had engaged Boris Karloff as the eponymous hero. The stories themselves were thin and more cerebral than dramatic, but Hannah didn't care. They could easily be rewritten, or new stories created; it was just a matter of writers. She also didn't care what name anyone used.

Manoff was busy writing for Russell, so Polonsky and I took on *Colonel March*. We decided to collaborate, since writing dramatic puzzles seemed easier for two than for one. We told Hannah, who also knew Polonsky, and it was fine with her. She was happy another blacklisted writer was getting work. She took off for England, but first she asked if I would meet Karloff and see what ideas he might have. I leaped at the chance, wondering if I should tell him how I had dived under the seat when he came to life in *The Mummy.* That had scared me even more than when he came to life in

Frankenstein. Actually I had pretended I had dropped something and was searching for it. My friends, glued to the screen, were not fooled.

Karloff lived with his wife on the top floor of an old and distinguished West Side apartment house. You took an elevator and then climbed a winding set of iron stairs. It seemed appropriate, like climbing to the bell tower where he held Gloria Stuart captive. I climbed, rang the bell and waited, not without apprehension. This man had terrorized my childhood and caused nightmares. Growing up provided no protection, only the illusion that you were safe. Life imitated art, and not the other way around. A certain wariness was called for.

The door was opened by a tall, elderly English gentleman wearing fawn-colored trousers and a houndstooth jacket. He had a clipped white mustache and the familiar stoop, and when he opened his mouth, there was the familiar lisp. It was Karloff all right. I felt as I had on meeting Bette Davis, that I already knew him. The movies had performed another one of their miracles; Karloff and I were old friends without having met. He invited me in and sat me down and offered tea. His manner was pleasant and courtly. His wife brought the tea and then left with a smile. They were both charming and very English. The apartment was like a small, neat upper-class English cottage. The rooms were bright and cheerful and had eaves and leaded windows. The sofa and chairs were covered with floral patterns. There were hunting prints on the walls. You were in the presence of a lot of chintz. It was like walking onto the set of an old MGM movie about Little England.

We talked briefly about Colonel March and Karloff had a few ideas about the character. He was modest about them, offering them merely as suggestions, but they were good suggestions. He knew what he was talking about. Once I had been on a set with Lillian Gish while a cameraman was lighting her and heard her quietly tell him how to do it, how Mr. Griffith had lit her. She showed him exactly where to place his lights. Afterward the cameraman told me she had been right. Miss Gish had been in pictures for half a century, since she was a child, and she knew the business. So did Karloff, who had also started back in the silents.

In our case he knew the pitfalls of making a detective story into a film, how the movie frequently became static at the end because the detective had to stop the action to explain the case. We talked about how we could make those endings active. Karloff suggested dryly that we not make them too active; he was not as young as he used to be. It turned out that he had entered movies the same year I had entered the world. We had a drink on that. It was the kind of coincidence that took on meaning the more you drank. I kept pumping Karloff about his career, whom he had worked with, the pictures he had made. He answered willingly; he was humorous, knowledgeable and self-deprecating and gave me more time than I deserved. I could have stayed there forever.

Colonel March had the same format as *Danger*, half an hour with an act break in the middle. Polonsky and I had a great time writing the shows. We discovered we were adept at creating the puzzle and our first acts usually ended on a high, expectant note of suspense. Unfortunately we then had to write the second acts. This proved much harder. Our puzzles were so good they were unsolvable. The question was not how to make the endings more active but how to end them at all. No one else seemed to worry about this, least of all Hannah. So long as she got something to shoot, she was happy. If the endings made no sense, that did not bother her. It didn't seem to bother Karloff, either. His part was not demanding and he performed it professionally and without complaint.

The show was moderately successful and enabled Hannah to start two new series, *Robin Hood* and *Ivanhoe*. She used blacklisted writers to write them and blacklisted directors to direct them. The writers were mostly in New York and included Oscar winners like Ring Lardner, Jr., and future Oscar winners like Waldo Salt and Ian McLellan Hunter. The directors were Hollywood fugitives like Joseph Losey, John Berry and Cy Endfield, who had settled in Britain or France. These shows, too, were successful, not least because Hannah commanded talent that normally the studios slavered over. For a while she had a small empire going. We all were grateful to her.

I was working, but the general atmosphere was still contaminated. In court trials and committee hearings, allegations still took the place of proof. Robert Oppenheimer was denied security clearance by the Atomic Energy Commission because of alleged Communist sympathy. Other scientists were kept from laboratories, teachers were still being fired, doctors denied hospital accreditation, all for the same reason. None was ever proved subversive or even delinquent in his or her work. My actor friends could not work in movies or television, but there was occasional work in the theater. Marty Ritt got a job acting in a play called *The Flowering Peach*, written and directed by Clifford Odets. He had known Odets from the Group Theater and they had marched together in May Day parades. Ritt was pleased when Odets showed up at rehearsal one day and informed the cast that he had just come from testifying before the House Committee on Un-American Activities and had really told them off. He had lectured them on freedom. He had made a ringing, eloquent speech, defending the right of artistic expression. Spectators in the committee room had to be gaveled down for applauding. He had also given names. Odets assured Marty that he had not given his name, only other friends from the Group Theater. Perhaps he had not wanted to spoil Marty's performance. The mind of Odets was a marvel of compartmentalization; he truly believed he had defied the committee. Marty was of two minds whether or not to quit, but a job was a job and he remained in the play, taking direction from an Odets increasingly insistent on the virtue of what he had done.

As usual, I was inconsistent in how I felt about the informers I knew, contemptuous of Kazan but only saddened by Maddow, understanding (if not forgiving) of Rossen but despising Harold Hecht. The difference seemed to lie in how personally aggrieved I felt. My former friend and mentor the devotedly left-wing Budd Schulberg had written a novel called *What Makes Sammy Run?* which had been stupidly savaged by the Communist press. He had visited the Soviet Union and disliked what he saw there. The committee called him and he testified that he was no longer a Communist and gave them names of those he had known. I had looked up to Budd, had wanted in college to fashion myself on him, and I felt betrayed. He had not only betrayed himself and his friends, he had betrayed *me*. If I had not known Budd, I would still have felt anger and scorn, but this went beyond that. I could not see beyond his capitulation. In my eyes, informing had warped his testimony so that anything he had said about communism or the Soviet Union was without value. There was nothing to be learned from it. There was nothing I wanted to learn from it.

Later Schulberg wrote a movie called *On the Waterfront*, which Elia Kazan directed. Brando played an ex-fighter who turns on the mob and testifies against them in court, facing the opprobrium of being a stool pigeon. He was transcendent. The picture was a great success and swept the Academy Awards. But all I saw was a rationale for Schulberg's and

Kazan's own informing. There were, it seems, good stool pigeons and bad ones, and they wanted to make clear which kind they were. Schulberg always denied this was the reason for making the film, but Kazan, a man never without a chip on his shoulder, asserted it with pugnacious defiance in his autobiography.

I kept waiting to be named. No one did so, at least not publicly. This did not keep me from still being blacklisted. *Colonel March* finished its run, but Susskind came through with a few more assignments. I rewrote a show for Sidney Lumet and the original writer went off with a Hollywood contract on the strength of it. By now I had convinced myself I was inured to this kind of thing. It even gave me secret satisfaction, another identity: Cardinal Richelieu operating behind the scenes, puppet master to the stars. Careers were made on my talent. Smugness loomed, a righteous superiority. My ulcer started to bleed, but that was normal in my business, blacklisted or not. Writers had ulcers, that was all, and they bled.

I was happily, if surreptitiously, employed, accepting of my situation, in touch with my anger. Losing a little blood was part of the tab you picked up. Then I lost a lot of blood. I lost half of it. Fortunately it took its secret time seeping out until I started to look interestingly translucent. I would stand in front of a mirror and see myself as Claude Rains, slowly turning invisible. Soon I would have to walk around bundled up in an overcoat, my invisible head swathed in bandages. I was probably delirious. Finally, when I could barely drag myself up the stairs to my apartment, I called a doctor friend and he came and sighed when he saw my condition and carted me off to a hospital. When I had been sufficiently transfused, he told me to get out of town for a while. His suggestion of lying on a beach somewhere, enjoying myself, got nowhere with me. What I knew and he didn't was that the bleeding stemmed from a lack of character. The real weakness was not in the duodenum but in the head. Somewhere, somehow, I had failed. What I had failed was not clear, but what else was my gut telling me? And so, ashamed and guilty, I did penance in a small, dark, unpleasant apartment in Cambridge, Massachusetts, found for me by Justin Gray, who was at nearby MIT studying to be a city planner.

Recuperating in Cambridge was satisfyingly miserable. I tried working but soon learned the physical basis of the will. You needed blood to work and I still didn't have enough. Gary Merrill and Bette Davis now lived on Cape Elizabeth in Maine and I often visited them. Their colonial house was big and beautiful with a stunning view of the ocean, but they were too busy fighting with each other to enjoy either the house or the view. They were basically incompatible and the abatement of passion had left them room to exploit this. She would attack his passivity and he would counter by attacking her need for discipline and control. Bette had had a daughter by a previous marriage and she and Gary had adopted two infants, a boy and a girl. The boy seemed fine, but the girl, now a lovely, heartbreaking three, had turned out to be retarded. There was a stubborn New England part of Bette that refused to accept this as anything more than a remediable impediment. She believed there was nothing a strong will could not affect. At meals she would exhort little Margo to sit up straight, improve her table manners, eat her food. Gary would remonstrate, Bette would continue, and he would sit and seethe. The child would try as best she could and the food would spill and Bette would not desist, could not, she had too much at stake.

They wanted me there as witness, referee and friend to them both. In the evenings we would sit by a fire and Bette would take out her knitting and we would drink and talk and listen to the surf crashing against the rocks. Those moments were the best. Gary was a Roosevelt Democrat, more interested in politics than acting, and even thought he might run for office someday. He had a concern for the world. Bette had no interest in ideas, but she had a sharp, moral intelligence and despised cant. I was always glad to come and usually glad to get away. Back in Cambridge I would see Justin and his wife or take the subway into Boston and go to the movies. By then no one was showing *You Were Never Lovelier* anymore, but I saw *The Barefoot Contessa* in an old theater where I was one of the few civilians. The rest of the sparse audience were sailors off a recently arrived destroyer. They had been at sea for months and they were horny and impatient. The picture baffled them. They could not understand why Rossano Brazzi was unable to have sex with Ava Gardner. They began to boo him every time he came on the screen. They called out obscene suggestions. Then the truth was suddenly revealed to a sailor sitting behind me.

"He's got no dick!" he shouted. "He's got no dick!"

That quieted them. They watched the rest of the movie in respectful silence, Brazzi more to be pitied than censured. I pitied him, too, but mainly for being in this bad movie at all, although I sneakily admired its lunatic pretension.

My blood slowly returned. I started writing again. After six weeks I felt shriven enough to go back home. Arnie and Abe welcomed me at Steinberg's, where Max, the waiter, insisted I have the protose steak, a suspicious mixture of soybeans that tasted like cardboard left out too long in the rain. He said it was good for the blood. But this time the three of us did not want to talk about scripts. We wanted to talk about the recent Twentieth Congress of the Communist Party of the Soviet Union.

The New York Times had just published extracts from a secret speech that Premier Khrushchev made to the congress.
What he had said was shattering—a detailed attack on the
dead Stalin as despot and dictator, a full and crushing account of his crimes: the purges, the trials, the frame-ups, the
executions, all that our enemies had been saying about him.
The effect was devastating. What had we believed all these
years? Did it come down only to the tyranny of a paranoid
dictator? Was it a man or the system that had failed? Was it
Marxism itself? For more than a hundred years people all
over the world had been inspired by the ideal of socialism.
They had fought and suffered and died for this ideal. And for
half a century the battle for socialism had become above all
else the need to support and preserve the Soviet Union, the
workers' state, the country of "already existing socialism."
Had it all been for a lie? I would not accept this, would not
relinquish what had inspired so much of my life, the socialism
in which I still believed, however corrupted it may have become. For we all accepted, without question, the truth of
these revelations. That was another revelation. We did not
doubt it for a moment. Perhaps we had been predisposed. Soviet anti-Semitism, the phony treason trials in Eastern Europe, everything that had created doubt but not defection,
had prepared us for this. Now our questions had been answered.

We discussed all this in Party meetings and at one another's
houses, and we were still discussing when the Russians invaded Hungary. The people of Hungary had risen up against
their own already existing socialism, calling for more freedom, more democracy, and Russia had sent in its tanks and
rolled over them and crushed the rebellion. That was it for
me. Doubt solidified into conviction. This was no longer a
Party I wanted to belong to. I left; so did all my friends. There

were no speeches or denunciations, no rending of garments. We left quietly, some with sadness, some with relief, without announcement. I simply stopped going to meetings. So did most of the others in my branch until the only ones left were those who still worshipped Stalin and the undercover FBI agents, although it was difficult to tell which was which. No one tried to urge me back. The Party was imploding. Two-thirds of its membership left within the year. I felt both sadness and relief. I would miss the connection to decent and committed people who believed as I did and were willing to risk much on those beliefs. No one I knew had ever been treasonous. Those who were friends would remain friends. The others would drop out of my life. I would not miss the dogma or the unthinking obedience to the Soviet Union. I reread those writings of Marx that had stirred me the most, looking, I suppose, to bolster my faith, and found they held the same powerful truths for me. I had left the Party but not the idea of socialism, the possibility that there could be a system not based on inequality and exploitation.

The immediate, nagging problem, though, was the fronts. Once again I didn't have one. Leslie was happily ensconced in City Hall, Leo was deeply involved in production, Howard had moved to Los Angeles, and I couldn't find anyone else. There were jobs to be had but no way I could take them. A story editor I knew visited me at home (he was more paranoid than I about phones being tapped) to say that his producer wanted me to write for his new dramatic series on NBC. I said I would when I found a front. Time passed and I still hadn't found anyone and he called again. I said I was sorrier than he was and would let him know as soon as I found someone. He called again a week later. He said his producer was furious with me.

"He thinks you're stalling," he said.

"Why should I be stalling?" I said. "I need the work. I just haven't found a front yet."

"He says he knows that you have."

In fact, he went on, the producer had been told by another producer that someone was roaming the halls of NBC claiming to be my front, available for assignments.

I did not know whether to be flattered or enraged. Had I achieved such eminence that someone could get work simply by claiming to be me? Suppose he did get a job? What could I do about it? The producer didn't believe me and I could tell from the story editor's face that he didn't, either. Maybe I should just find this person and see if he would really front for me. I would forgive his transgression; like the rest of us, he was just trying to make a buck. But suppose he wouldn't? After all, this way he was keeping 100 percent instead of the measly 10 or 20 he would get fronting. Who needed me? Who was I, anyway? Could there be another me somewhere, a doppelgänger ready to take my place? Why not? I had just seen *Invasion of the Body Snatchers*. Who knew?

I watched television, waiting to see if a show came up with my name on it. None ever did. Knowing my predicament, both Leslie and Leo volunteered one more time. I chose Leo as the safer choice for both of us and wrote a script that mollified the producer. My impostor was not heard from again, but I was sure he still lurked in the shadows, waiting his chance. Maybe there was more than one of him; after all, this was America, land of opportunity. My problems remained the same, although the atmosphere seemed to be improving. The FBI stopped accosting me but still telephoned once a month. The same man always called, first carefully giving his name, Special Agent Graubard. He would ask if I was ready to talk and I would say no and he would thank me and hang up. I tried to picture him at his desk, going down his list of

subversives, hoping someone would talk to him. He would be
in his suit and tie, since Mr. Hoover insisted his agents be
jacketed at all times. A few other agents would also be on
phones, but the lucky ones would be going out into the field
for the daring face-to-face work. Possibly, like me, Graubard
hated wearing a tie.

I began to feel sorry for him. He was always polite, even
apologetic for disturbing me, and after a while he started calling me Walter. It turned out he was Walter, too. We had a
good chuckle over that. He said that his friends called him
Wally. I said I never allowed anyone to call me Wally. Well,
maybe Sidney Lumet. He knew I knew Sidney. He knew
everyone I knew. I said that was unfair, that I knew nothing
about him, and he told me he was married and had two children, a boy and a girl, and they were thinking of having another but were not sure they could afford it. I said I, too, had
a boy and a girl. He knew that, of course, but it cemented our
relationship even further.

The cold war continued, but at a less hysterical pace.
Joseph McCarthy died, but he had done his work. Fear became internalized and a pall of conformity settled on the
land. Public discourse became bland and timid. There was
some agitation about the atom bomb, but little critical evalu-
ation of anything else. The colleges were quiet. The scientists
kept their mouths shut. Intellectuals stopped questioning society and stuck to questioning one another, except those doing piecework for the CIA. The movies settled for Cinerama
and costume pictures and musicals and stories about great
men. There was *The Glenn Miller Story, The Eddy Duchin
Story, The Monte Stratton Story*. The studios had always done
biographies. They had done Thomas Edison and Alexander
Graham Bell and Stephen Foster and Lou Gehrig and Jesse
James and, naturally, Abraham Lincoln. They had also done

Juárez and Zola and Louis Pasteur. The new biographies were different from the old ones. For one thing, all the men seemed to have been married to June Allyson. For another, they achieved a stupefying dullness that the old movies rarely approached, although many came close.

The various witch-hunting committees were also starting to run low on witches. There were fewer and fewer Communists to go after and the liberals had either been purged or cleansed themselves with an acceptable anticommunism. The committees had also been rocked by some unexpected Supreme Court decisions—unexpected because it was considered a conservative court, headed by the former Republican governor Earl Warren. In two of the decisions the Court supported the First Amendment positions of men fired from their jobs or denied admission to the California bar for past activities such as supporting causes like Loyalist Spain. In another, the Court ordered the acquittal of five Communist Party officials convicted under the Smith Act, saying the evidence was insufficient. In a third, the Court asserted that Congress was not a "law enforcement or trial agency" and could not expose for the sake of exposure in the areas of ideas protected by the First Amendment.

There were other decisions, all stressing the right to academic freedom and political liberty. They asserted that the Court would not uphold contempt citations based only on an investigator's idea of what was un-American. The committees continued to function, continued doing their damage with informers and intimidation. If you refused to cooperate, you still lost your job even if it was harder now to jail you for contempt. But now they were restricted to more stringent rules of evidence. There were rumors that the blacklist was breaking up. The director-producer Otto Preminger was said to have hired Dalton Trumbo to write a script for him under his own name. Preminger was an interesting contradiction, a Nazi on the set and a kind, generous, cultivated man in private life. When FBI agents had come to question him about his hiring practices, Preminger had thrown them out of his office. He was also a shrewd businessman, and if he had hired Trumbo, it was because he knew he could get away with it. These were all hopeful signs. Maybe the ice was melting. We were wary, not yet willing to trade hope for belief, but our gatherings now had a kind of pleasant giddiness. Our jokes were less bitter. For the first time we allowed ourselves a cautious optimism.

The first of my friends to get work openly was Martin Ritt. He was hired by David Susskind to direct a movie called *Edge of the City*. It had been done initially as a television show called *A Man Is Ten Feet Tall*, written by Robert Alan Aurthur, who had also written the screenplay. It had received excellent reviews and its success had enabled Susskind, the producer, to make a movie deal with MGM. Certain he would have a fight on his hands, he had proposed Marty as the director, but no one at the studio objected. They were too busy fighting off a takeover attempt and had no time for politics. Their only concern was that Marty was a first-time movie director and Susskind should keep close watch to see that he didn't go over budget.

We had a party to celebrate. Everyone was happy for Marty. There was a little envy, but not much. We all felt it was a harbinger of good news for all of us. There were also no smoke signals from Syracuse. Perhaps the tide was turning, the networks getting bolder, the movie studios sensing where more money could now be made. Marty directed the movie without incident. Word spread that it was good and he was offered a job by NBC in Hollywood. We celebrated again; first the movie walls, then the television walls were tumbling

down. *Edge of the City* opened to laudatory reviews and
Marty climbed up another rung. Twentieth Century–Fox offered him a directing job. The studio had a stable of young
actors that included Joanne Woodward, Tony Randall
and Anthony Franciosa and a script for a movie called *No
Down Payment* about young suburban marrieds, and it
wanted Marty, another young comer, to direct. No one
knew that the script, attributed to Philip Yordan, had actually been written by Ben Maddow. Even Marty did not know.
He signed a contract—and Spyros Skouras, the head of Fox,
received a call from Ward Bond asking what did Skouras
think he was doing, hiring a Communist?

Bond was part of an extreme-right-wing Hollywood group
that included Adolphe Menjou, John Wayne, Robert Taylor,
Victor McLaglen and several other actors and directors.
McLaglen financed his own private troop of cavalry which he
trained for use in case the Communists started anything.
Menjou had testified as a friendly witness before the House
committee and urgently asked them what it was doing about
the thousands of Communists pouring across the Mexican
border disguised as farm laborers. They were a nutty, rabid
group, but power had been ceded to them by the studios and
their word was often law. Bond, in particular, was a bully. He
was also a good actor and a fixture in John Ford movies.
When he died, Ford closed production on the movie he was
making and went to his funeral. His cast was lined up waiting for him when he returned. They knew Ford's long connection to Bond and expected a few heartfelt words. Ford did
not disappoint them. Stepping out of his car, he turned to
Andy Devine and said, "Now you're the biggest shit I know."

Bond's call to Skouras got the attention he wanted, if not
the result. Marty was summoned to New York for ten days of
private meetings between him, his lawyer, his agent, Skouras

and other Fox executives. Marty's lawyer, Sidney Cohn, was known for having represented the writer-director Carl Foreman before the House committee. Foreman did not intend to be a friendly witness, but taking the Fifth Amendment, refusing to answer because the answer might incriminate him, would make him unemployable. Cohn had come up with a solution that became known as the Diminished Fifth. Foreman partially answered some questions about himself and did not name anyone else. That he got away with it was an indication of changing times. Joseph McCarthy was dead along with the worst excesses of his time. The cold war had simmered down. Foreman's success was also an indication to some people that maybe there had been a little hanky-panky. His movies had been highly profitable for Columbia Pictures and it wanted to keep him working. Possibly money had changed hands. There was no proof of this, only supposition. In any case, what had worked for Foreman now worked for Marty. He signed a statement for Fox disavowing any present Communist ties. He gave no names. His statement was enough for Skouras to stand up to Bond, and Marty was finally, unconditionally, free to work.

But we were unaccustomed to anyone's being cleared without informing. There were mutterings that maybe Marty had given names; no one really knew what went on in those meetings. When he and his wife returned to California, old friends came around, and while no one asked directly, there were subtle probings. I knew Marty and knew he would stay blacklisted forever rather than inform. I also knew he would deck anyone who suggested he might. I thought there might be some envy involved here. Marty was working under his own name. He was acceptable again, back in society's bosom. The rest of us were still outside, noses pressed against the glass.

Dalton Trumbo was indeed openly hired by Otto Preminger to write *Exodus* and then by Kirk Douglas to write
Spartacus. Some blacklisted actors were hired under their
own names. Their parts were smaller than those they had gotten before being blacklisted, their pay was less, and they either received no billing or a mention low down in the credits,
as though the producers didn't want to call attention to what
they had done, but their faces were up on the screen again
and it still took a certain courage to hire them.

And I got a call from Sidney Lumet. He had been hired by
Carlo Ponti, husband of Sophia Loren, to direct a movie with
her. Sophia had just done her first Hollywood film with Cary
Grant and now she was to do her next in New York. Paramount had bought a World War Two short story about a kept
woman who falls in love with a young soldier waiting to go
overseas. It sounded like *Shopworn Angel*, made first with
Nancy Carroll and Gary Cooper and then remade with Margaret Sullavan and James Stewart. Those had been about
World War One, but any war would do when it came to kept
women and virginal soldiers. The story had worked then and
there seemed no reason why it shouldn't work now.

Ponti had asked Sidney to suggest a writer and he had suggested me. He said he had worked with me in television, I had
been in the war and knew soldiers, if not kept women, and he
thought I would be perfect for this script. He said nothing
about the blacklist and Ponti didn't ask. He hired me. I
waited for the other shoe to drop. Paramount had the same
screening procedures as other studios. It submitted names to
clearing agencies. It was sure to have the same list as my
friend Special Agent Wally Graubard and it would find my
name there and that would be that. But nothing happened. Irwin Shaw spoke to his agent, Irving Lazar, who agreed to represent me, and he negotiated my deal with Ponti.

I was working again. As myself. After eight years I was no longer blacklisted. At least in movies. On the East Coast. For the moment. I could not let myself believe it was really true or would really last. But there it was: a job under my own name. Then why didn't I feel any different? I had money; I could pay some bills; I didn't need a front anymore. There could be other jobs after this; I might even have a future. I could have a career. People would answer my phone calls. They would not cross the street to avoid me. Al Levy saw me in a restaurant and called afterward to say I looked different. He said I had walked in as though I owned the place. I thought I had slunk in as usual. Maybe I did look different. I didn't feel different. Sidney and I were working together, as we had done before; there was no change in that. Wally Graubard still called. He didn't mention my new job and I didn't tell him. Maybe the FBI didn't know everything. My friends, my politics, my apartment, my life remained the same. So did my anger. So did my feelings for the people who had gone through this with me. Love and kinship had helped sustain me in those years, opened my heart. The time had not been entirely wasted. I tried to feel guilty at having been cleared while others weren't but couldn't quite manage it. They would be next and it wouldn't be too long. My clearance would be the first of many. The ice was truly melting. Not only that; now I could really strike a blow for the cause. I could be a front.

Neither Polonsky nor Manoff had been cleared and Manoff had written a charming script on his own. He had shown it to Marty Ritt, who liked it and thought he might get it produced. Paul Newman would play the lead and Marty would direct. But Arnie needed a front. He and Abe and I discussed the problem in Steinberg's while Max hovered with the dreaded protose steak. The solution was obvious. It made

us laugh. It had a satisfying, joyful sense of completion. It
even had irony, a quality we cherished. I would be Arnie's
front. I sent back the healthy soybean and ordered a triple
portion of the Steinberg Special Platter of smoked salmon,
whitefish and sturgeon with coleslaw, potato salad, olives,
radishes, sliced tomato and Bermuda onion. We ordered extra onion rolls along with the toasted bagels. We spurned the
regular cream cheese and ordered cream cheese with chives,
knowing the chives were really scallions, but no matter, this
was no time to quibble. The sky was the limit. The decision
was so natural it seemed like no decision at all. My name had
been purified. It carried weight; it was free of entangling al-
liances. It could be used.

That was when I felt different: when I saw my name on the
cover of Arnie's script. Maybe it was seeing it from the other
side of the looking glass. Blacklisted, I had needed a front, a
person; the name was taken as a matter of course. But now I
saw the name was everything. Your name was who you were
and how you used it told what you were. No wonder we despised the informers. Not only for turning in friends, for prof-
iting from their misfortune, but for turning over their own
names and thus giving sanction to what was contemptible.
The power I now had was not only that I could compete
equally on the open market. It was the power to give my
name.

The script for Sophia Loren was called *That Kind of
Woman* and Ponti decided I should write it in Hollywood,
where he and his partner, Marcello Girosi, had their offices.
He was going back to Italy, but Girosi would be there to
keep an eye on me. I was reluctant to leave my children, but
they could come on holidays and for the summer if I stayed
out there that long. The idea of living permanently in Hollywood did not occur to me, partly from predilection and

also because I was still waiting for the other shoe to drop. But I lent my apartment to a friend and flew out and rented a car and a little house in Beverly Hills from which you could see both the ocean and the mountains across the valley. The house was the pool house belonging to an estate and I had privacy and the use of the pool. There were worse ways of returning to Hollywood. Girosi was an affable, cosmopolitan man who urged me not to work too hard, just do my three pages a day and everything would be fine. But when I turned in my first several pages, he became apprehensive. I had written them with only the dialogue and indications of the action and he was worried I did not know how to write a movie. I was worried I was going to be fired and consulted my friend Bob Parrish, who by then had become a director. He told me not to worry, just to write in shots and camera angles and Girosi would think I knew what I was doing.

"The director won't pay any attention to them, anyway," he said consolingly.

I did what he said, inserting long shots and close-ups and reverse angles, and as Bob had predicted, Girosi was happy and impressed with how soon I had learned film technique. He consulted Ponti in Italy and they offered me a contract to continue writing other scripts for them after this one. Again, Irving Lazar was to make the deal, this time directly with Paramount, which was putting up the money for Sophia's movies. I was having a very good time. I missed Abe and Arnie and Steinberg's, but there were close friends like the Ritts, the Parrishes and Charley Russell, who was hanging on by his teeth. Marty and I were able to play more tennis than we'd ever dreamed of. There were always courts available and they were free. I would pick him up early in the morning (he was ready at six, but I refused to appear before eight) and first he would buy the *Racing Form* and then we would find one of the many public courts. Success had mellowed Marty and he rarely threw his racket anymore, making our games somewhat less interesting.

I made other friends, male and female. The blacklist was behind me. Its pain was in the past, remembered but unfelt, pain's only blessing. I knew something was missing, had left my life a little emptier, but I thought it was only New York. I missed the city, my city, missed its energy, its hipness, missed walking. If you walked at night in Beverly Hills, you would be stopped by cops in a patrol car, who would ask you politely where you lived and then politely drive you there. The Beverly Hills cops were more polite even than the FBI, but you had the feeling that if you refused their kind offer of a lift, they would just as politely shoot you dead on the spot. So, in the evenings when I was alone and longing for sidewalks, I would drive into Hollywood and walk along real streets, feeling the comfort of solid pavement under my feet. I would buy a magazine at the out-of-town newspaper stand and go to Don the Beachcomber and read in the dim light designed for lovers and drink navy grogs and eat egg rolls and spareribs and feel pleasantly content.

Then the other shoe dropped. Lazar called. "Paramount's not signing your contract," he said. I asked why not. "Because," he said, "they know the committee's got a subpoena out for you."

"How do they know that?"

"How do they know?" he asked rhetorically. He sounded irritated. "They know. And they won't sign your contract until you do something about it."

I knew what that something was. I would have to go and be a friendly witness. No one was offering me any other kind of deal. If I did not do that, if I took the Fifth Amendment or otherwise defied the committee, I was back to being black-listed.

I was not sure if I would take the Fifth. It was an honorable position, but I had felt for some time that it was not for me. I don't know why. Perhaps some ego-driven need for self-revelation or a misguided belief that I could show the committee what we patriotic Commies were really like. Or maybe a masochistic urge to go to jail, the ultimate in being black-listed. I was prepared to tell the committee about myself but not about anyone else. At any rate, that is what I thought I would do. The hard truth was that refusing to tell about any-one else meant a contempt citation, and even with the recent Supreme Court decisions, it still could mean a year in prison. The goal was not to testify at all. I thanked Lazar and packed my bags and called Girosi to tell him I had to return home temporarily on urgent family business and would continue writing there. He was puzzled but sympathetic. Then I went on the lam. I flew to New York but stayed with friends in-stead of going back to my apartment. I consulted a lawyer friend, Leonard Boudin, who had represented other people before the committee, and he checked with its chief investiga-tor and reported back that it was true. A federal marshal was out with a subpoena, summoning me to present myself before the House Committee on Un-American Activities.

I needed a place where I could live and work and not be found. It had to be close to New York so I could consult with Sidney on the script. It had to be secret. I was not the first to have had this problem and there were Party members and ex-members and sympathizers who could be called on to help. I ended up in Little Compton, Rhode Island, a guest of Harvey and Jesse O'Connor. Harvey was a journalist who had writ-ten several muckraking books about the oil and steel indus-tries and the financier Andrew Mellon. He had now pretty much retired, but both he and Jesse were active in progressive causes. Jesse came from Chicago money and they lived in a large Victorian house overlooking the ocean, the kind of house called a cottage across the bay in Newport. They were a close-knit couple, sharp-tongued and affectionate with each other, finding it a little hard to get around now, but spry in heart and mind. They also owned a tiny two-room shack along the water, which they offered me for as long as I wanted. There would be no charge, of course. They never asked why I needed it and I never told them. They were involved enough as it was. All they knew was that a friend had told them he had another friend who needed a place to stay for a while. That was enough for them. They took helping for granted and accepted the risk as natural and familiar.

The shack was notable for having been put together out of thirty-two doors from houses that no longer needed them. Windows were cut in at random. The effect was disconcerting. Nothing quite fitted together, and when the doors were not warping, they were sagging. It was a little like the set for *The Cabinet of Dr. Caligari*. But the weather was warm and there were large rocks outside encrusted with mussels that I could pick and bring back to steam and eat on the rickety porch. Harvey gave me an open invitation for cocktails and occasionally, at the end of the workday, I would walk down the beach and join him on his spacious veranda, where he sat with a pair of binoculars and a pitcher of martinis and we would drink and take turns looking out to sea.

I stayed in Little Compton for about six weeks, finishing the script, taking occasional trips into New York to consult with Sidney. The House committee held its hearings without me. All the unfriendly witnesses took the Fifth Amendment and I wondered if out of solidarity, I would have done the same. I was glad not to have had to make the decision. These hearings lacked the brio of the previous ones. They had a tired air and went quickly, by rote, as if everyone just wanted to get them over with. The Hearst papers obediently put them on the front page, but below the fold. No further hearings were scheduled, not even executive sessions, and I figured I was home free. There was no reason to serve me with a subpoena if there was no place for me to testify. Leaving Little Compton, though, was not easy. It had been an unexpected paradise, a one-man artist's colony, a retreat where I had had day after peaceful day to work and read and listen to music and eat uncounted mussels. A pool house in Hollywood didn't even come close.

I said a sad farewell to the O'Connors, thanking them as best I could, wanting them to know how much they had done for me, and headed back to New York. Production had started on *That Kind of Woman* with Tab Hunter playing the young soldier Sophia improbably falls in love with. Not improbably because she was leaving her rich benefactor for the doomed boy; in the movies the improbable would have been if she hadn't left him. Doom was one of film's great aphrodisiacs. But Tab, sweet and shy, with the weak good looks of many young leading men in the fifties, was just not in her league. He might hold his own with Sandra Dee; he was no match for Sophia. If they married, you knew who would carry whom over the threshold.

But Sidney thought he could make a sexual attraction work and the atmosphere on the set was jolly and optimistic. During the lunch break we would send out for hero sandwiches and bottles of Soave. Every so often, if a stranger appeared, I would feel caught out, as if I should be hiding in another room, but the feeling disappeared after a while. Sidney wore funny hats and had a mania for bringing in his films under schedule so that the shooting moved crisply along. He was full of talent and nervous energy, always on the move. Ideas did not interest him as much as action. Like Marty Ritt, coming from the same background, Sidney loved actors and they responded to him. With Sophia, he was supportive and encouraging. She was friendly and nervous. Her English was not fluent and she missed Ponti. He had found her when she was only sixteen; he was tutor and protector as well as husband. She felt lost without him there but at the same time excited by the freedom. She worked hard and took direction willingly. She had no airs. Everyone liked her.

Paramount still refused to sign my contract. Lazar told me this in his hotel room; he had come to New York on other business. The studio said it didn't care that the hearings were over; I would still have to go before the committee. So far as it was concerned, the subpoena was still up and running. I said that was crazy. Lazar agreed. It was a disgrace. He said he wouldn't stand for it and picked up the phone and called a high executive at Paramount. He was genuinely angry as he got the man and started berating him. I listened with pleasure; for the first time someone was openly fighting on my behalf. Lazar was a fighter. I remembered when I had first met him. Back in 1947 I would spend Sundays at Irwin Shaw's beach house in Malibu. There would be other guests and we would play ball on the beach and swim and then have a long, delicious lunch with a great deal of wine. Irwin also had a rubber life raft and we would take it out beyond the breakers and ride the waves back in. The surf was very heavy and the raft always pitched over and sometimes you would get picked up and whirled around by a wave and slammed down hard on the seafloor. You had to be in pretty good shape, but we were young and still fit from the war. Lazar came out a few Sundays, small and bald and older and unathletic, and would insist on going out on the raft with us.

This meant searching for him after the raft overturned. We usually found him facedown in the shallows and had to pump the water out of him. But he would bound up briskly and insist on going out again. He had nerve and I watched him now, yelling at the Paramount executive, and felt a glow of trust.

"He doesn't have to go!" he shouted at the man. "There's no reason! I'm not going to let him, you hear me? I'm telling you! He doesn't have to go!"

He went on like this for a while, full of fight and fury, and then stopped as the executive replied. I couldn't hear what he said, but Lazar listened for a long time. Then he hung up the phone and turned to me with a shrug.

"You have to go," he said.

His anger was gone. He had made his pitch and it hadn't worked. The executive had set him straight. If I wanted to work, I would have to go. That was the end of it as far as Lazar was concerned. I wasn't going and I told Lazar that. He shrugged again. He knew where the power was. I thanked him for trying and left.

Carlo Ponti returned from Europe for the end of shooting on *That Kind of Woman* and wanted to know what was going on. We met in a conference room at Paramount's New York office. Ponti and an interpreter sat on one side of a long table; Ponti was not yet fluent in English. Leonard Boudin and I sat across from them. Ponti was a short, stocky, balding man, cultivated and intelligent. He resembled a more sophisticated Harry Cohn. He had a commanding presence, and when he wanted to, he could be charming. Leonard spoke first. He told about the subpoena, what it meant and what I would do if I had to testify, the bottom line being that I would not give names. The interpreter translated for Ponti, who listened impatiently, then rattled off a long stream of Italian.

The interpreter then turned to us and said, "Mr. Ponti would like to know who has to be fixed and for how much."

"Is politics," Ponti said, waving his hands dismissively. "Is politics."

He could not understand why such a fuss was being made. It was just getting in the way of what was infinitely more important, making a movie. If politics was involved, someone certainly could be bribed. Politicians were politicians, whether Italian or American. Grease a few palms and get on with what had to be done. He had a Renaissance grasp of knavery. But like most producers, he regarded putting up his own money as a mortal sin and was not about to hire me himself. He was sympathetic, he wanted me to work for him, he regarded the Red scare as a bad American joke, product of a frightened, provincial people, but basically I was out of luck.

I needed a job. Marty was getting nowhere with the Manoff script, but that wasn't for me, anyhow. I was only the front. We worried that my name on that script would now be a liability and decided not to send it around for a while. Marty was also planning to produce a remake of the Japanese film *Seven Samurai* that Yul Brynner was going to direct for United Artists. This would be Yul's first film to direct and he was excited at the prospect. He said he wanted to get out of acting and into something that used his brains. He and Marty had asked me to write the script, now called *The Magnificent Seven*, but I was then involved with Ponti and Girosi. Now I was uninvolved, but the job had since gone to Bob Aurthur. Even if it were open, I was not sure any studio would hire me now that Paramount wouldn't. Lazar confirmed this. He said he couldn't get me work since word had spread about my subpoena and other studios were taking the same position as Paramount. I was blacklisted all over again.

The dressing room lunches with sandwiches and white wine were finished. It was back to Steinberg's and the protose steak. Abe and Arnie would be there, ready with tart comfort. Max, the waiter, would bring us glasses of tea. We would laugh and make plans and help each other. We would discuss possible fronts. I would be back where I belonged, ready to bleed again.

Then Marty called from Hollywood. Bob Aurthur had withdrawn from *The Magnificent Seven* so that I could get the job. He had told Marty that he could easily get another movie, he already had several offers, and he knew what had happened with me and Paramount and thought I needed the job more than he did. He knew I had been offered the movie first and he thought it only fair.

Once again I was overwhelmed by someone's generosity. I knew Aurthur only slightly. Maybe he had other offers or maybe he didn't; the gesture was selfless. He was not just being fair. I called him up and thanked him, and he insisted his other offers were real, he could get another job tomorrow. He would not accept that he had done anything much. Now I had to be approved by United Artists. UA was a small, independent company with a rich history. Started by Chaplin, Pickford, Fairbanks and Griffith when they decided they didn't need the established studios, it had shrunk over the years until now it was owned by a small group of New York lawyers headed by Arthur Krim. It had been very successful bankrolling stars like Burt Lancaster and Frank Sinatra, who had their own production companies.

By Hollywood standards, UA was suspiciously liberal. Krim himself was a leading Democrat and friend of Lyndon Johnson's. If I had a chance anywhere, it was there. Marty and Yul pleaded my case, but it was not really necessary. Krim and his colleagues had no use for the blacklist but had of necessity gone along when it was most virulent, looking the other way when they knew Lancaster and Belafonte were using blacklisted writers under other names. They were ready to take advantage of the fact that the times were changing. Their attitude was that officially they knew nothing of any subpoena. They were not about to force anyone to testify. I was simply a writer like any other writer and should be considered on my merits.

So we lifted our glasses of tea to my luck and I flew back to my little pool house. I screened *Seven Samurai* a few times and then tried to forget it. Kurosawa's movie was a masterpiece. All I could try to do was a pastiche set in our cowboy West. I wrote a first draft and was in the middle of script conferences with Marty and Yul when Lazar called. Paramount had called him. It had heard I was working for United Artists and, urged by Ponti and Girosi, wondered if I would come in and meet with the head of Paramount. Possibly an agreement might be reached.

The head of Paramount was a tall, courtly southerner named Y. Frank Freeman. I never did find out what the Y stood for; no one else seemed to know, either, or else people weren't telling. All I knew about him was that he came from the business side and his politics were somewhat to the right of Ward Bond. I had no great hopes but figured there was nothing to lose.

When I entered his office, Freeman stood up and gravely shook my hand. He asked if I wanted something to drink. When I declined, he said nothing for a moment, then sighed and remarked upon how difficult the times were, so many good people hurt, so much damage done. He talked about a recent strike of technicians against the studios. The strike had been lengthy and vicious. The Paramount strikers, most of whom he had known for years, loyal employees of the studio, were picketing right out in front of his office window. Freeman knew he could bring them back in, settle the strike just by talking to them, they were his boys, after all, but when he tried a few times, went out to make the attempt, Russian-looking men kept interfering. He shook his head sadly. He was not joking. He said he liked helping people in my unfortunate position and named a few he had helped. They all turned out to be informers. Then he asked if I minded answering a few questions. He had a file on his desk. It turned out to be my complete political dossier. It went all the way back to Dartmouth and the YCL. It included the trouble I had at Fort Benning when I was discovered living off the post. It had information about my Red aunt Sara. It would have been silly to ask him where it came from. I could only admire its thoroughness.

Freeman thought he would start from the top and ask me if these associations were true and, if so, what I thought of them now. Or, if organizations still existed, if I still belonged to them. If I didn't mind. His courtesy never flagged. He was consistently polite, not as polite as the Beverly Hills cops but probably just as deadly. I said I wouldn't mind at all. I really didn't. There was not much more the studios could do to me than what had already been done. They could continue to blacklist me, but I had survived that once and knew I would again. The thought made me light-headed, as though I could float, released from some self-imposed restraint. A movie contract was, after all, only a movie contract. I wanted it, but there was another life out there that I had felt good living, that had nothing to do with movie contracts, even if it was all tied up with movies. Y. Frank Freeman, the courtly southern gentleman, was giving me a choice. I could celebrate that life or lie about it or just keep my mouth shut. It was up to me.

I told him to ask his questions and I would answer. He went

down the list carefully, making notes as he went. I felt like the star guest of *This Is Your Life*. When we came to Yugoslavia, Marshal Tito would bound out from the wings, grinning at my amazement. The audience would applaud. The causes rolled by, bearing their load of nostalgia. How noble this one was, how misguided that one, how could this other one be both noble *and* misguided? How stupid I was to join this, how lucky to have been part of that! These causes were what had shaped my life, given it purpose, enriched it, impeded it, gotten me blacklisted for eight years. They belonged to a time when I had hope and belief in what they represented. Most of them had ended in defeat and some in corruption, but there were many that I still believed in, would join their equivalents again if they existed, even if they were thought subversive, even if I knew their time had not yet come.

I told Freeman that and, when he had finished, he thanked me for being frank. He said he would take the matter up with a friend who advised him on such things, a man named O'Neill, head of the American Legion. I would hear from Paramount. He appreciated my coming in. We shook hands again and he walked me to the door and asked what I would do if I had to testify before the committee. I told him I might or might not take the Fifth Amendment, but I wouldn't give names.

"Then don't go," he said.

His answer surprised me since Paramount had been the one insisting I go. But he was serious. He said there was no point going if that was my position. I would only be making more trouble for myself. He may have been idiotic about the "Russian-looking men," but he was shrewd about the committee. Either go and be friendly or don't go at all. He seemed concerned for me, as he had been about his boys, the strikers. I thanked him for the advice and left.

Two weeks later I got a call from Lazar. "Whatever you did, it worked," he said. "They'll make the deal with Ponti. You're cleared, kid."

I went outside and stood by the pool and looked out across the valley. I was cleared, finally cleared—this time, it seemed, for keeps. My mind tried to fasten on what this meant, but all I could feel was an emptiness, an absence of something unde-fined but precious. I had felt like this when the war ended and the staff of *Yank* had dispersed. My friends would still be my friends, but we were no longer held together by the cement of repression. We were no longer a community. I had broken out, but at a price, the loss of the bonding, the group support, the liberating affection. The absence I felt was the absence of love.

But I had what I wanted. I was working again in movies, a cooperative enterprise. I would find a community there. I still lived in a country where there was no shortage of injustice and inequality, and so there would be people to join with to fight against this. Repression had not been our only bond. We had also been bound together by a common cause, our friendships built on the belief that there was a better world to be made. I was only as alone as I wanted to be.

Tomorrow morning, first thing, I would apply for a pass-port. I would get it now. The American Legion had certified me as no longer unclean. When the Legion spoke, committees listened. I could go anywhere, work anywhere, subject only to the vagaries of the marketplace, welcomed back to the world of dog-eat-dog. The trick now was not to act like a dog.

The mountains shimmered in the distance. The air was still, without fragrance, the silence soothing, broken only by the occasional soft hum of tires as a car swept by on the road below. Here, you could really rest in peace. I stripped down and dived naked into the pool, swimming back and forth under water, holding my breath until life forced me to the surface.

I SIT ON the set of a movie about to start shooting. The name of the movie is *The Front*. Woody Allen has the title role. Martin Ritt will direct and I have written the script. The movie is a comedy. It is the only way this studio, Columbia Pictures, will do a picture about the blacklist. It has also insisted on a star and suggests Robert Redford or Warren Beatty but has agreed to our choice of Woody. He is not a star of their magnitude, but he is on the way.

I feel calm, but my face is dotted with bits of Kleenex where I have cut myself shaving. I look like someone to be avoided. On the set Marty talks quietly with Woody. Zero Mostel is also in the cast and he walks arm in arm with the lovely Andrea Marcovicci. He is singing softly to her, an aria from *Don Giovanni*. "*Là ci darem la mano*," he sings, a song of seduction. Take my hand. You will say yes. I marvel again at Zero's grace, his dancer's movements. We have cast him because he is right for the part and because he had been blacklisted. We have cast all the parts we could that way, deliberately. It is our revenge.

I watch Zero and Joshua Shelley, who came to our touch football games in his camouflage suit, and Lloyd Gough, who used to play the concertina and sing at cause parties, and Herschel Bernardi, whose sister, the cabdriver, came in to sing at Berkowitz's restaurant. They all were blacklisted, but they have survived, however well, and now they are working again. I have trouble seeing them clearly; something is in my eye. The first assistant goes up to Marty and whispers in his ear. Marty nods and pats Woody on the shoulder. Woody does not like to be touched, but he accepts this. The actors take their places. Marty comes back to where I sit. We look at each other.

"Well?" he says.

I nod. There is nothing to say. We have come a long way for this and now it is time to do the work. Marty turns back to the set. The cast and crew are waiting. I can see clearly now, everything in focus.

"Action!" Marty calls.

The movie begins.

Acknowledgments

The idea for this book originated with Jonathan Segal, who then bravely stuck with it through its interminable gestation. I cherish him as editor and friend. My agent, Arlene Donovan, was always there with encouragement. Abe Polonsky, John Berry and Dick Sasuly provided facts, anecdotes, wisdom and, as usual, passionate, necessary argument. Bob Conquest came back into my life after fifty years, bringing warmth and affection along with remembrance of much that I had forgotten. Finally, my wife, Gloria Loomis, would not let me be satisfied with anything less than the best I could do. This work would not have been remotely possible without her care, her urging, her judgment and her love.

Index

Abbott and Costello Meet Jekyll and Hyde, 232
ACLU, 149
actors, effects of blacklisting on, 26–7, 173–4, 175, 184–5, 197–8
Actor's Laboratory Theater, 10, 208
Ada (front), 240
AFTRA, 26–7
Agronsky, Gershon, 78–9
All About Eve, 224
Allen, Woody, 278
All Quiet on the Western Front, 131
All You Need Is One Good Break, 208
Allyson, June, 258
American Business Consultants (ABC), 25–6
American Civil Liberties Union (ACLU), 149
American Legion, 12, 140–3, 147, 276, 277
   magazine, 154
American Student Union, 45
American Veterans Committee, 140
anticommunism, 144, 181, 258
   in movies, 177–8
Anzio, 121
Aragon, Louis, 51
Argosy, 158
army, segregation in, 126
Asphalt Jungle, The, 9
Astaire, Fred, 85, 93, 96
atom bomb, 130–1

Attorney General's list of subversive organizations, 144, 145
Auden, W. H., 48
Aurthur, Robert Alan, 259, 272, 273
Aware, Inc., 152

Ball, Lucille, 141
Barefoot Contessa, The, 253
Bari, 99, 118–19
Barthelmess, Richard, 29, 31, 68
baseball, in Central Park, 133, 233–4
Baum, L. Frank, 173
"Bauman, Paul" (author's pseudonym) 22–5, 151, 154–7, 210
Belafonte, Harry, 241, 274
Bell, Tommy, 163
Bendix, William, 67
Bentley, Elizabeth, 19, 20, 181
Berkowitz's (restaurant), 210–11, 278
Berlin, Irving, 63, 64
Berman, Harold, 47
Bernardi, Herschel, 212, 278
Bernstein, Walter
   bar mitzvah, 35–6
   blacklisted in 1950, 163
   blacklisting ends, East Coast, 263
   blacklisting extended by Hollywood studios, 272
   blacklist newsletter, 202–3, 205
   childhood, 28–36

Bernstein, Walter (*cont'd*)
    college years, 37–52
    Communist Party membership,
        134, 136, 254–5
    family members, *see* Bernstein
        family
    FBI dossier on, 275
    FBI interrogations of, 19–20, 155,
        174–6, 227, 256–7
    foreign correspondent for *Yank*,
        12, 69–122
    friendships with blacklisted people,
        186, 199–200, 210
    fronts, search for, *see* fronts
    in Hollywood, 4–12, 242–5,
        264–6
    illness and recuperation, 251–2
    marriage during wartime, 61–2
    military service in World War Two,
        56–130
    as *New Yorker* staff writer, 4,
        131–3, 155
    postwar return to civilian life,
        131
    pseudonym used by, 22–5, 151,
        154–7
    sports writing, 15, 158–63
    subpoenaed by HUAC, 266–72,
        276
    teaches scriptwriting class,
        193–4
    television scriptwriting, 21–2; un-
        der blacklist, 23–7, 150–7; with
        Manoff and Polansky, 209–10,
        212–23, 235–6
    television shows written by: for
        Susskind, 239–40; for Weinstein,
        245–49
    vacations in Maine, 130, 223–4
    veterans' organization activities,
        140–3
Bernstein family
    aunt, in Communist Party, 31–2,
        123, 228, 275
    brother, 218
    daughter, 85, 178–9, 233
    father, 32–4, 37–8, 128

    father's family, 31–3
    mother, 129–30, 196–7
    mother's family, 29–31
    sister, 194
    son, 13, 184, 233–4
    uncle Irving, 50–1
    uncles' clothing business, 31, 68–9
Berry, John, 249
Beverly Hills, 266
Big Parade, The, 131
blacklist
    cold war purposes of, 11, 19, 181
    compiled by American Business
        Consultants, 25–6
    expansion of, 231
    in magazines, 158
    newsletter about, 202–3
    professionals, effects on, 190
    Red Channels, inclusion in, 26
    signs of breaking up, 258–9
    in television, 152, 156
    in theater compared with movies
        and television, 17
blacklisted actors, 26–7, 173–4, 175,
    184–5, 197–8
blacklisted writers
    departure of, 227
    pseudonyms used by, 156
    television's acceptance of fronts,
        240
Block, Mel, 152–3, 153–4
Body and Soul, 6, 11, 209
Bogart, Humphrey, 6, 67
Bond, Ward, 260, 261
Boudin, Leonard, 267, 271
boxing, 15, 133, 158–63, 202
    in the army, 57, 72–3, 75–6
Bradley, Gen. Omar, 141
Brando, Marlon, 214, 250
Brazzi, Rossano, 253
Bride of the Gorilla, 201
Bridge of San Luis Rey, The, 239–40
Brodkin, Herbert, 22
Bromberg, J. Edward, 198
Brooklyn Navy Yard, 70–1
Browder, Earl, 48
Bryan, William Jennings, 173

Brynner, Yul, 22, 272, 273, 274
Buchalter, Louis ("Lepke"), 163
Bund, Yorkville demonstration
    against, 54
Burr, Raymond, 201

Cabin in the Cotton, 225
Cagney, James, 6, 39, 68, 176, 177
Cairo, 80–1, 86–8, 95, 96
    Yank's bureau officer in, 98–9
Camp Upton, 63
Capa, Robert, 93, 104
Catskills hotels, 190, 200
CBS
    Danger, 22, 24, 210, 216, 219
    response to blacklisting, 24–5, 27,
        154, 156, 164–5, 203, 219
    You Are There, 217, 220–3, 233,
        234, 237
Chagall, Marc, 191
Chaplin, Charlie, 182, 273
Charlie Wild, Private Eye, 21–2
Chayefsky, Paddy, 241
Cheever, John, 133
Christians, Mady, 198
Churchill, Randolph, 116–18
Churchill, Winston, 11, 142
CIO, 163
Clark, Gen. Mark, 88
Clurman, Harold, 199
Cobb, Lee, 230–1
Cohn, Harry, 7
Cohn, Sidney, 261
cold war
    beginning of, 11
    blacklist necessary to, 19, 181, 197
    after McCarthy, 257, 261
Collier's, 158
Colonel March of Scotland Yard,
    246, 248, 251
Columbia Broadcasting System, *see*
    CBS
Columbia Pictures, 4, 6, 261, 278
Committee for the Arts, Sciences and
    Professions (ASP), 15, 245–6

Communist Manifesto, The, 51
Communist Party, 11–12, 14, 123–4,
    134–9
    art criticism in, 138–9
    branch meetings, 134–8, 180,
        181–2, 197, 199, 201, 212
    defection from, 254–5
    defensiveness of, 212
    detention program, effect of, 150
    membership in, 12, 60, 134, 136
    questions concerning Soviet Union,
        137–8, 180, 199, 212, 230, 254
    Smith Act, convictions under, 136,
        163, 258
    Stalin's death mourned by, 227–8
    trust in principles of, 54
    Twentieth Congress, CPSU, 253–4
    Wallace campaign supported by,
        18
    wartime meeting in Naples, 90
    World War Two policies of, 52,
        56, 58
    Young Communist League, 45, 52,
        60
Communists and communism
    belief in cause, 138
    cold war attitudes toward, 19
    Detention of Communists Program
        (DETCOM), 150
    in Eastern Europe, 137, 180
    European students, prewar, 40–1
    Internal Security Act, effect of, 172
    movie portrayal of, 177–8
    movie studio writers, 7
    New Yorker writers, 20
    persons named by Matusow as,
        153–4
Concord Hotel, 190–3
Conquest, Robert, 41–4
Cooper, Gary, 132
Corsair, 32
Costello, Lou, 232
Costello's (bar), 67
Counterattack, 25, 152, 153, 154
Crawford, Joan, 232
Crime and Punishment, 88
Crisp, Charles, 13

Croatian fascists (Ustachi), 104–5, 131
Cronkite, Walter, 217, 221

Daily Worker, 14, 46, 205
Danger, 22, 24, 151, 152–3, 164
  format, 248
  fronts writing for, 168, 169–70,
    188, 194, 203, 210, 213, 216,
    218–19, 223, 235
Dartmouth College, 20, 37, 44–45
  student life at, 44–52
Davis, Benjamin, 99
Davis, Bette, 6, 224–6, 247, 252–3
Day, Doris, 238
Dead End, 22
Dean, James, 18, 177
Death of a Salesman, 17
de Carlo, Yvonne, 144
Dedijer, Vladimir, 96, 97, 98, 100,
  119, 139, 181
Dennis, Eugene, 124, 139
Destination Tokyo, 67
Detention of Communists Program
  (DETCOM), 150
Devine, Andy, 260
Dewey, Thomas, 150
Donlevy, Brian, 67
Dorso, Dick, 238
Dos Passos, John, 51
Douglas, Kirk, 262
Dowling, Doris, 144
Downey's, 200
Dozier, William, 24, 217, 219–20,
  221, 222, 233, 234, 237
Dreiser, Theodore, 51
Duncan, Greg, 140
Duryea, Dan, 144

Earrings of Madame De, The, 232
East of Eden, 18, 177
Eddy Duchin Story, The, 257
Edge of the City, 259–60
Einstein, Albert, 229
Eliot (front), 214–15
Endfield, Cy, 249

Equity, 185
Erasmus Hall, 35, 36, 45
Exodus, 262

Facts About Blacklist, 202, 205
Fairbanks, Douglas, 273
Farrell, James T., 138
Fast, Howard, 142
FBI, 165, 197
  agents, 19–20, 155, 174–6, 227,
    256–7, 259
  dossier on Bernstein, 275
  informers, 182
Ficarra, 84
Fighting Sixty-ninth, The, 68
films, *see* movies
Flight into Egypt, 193
Flowering Peach, The, 249
Flynn, Errol, 6, 67, 239
Fontaine, Joan, 9, 24
football, in Central Park, 133
Forbidden Games, 232
Force of Evil, 209
Ford, John, 51, 260
Foreman, Carl, 261
Forsberg, Col., 66
Fort Benning, 57, 59, 63
Fox, William, 33
Franciosa, Anthony, 260
Freeman, Y. Frank, 274–6
Front, The, 278–9
Fronts, 157–8, 166, 193–4, 213,
    236, 239–40, 255–6
  Ada, 240
  Eliot, 214–15
  Howard, 203–5, 239, 255
  Leo, 186–90, 213–14, 239, 255, 256
  Leslie, 218–20, 236–7, 239, 255, 256
  for Manoff, 213, 263–4
  Monash, 168–9
  Rita, 169–72
  Shirley, 194–5
  writers presumed to be fronts for
    Bernstein, 240–1
  for *You Are There*, 218, 220–1, 233
Fusari, Charley, 160–1

Gardner, Ava, 144, 232, 253
Garfield, John, 6, 16, 198–9, 209
Gates, John, 140
Gavilan, Kid, 159
Gellhorn, Martha, 99
Gentleman's Agreement, 17
Girosi, Marcello, 264–5, 267, 274
Gish, Lillian, 248
Glenn Miller Story, The, 257
G Men, 176
Goldbergs, The, 185
Golden Boy, 13, 198–9
Gough, Lloyd, 278
Graham, Billy, 158–9
Grant, Cary, 67, 110, 262
Grapes of Wrath, The, 128
Graubard, Walter, 256–7, 262, 263
Gray, Justin, 126–7, 130, 132,
    141–3, 252, 253
Graziano, Rocky, 158, 159–61
Greenberg's Romanian Casino, 211
Greer, Jane, 144
Grenoble, University of, 37
    student life at, 38–41
Griffith, D. W., 273
Group Theater, 13, 16, 17, 153, 198,
    199, 249, 250
Guthrie, Tyrone, 241

Hargrove, Marion, 71, 140, 142, 143
Hart, Moss, 62
Hayden, Sterling, 100
Hayes, Helen, 177
Hayworth, Rita, 85, 93
Hecht, Harold, 8, 10, 250
Hellman, Lillian, 68
Hepburn, Audrey, 232
Herman, Babe, 234
Hickory House, 210
Hindenburg, 41–2
Hiss, Alger, 164
Hitler, Adolf, 52, 56
Hollywood, 5, 10–11, 242–3, 266
Hollywood Ten, 7, 11, 12
Hoover, J. Edgar, 135, 163, 165, 257

horse racing, 14, 205–6
Hotel Lombardy, 218
House Committee on Un-American
    Activities (HUAC), 11, 26, 153,
    172, 201, 231
  Bernstein subpoenaed by, 266–72,
    276
  Cobb's testimony, 230
  Foreman's testimony, 261
  Garfield's testimony, 198, 199
  Hollywood Ten called before, 7, 11
  Kazan's testimony, 17, 193
  Maddow's testimony, 243–4
  Manoff named before, 208
  Menjou's testimony, 260
  Mostel subpoenaed by, 184
  Odets' testimony, 249–50
  Rossen's testimony, 8
  Schulberg's testimony, 250
Howard (front), 203–5, 239, 255
Huckleberry Finn, 173
Hungary, Soviet invasion of, 254
Hunter, Ian McLellan, 249
Hunter, Tab, 269
Hustler, The, 8
Huston, Walter, 68
Hyman, Stanley Edgar, 38, 49, 55

Internal Security Act (McCarran
    Act), 163, 172
Intruder in the Dust, 9
I Remember Mama, 198
Italy, Allied campaign in, 91
    coverage of, 92–5, 121
Ivanhoe, 249

Jackson, Shirley, 49, 55
Jaffe, Sam, 185–6
Japan, 129
    atom bomb dropped on, 130–1
Jean Christophe, 51
Jerusalem, 76–8
Johnny Guitar, 243

Johnny O'Clock, 6
Johnson, Laurence, 152–3, 203, 219
Jolson, Al, 81–2

Karloff, Boris, 232, 246–8
Kaye, Sidney, 200
Kazan, Elia, 15–18, 193, 243, 250–1
Kelly, Gene, 141
Kesselring, Gen. Albert, 88
Keynes, John Maynard, 167
Khrushchev, Nikita, 254
King and I, The, 22
Kiss the Blood off My Hands, 9
Kohlberg, Alfred, 25
Korean War, 164, 166, 236
Krim, Arthur, 273–4

Ladd, Alan, 144
Lady in the Dark, 62
La Motta, Jake, 158, 163
Lancaster, Burt, 8, 10, 144, 232, 273, 274
Landy (Communist Party figure), 124
Lardner, Ring, Jr., 249
Laski, Harold, 48
Lazar, Irving, 262, 265, 266–7, 270–1, 272, 274, 277
Leo (front), 186–90, 213–14, 239, 255, 256
Leslie (front), 218–20, 236–7, 239, 255, 256
Levy, Al, 237, 238, 263
Liebling, A. J., 15
Life, 153, 158
Lindbergh, Charles A., 54
Little Compton, R.I., 267–9
Little Red Schoolhouse, 233
Lobrano, Gus, 166
Loeb, Philip, 185, 197
Loren, Sophia, 262, 264, 269–70
Losey, Joseph, 249
Lost Horizon, 20, 46
Lost Patrol, The, 51

Louis, Joe, 202
Love, Montagu, 29
Lukin, Pavo, 101–2, 104, 105, 181
Lumet, Sidney, 22, 153, 154, 235, 251, 257
  Danger, 22, 151, 170, 188, 195, 216
  That Kind of Woman, 262, 263, 268, 269–70
  You Are There, 222, 223
Luxemburg, Rosa, 134

Maddow, Ben, 9–10, 243–5, 250, 260
Magnificent Seven, The, 272, 273
Mainstream, 26
Maltz, Albert, 138, 139
Man Is Ten Feet Tall, A, 259
Manoff, Arnold, 206, 207–13, 216, 235, 245, 246, 253
  front for, 213, 263–4
  in Hollywood, 242
  and Susskind, 241, 242
Marcovicci, Andrea, 278
Marked Woman, 225
Marshall, Gen. George C., 65–6
Marx, Karl, 50–1, 73–4, 255
Marxism and the Democratic Tradition, 124
Massey, Raymond, 177
Matusow, Harvey, 153–4
McCarran Act (Internal Security Act), 163, 172
McCarthy, Joseph, 153, 164, 172, 201, 231, 235–6, 257, 261
McLaglen, Victor, 260
Menjou, Adolphe, 93, 260
Merrill, Gary, 224–6, 252–3
Messina, 86
Meyers, Blackie, 17
MGM, 6, 259
Midsummer Night's Dream, A, 39
Mihailovič, Gen. Draža, 20
Minor, Worthington, 154–5, 157
Mission to Moscow, 68, 227
Mitchum, Robert, 144
Monash, Paul, 168–9

Monte Cassino, 93
Monte Stratton Story, The, 257
Montgomery, Gen. Bernard, 91
Moore, Sam, 202
Morris, Chester, 32–3
Mostel, Zero (Samuel), 17, 182–6,
    190–3, 230–1, 278
movies
    anticommunist, 177–8
    biographical stories, 257–8
    childhood recollections of, 28–9,
        31, 32–3
    enjoyment of, 176, 200–1, 232
    foreign films, 205
    making of, 143–4
    postwar, 144, 177, 232, 257–8
    revivals, 176
    Russian, 51, 111
    Technicolor compared with black-
        and-white, 127–8
    war movies, 67–8, 177
    women in, 144, 177, 232
Mulligan, Robert, 240
Mummy, The, 246
Muni, Paul, 6
Murrow, Edward R., 222
My Son John, 177

NAACP, 149
Naples, 95, 99, 121–2
    German retreat from, 88–90
Nation, The, 149
National Broadcasting Company
    (NBC), 255, 259
National Security Act, 150
Native Land, 9
Nazi Bund, 54
NBC, 255, 259
New England, 44, 48
Newman, Paul, 263
New Masses, 26, 138, 139
New York City
    anonymity of living in, 232
    Lower East Side restaurants,
        210–11

Metropole bar, 55
    Ninth Avenue shops, 14–15
    returning to, in 1947, 13
    Steinberg's, 210, 253, 263–4
    working at *Yank* in, 66–7, 124–5
New Yorker, The, 12, 20–1, 166
    articles written for, 15, 65, 87, 117
    assignment in Yugoslavia, 20–1
    staff writer, 4, 131–3, 155
New York Times, The, 59, 120, 141,
    153, 254
    Kazan's ad in, 17
Nex, Martin Andersen, 51
Nixon, Richard, 144
No Down Payment, 260
Noose, The, 29
Norris, Frank, 51
North Star, 68, 227
Nova, Lou, 133

Objective Burma, 67
O'Connell, Arthur, 143
O'Connor, Harvey, 267–8
O'Connor, Jesse, 267–8
Odds Against Tomorrow, 241
Odets, Clifford, 249–50
Oedipus Rex, 241
Only Angels Have Wings, 110
On the Waterfront, 250
Oppenheimer, Robert, 249
O'Shea, Dan, 24
OSS: Special Balkan Section (SBS),
    99–100, 101, 119, 120

Palestine, *Yank* assignment in, 76–80
Panic in the Streets, 16, 184
Paramount Studios, 262, 265
    contract negotiations, 266, 270–2,
        274–7
Paris, Pete, 140
Parker, George, 162
Parrish, Robert, 11, 265
Patent Leather Kid, The, 31, 68

Pearl Harbor, 59
Peekskill, 146–50
Pelle the Conqueror, 51
Perth, 73
Pickford, Mary, 273
Pigtown, 34, 48
Plummer, Christopher, 239
Polonsky, Abraham, 206, 207,
    209–10, 212, 235, 239, 253, 263
  Belafonte and, 241
  Colonel March, 246, 248
  front for, 213, 215–16
  You Are There, 221, 233
Ponti, Carlo, 262, 264, 270
  contract negotiations with, 271–2,
    274, 277
Popovic, Milentje, 96, 97
Preminger, Otto, 258–9, 262
Prince and the Pauper, The, 239
Progressive Party, 18–19
pseudonyms, 156, 210
  "Paul Bauman," 22–5, 151, 154–7
psychiatrists, 186

Radio Writers Guild, 202
Raimu, 182
Randall, Tony, 260
Randolph, John, 219
Red Channels, 26, 173, 185, 190
Reinhardt, Max, 39
Remington, William, 19–20, 47, 155,
    181
Riesel, Victor, 153, 154
Rise of the Goldbergs, The, 185
Rita (front), 169–72, 188, 189
Ritt, Adele, 13–14, 15, 229–30
Ritt, Martin, 13–14, 21, 22, 229–30
  Danger, 22
  Edge of the City, 259–60
  The Front, 278–9
  in Hollywood, 265–6
  James Dean and, 18
  Kazan and, 15–17
  The Magnificent Seven, 272, 273,
    274

Manoff's script with, 263–4, 272
Odets and, 249–50
at racetrack, 14, 205–6
Twentieth Century–Fox contract,
    260–1
Robeson, Paul, 146–8, 163
Robin Hood, 249
Robinson, Edward G., 6
Robinson, Sugar Ray, 161–3
Rolland, Romain, 51
Rooney, Mickey, 39
Roosevelt, Eleanor, 125
Roosevelt, Franklin D., 128–9, 246
Rosenberg, Ethel, 228–30
Rosenberg, Julius, 228–30
Ross, Harold, 20–1, 65–6, 117, 132
Rossen, Robert, 4, 5–8, 250
Russell, Charles, 22, 154–5, 157,
    209–10, 216–223, 234–5, 237
  Danger, 22, 24–5, 151, 164, 168,
    169–70, 188, 194, 210, 213,
    216, 218–19, 223
  in Hollywood, 237, 242–3, 265
  Susskind and, 238, 239
  You Are There, 217, 220, 221,
    222, 223, 233, 234, 238
Russian movies, 51, 111
Russian Tea Room, 200, 240
Ryan, Robert, 241

Sahara, 67
Salerno, 88
Salt, Waldo, 249
SBS (Special Balkan Section, OSS),
    99–100, 101, 119, 120
Schulberg, Budd, 45, 49–50, 250–1
Schulman, Arnold, 220
Seeger, Pete, 147
See Here, Private Hargrove, 71
Seven Samurai, 272, 274
Shaw, Irwn, 79–81, 87, 96, 133, 139,
    166, 262, 270
Shawn, William, 133, 155
Shelley, Joshua, 278
Shirley (front), 194–5

Shopworn Angel, 262
Sicily, invasion of, 81–6, 88, 91
Sillen, Samuel, 139
Sinatra, Frank, 273
Sinclair, Upton, 51
Singing in the Rain, 201
Skouras, Spyros, 260–1
Smith Act, 136, 163, 258
Socialist Workers Party, 163
Sokolsky, George, 26
Somerset Maugham Theatre, 21
Soviet Union
    anticommunist view of, 144–5, 197
    anti-Semitism in, 137, 181–2
    belief in ideals of, 53, 55, 126,
        134, 180
    Communists' defense of, 136–8,
        199, 202, 212, 230
    under Khrushchev, 254
    nonaggression pact, 52, 56
    under Stalin, 53, 227–8
    wartime movies about, 227
Spanish Civil War, 26, 44, 45, 97
    Capa photographs of, 93
    Loyalist songs, 53, 103
Spartacus, 262
Spiegel, Sam, 22
Sports Illustrated, 158
sports writing assignments, 15, 158–63
Stack, Robert, 5
Stage Struck, 237
Stalin, Josef, 53, 227–8
    Hitler-Stalin Pact, 52, 56
    split between Tito and, 180
Stanton, Frank, 156
Stars and Stripes, 65, 66, 89, 129, 140
Steffens, Lincoln, 51
Steinbeck, John, 51
Steinberg's Dairy Restaurant, 210,
    253, 263–4
Stevens, George, 79
Stopcock, Saunders, 166
Streetcar Named Desire, A, 17
Stuart, Gloria, 247
Studio One, 154
Supreme Court decisions, 258
Susskind, David, 237–42, 251, 259

Tabori, George, 193
Taylor, Albert, 24
Taylor, Robert, 260
Teheran, *Yank* mission to, 69–76
Tel Aviv, 79–80
Telegram from Heaven, 208
television networks, response to
    blacklisting, 152, 155–6, 240
television shows, live, 21
That Kind of Woman, 264, 269, 271
    Lumet's direction of, 262, 269–70
This Is the Army, 63, 64–5, 224
Thurber, James, 67
Time, 153, 154
Tito, Mshl. Josip Broz, 96, 97
    headquarters in Drvar, 105, 109
    interview with, 12, 98, 100,
        114–20, 123–4, 139
    split with Stalin, 180–1
Toland, Gregg, 9
Torch Song, 232
Truman, Harry, 18, 19, 144, 164
Trumbo, Dalton, 173, 258–9, 262
Tuskegee squadron, 99
Twentieth Century–Fox, 243, 260, 261

United Artists, 272, 273, 274
Universal studio commissary, 10
Ustachi, 104–5, 131

veterans' organizations, 140, 147
Vis, 101–2

Wake Island, 67
Walker, Robert, 177
Wallace, Henry, 18
Wanger, Walter, 50
Warner Bros., 6
Warren, Earl, 258
Wayne, John, 67, 260
Weeks, Maj., 66

Weinstein, Hannah, 245–6, 248–9
Westerner, The, 132
Westinghouse Summer Theatre, 194
What Makes Sammy Run, 50, 250
White Heat, 177
William Morris (agency), 151, 236,
   244
Winchell, Walter, 163
Wise, Robert, 241
Wizard of Oz, The, 173
Woltman, Fredric, 26
Woodward, Joanne, 260
World War Two, military service in,
   56–130
Wycherly, Margaret, 177

Yank, 66–7, 125–6, 130, 140, 147
   assignments overseas, 12, 69–81,
      87, 95, 121, 129
   foreign correspondents, 71, 75, 76,
      81, 127
   Middle East correspondent, 76–81
   return to work in New York at,
      124, 125
   staff discharged, 134, 277
   Tito interview, report of, 98–9,
      103, 117, 120

Yiddish theaters, 210–11
Yordan, Philip, 243, 260
You Are There, 217, 220–3, 233,
   234, 235, 237, 238
Young Communist League, 45, 52,
   60
Young & Rubicam, 22–3
You Were Never Lovelier, 84–5, 93,
   95–6, 121, 128, 176, 253
Yugoslavia, 96–120, 123, 131, 139
   British mission in Drvar, 109,
      116–18
   Chetniks, 20, 96
   New Yorker assignment in, 20–1
   partisans, 96–8, 115, 117–19, 123,
      131
   partisans, traveling into Yugoslavia
      with, 100–11
   Tito, interview with, 12, 98, 100,
      114–20, 123–4, 139
   Tito's headquarters, 105, 109
   Tito's split with Stalin, 180–1
   Ustachi, 104–5, 131
   youth congress, 105, 111–14

Zanuck, Darryl, 209
Zweig, Stefan, 104

A Note About the Author

WALTER BERNSTEIN was a staff writer for *The New Yorker* and a correspondent for *Yank* during World War II before turning to screenwriting. A collection of his wartime writings, *Keep Your Head Down*, was published in 1946. Beginning in 1950, he was blacklisted for his political beliefs for eight years, during which time he wrote pseudonymously for television shows, including *Danger*, *You Are There*, *Studio One*, and *Philco Playhouse*, winning awards he could not claim. Bernstein has directed films, written movies, such as *The Front*, *Fail Safe*, *The Molly Maguires*, *Semi-Tough*, and *Paris Blues*, and written and directed original screenplays for HBO. He lives with his wife in New York City.

A Note on the Type

The text of this book was set in Sabon, a typeface designed by Jan Tschichold (1902–1974), the well-known German typographer. Based loosely on the original designs by Claude Garamond (c. 1480–1561), Sabon is unique in that it was explicitly designed for hot-metal composition on both the Monotype and Linotype machines as well as for filmsetting. Designed in 1966 in Frankfurt, Sabon was named for the famous Lyons punch cutter Jacques Sabon, who is thought to have brought some of Garamond's matrices to Frankfurt.

Composed by American–Stratford Graphic Service,
Brattleboro, Vermont
Printed and bound by Quebecor Printing,
Martinsburg, West Virginia
Designed by Anthea Lingeman